Developing
Competency
to
Manage
Diversity

Other Books by Taylor Cox, Jr.

Cultural Diversity in Organizations:
Theory, Research, and Practice

Developing Competency to Manage Diversity

Readings, Cases & Activities

Taylor Cox, Jr., & Ruby L. Beale

Berrett-Koehler Publishers, Inc.
San Francisco

Berrett-Koehler Publishers, Inc.
450 Sansome Street, Suite 1200
San Francisco, CA 94111-3320
Tel: (415) 288-0260 Fax: (415) 362-2512

ORDERING INFORMATION

Individual sales. Berrett-Koehler publications are available through most bookstores. They can also be ordered direct from Berrett-Koehler at the address above.

Quantity sales. Special discounts are available on quantity purchases by corporations, associations, and others. For details, contact the "Special Sales Department" at the Berrett-Koehler address above.

Orders for college textbook/course adoption use. Please contact Berrett-Koehler Publishers at the address above.

Orders by U.S. trade bookstores and wholesalers. Please contact Publishers Group West, 4065 Hollis Street, Box 8843, Emeryville, CA 94662. Tel: (510) 658-3453; 1-800-788-3123. Fax: (510) 658-1834.

Printed in the United States of America

Printed on acid-free and recycled paper that is composed of 50% recycled fiber, including 10% postconsumer waste.

Library of Congress Cataloging-in-Publication Data

Cox, Taylor, 1949–
    Developing competency to manage diversity : readings, cases, and activities / Taylor Cox, Jr., Ruby L. Beale.
       p. cm.
    Includes bibliographical references and index.
    ISBN 1–881052–96–6 (alk. paper)
    1. Diversity in the workplace.   I. Beale, Ruby L., 1949–
II. title.
HF5549.5.M5C69   1997
658.3'008—dc21   97–19978
                                          CIP

First Edition

99 98   10 9 8 7 6 5 4 3 2

Book Production: Pleasant Run Publishing Services
Composition: Classic Typography

To my children, Stephanie, Aaron, and Ty. Thanks for your understanding and love.

Taylor Cox, Jr.

To God, for opportunity, guidance, and, most of all, grace. To my sons, Clayton and Paul, and to my extended family, wishing for you a future of investment in, and opportunity for, the growth and development of all humankind.

Ruby L. Beale

Contents

Preface

Three years ago Taylor Cox, Jr., authored the book *Cultural Diversity in Organizations: Theory, Research and Practice* (1993). That book (which we will refer to here as the "theory" book) provided a conceptual foundation for thinking and learning about diversity in the context of organizations. The book was well received, and the author continues to hear of individuals and organizations that have benefited from it in their efforts to understand the dynamics of diversity and how to manage it. However, that book, as the name implies, was devoted to explaining a theory of the effects of diversity and to discussion of the empirical research that supported the theory.

From conversations with workers and managers who are involved in processes of organizational change to meet the challenge of diversity, we have identified a need for help in translating the theory and research in the previous book into teaching and learning tools. A question that we are often asked is: How do I develop competency to respond to the dynamics of diversity in organizations?

This book (the "competency" book) is designed to respond to this question. We wish to complement the earlier work by shifting the focus from intellectual foundations to translation of those foundations into a learning process leading toward individual and organizational competency. Whereas the content of the theory book was roughly 75 percent concepts, theory, and empirical research and only about 25 percent tools for application, this book reverses those percentages. *Thus, the purpose of this book is to provide a tool to assist individuals and work teams in developing personal and organizational competency to manage diversity.* As will be stated again in Chapter One, our definition of *managing* is not limited to the actions of people who supervise others. All members of organizations take part in creating a climate in which all people are treated fairly and can achieve and contribute to their full potential, and where diversity, as an organizational resource, can be fully leveraged to enhance organizational performance.

In order to make it easier to use the two books together, many of the chapter titles that were used in the theory book will also be used here. Following an introductory chapter that explains our approach to diversity competency, the book is organized into three major segments: (1) foundations for competency, (2) developing individual competency, and (3) developing organizational competency. Part One relates closely to Part One of the theory book, Part Two is coordinated with Parts Two and Three of the theory book, and Part Three is related to Parts Four and Five of the theory book. Within each of these parts, a combination of carefully selected readings (some by us and some by others), cases, and activities are assembled that address topics that were included within that section of the theory book. For example in Part Two of this book, you will find readings, cases, and activities that will help you to develop competency by understanding and changing behaviors related to stereotyping and prejudice. In Part Three, you will find learning aids to develop competency in understanding and changing organizational culture, and so on. In most cases, the readings we have included that were authored by others are presented here in an excerpted form. In shortening these writings, our goal was to create versions that could be read more easily while still preserving the essential messages of the authors.

Because of space and other considerations, we have not attempted to provide material in this book to correspond to every topic included in the theory book. Instead, our goal was to provide learning aids for each of the five major parts. In addition, we realize that the book does not give equal attention to all dimensions and important issues of diversity. Ideally, material on a broad scope of diversity dimensions could be provided in each part. However, this would require a very long and expensive book. We have decided instead to provide as much breadth as possible within the bounds of space and time, to allow us to maintain a modest price and a reasonable timetable for completion of the book.

One final point is that we view the quest for understanding how to be competent to manage diversity as a lifelong learning process. Therefore, as we update the book, we will seek to add more depth and effectiveness to this learning tool. Toward that end, we invite you to send us any ideas or feedback that you may have for making the book more useful to readers in the future. In the meantime, we hope that this initial effort will meet some of your important needs.

May 1997   Taylor Cox, Jr.
Ann Arbor, Michigan   Ruby L. Beale

Acknowledgments

No one creates a book like this without the direct or indirect help of many people, too many to name here. Special thanks to Marilyn Bernhardt, Dianna Romas, and Shelly Christian Sherman for their wonderful assistance with the preparation of the manuscript. Also thanks to the clients in our consulting partnerships, from whom we have learned so much about this topic.

We likewise acknowledge the support and input of our colleagues at the University of Michigan and throughout the management and organizational sciences and of Steven Piersanti and the other members of the Berrett-Koehler family.

Special thanks to Nancy DiTomaso, Bernardo Ferdman, and Julie O'Mara for their excellent reviews of the book, which greatly improved its quality.

Finally, we appreciate our family and friends, who have provided lifelong emotional support and encouragement.

1

A Framework for Understanding Competency for Managing Diversity

In this introductory chapter, we outline our approach to the subject of competency to manage diversity. We define key terms including *diversity competency,* and we explain how our approach to defining competency is used to frame the material that is presented in the rest of the book.

FOUNDATIONAL TERMS

We have learned that any useful discussion of the topic of diversity must be very conscientious about clarifying terms. The term *diversity* itself has a multitude of interpretations. In the broadest sense, our definition of diversity is a modification of one given in Cox (1993, p. 6): "a mix of people in one social system who have distinctly different, socially relevant group affiliations."

A social system may be defined on many levels: countries, cities, organizations, work teams, product markets, industry channels of distribution, and so on. Likewise, there are many kinds of group affiliations, such as gender, nationality, age cohort, levels or types of physiological abilities or disabilities, racioethnic identity, religion—and the list goes on. A socially relevant group affiliation is simply one to which some meaning is often attached when people interact together. For example, people differ in shoe size, but the social importance of this is very limited compared to, say, political party or occupation. When these group affiliations not only are socially relevant but also have cultural significance—that is, when they differentiate groups based on behavioral norms, values, language, goal priorities, and tendencies toward certain ways of thinking or views of the world—we speak of "cultural" diversity. Although we recognize that people can be diverse on a nearly infinite number of dimensions, in this book we are primarily concerned with cultural diversity.

Again using a modification of Cox's definition (Cox, 1993, p. 11), we will define *managing diversity* as "creating a climate in which the potential advantages of diversity for organizational or group performance are maximized while the potential disadvantages are minimized." We wish to emphasize that this definition implies that "managing" diversity can be done by anyone and is not limited to those in supervisory jobs. Finally, we will use the term *diversity competency* as shorthand for *competency for managing diversity*.

DEFINING DIVERSITY COMPETENCY

Having now defined the basic terms for a study of diversity, we turn our attention to the key concept in this book, diversity competency. Perhaps the best way to introduce our approach to this topic is to tell a story. The first draft of this book had a different title, *Developing Skills to Manage Diversity*. The responses of reviewers were predictable and coincided with many conversations that we've had while consulting with organizations on educational programs for diversity. The recurring response was to ask us to specify explicitly the *list of skills* that one must develop to manage diversity. This reaction to the title of our book, as well as to some of the consulting work we've done, helped us to reflect more deeply on our own thinking about the meaning of diversity competency. What we discovered as a result is that we do not think of competency to manage diversity as acquiring a list of skills; rather, we define *diversity competency* as "a process of learning that leads to an ability to effectively respond to the challenges and opportunities posed by the presence of social-cultural diversity in a defined social system."

Many of the words in the above definition deserve elaboration. First is the word *process*. This signifies our belief that diversity competency occurs by following a sequence of steps through which individuals and organizations move from ignorance of the topic to the point where they understand how the dynamics of diversity affect organizations, their people, and their outcomes, and how to change their own behavior to take these effects into account. This learning process is the core of our approach and we will return and say more about it shortly.

Next is the word *effectively*. Diversity competency means developing the extra knowledge and behavioral repertoire that is required to perform tasks and fulfill responsibilities at a high level of performance *in light of the special conditions that diversity creates*. Third is the phrase *challenges and opportunities*. The presence of diversity brings both, and the competent person is able to not only avoid diversity-related problems but also tap into the potential of diversity to enhance team performance. Finally, the phrase *defined social system* must be given due consideration. Although we strongly believe that much of the learning that is useful for diversity competency is generic to many forms of difference, we are also aware that there are limits to this overlap. Different forms of diversity affect work-related interactions in ways that have both similarities and points of divergence. Therefore, the specific learning needed for competency will depend to some degree on the composition of the social system or systems in which the learning is to be applied. For example, the knowledge that in many West, Central, and North African nations the individual self has no meaning apart from the tribe to which he or she belongs may be very useful in establishing competency in a global marketing person or firm or even a firm with a large percentage of African American employees, but it would be of less value to a small firm doing maintenance work with crews of local people who are 99 percent Anglo-American.

The Learning Process

Let us return now to a point made earlier. We have said that we do *not* view diversity competency as acquiring a list of skills but rather as working through a process of learning. We need to say more about what this process looks like. What exactly does it take to create the "ability to effectively respond to the challenges and opportunities" of diversity? We believe that the learning process has three phases of development: (1) awareness, (2) knowledge and understanding, and (3) behavior and action steps.

Awareness

Awareness means recognizing that diversity has very genuine effects on organizational behavior and work outcomes. It is a basic acknowledgment of the need for learning. For example, a person may believe that identity differences like gender and cognitive style have no effect on whether or not people can communicate effectively. Such a person will not be motivated to engage in development to understand how diversity affects communication. Often, showing this person even one concrete example of how gender or cognitive style affect communication is enough to ready him or her for further learning in this area. Once the assumption that diversity is irrelevant to communication effectiveness is refuted, the path is opened for phase two of the development process: understanding.

Understanding

Phase two of development toward diversity competency—understanding—occurs through the acquisition of knowledge. Here the person acquires a deeper cognitive grasp of how and why diversity competency is relevant to the good performance of individuals, groups, and organizations. Extending the previous communications example, the person may now read or hear extensively about cross-gender differences in communication styles (for example, Tannen, 1990, 1995) or about the impact of cognitive style on how people respond to information (for example, Whetten & Cameron, 1991). Rather than a single example that opens our eyes, we now have enough understanding of these phenomena to actually change our behavior, thus leading to the final phase of development—action.

Action Steps

Once individuals or organizations have awareness (the motivation to change) and understanding (the knowledge base that helps to determine the specific changes that might be helpful), they are positioned to take action to actually change behavior. Continuing again with the communications example, the person may now decide to take an action such as teaching others about the communication implications of different genders and cognitive styles or showing more patience when listening to people with reflective styles of information processing versus her or his own action-oriented style. When people or organizations have worked through the three stages of development shown in Figure 1.1 with respect to a broad range of tasks or activities, then they have developed diversity competency.

Figure 1.1. Learning Process for Diversity Competency

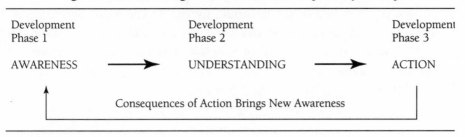

The Level of Analysis

It should be noted that our definition of diversity competency can be applied to individuals, work teams, organizations, and even countries. Therefore, an important question has to do with the level of analysis at which we wish to examine competency. In this book, we want to consider both individual and organizational competency. We will not directly address the work-group or societal (national) levels of competency except to say that we believe that the work-group level is simply a smaller version of the conditions necessary for organizational competency to manage diversity, and that societal competency is largely determined by the combination of individual and organizational competency that exists in that society. Individual and organizational competency also overlap, but we see enough distinction between these two levels of analysis to treat them separately in the book.

A key point of difference between these two levels of analysis occurs in the meaning of "effectively respond to the challenges and opportunities" of diversity. For individuals, diversity competency means learning to the point where they know how to change their personal behavior as they perform the daily tasks and responsibilities of work and supervision. For organizations, diversity competency requires the presence of two interdependent conditions: having a large proportion of individual members who are personally competent and having the appropriate infrastructure in place to support individuals who are seeking to display competency in managing diversity. Thus, we view the three-step process as applicable at both levels of analysis. What differ are the work activities or content areas of organizational practice to which the process is applied.

This is explained further in the next section of this chapter, but first, one additional point should be made about Figure 1.1. The loop connecting action back to awareness indicates that we gain additional awareness from our behavior and its consequences. These new insights can then be pursued to get a greater understanding. Ultimately, new behaviors may be tried as a result of this recycling of the learning process.

THE DIVERSITY COMPETENCY MODELS

We have prepared the diversity competency models shown in Figures 1.2 and 1.3 as a way to summarize our approach to diversity competency as explained in the preceding paragraphs. You will recall that this approach requires people to work through the three phases of development in order to understand how diversity affects performance in a variety of tasks and to identify specific action steps that can be taken by them (together with others) or by the organizational leadership to change behavior in some specific way. The figures illustrate some of the specific areas of work activity where we believe that the process of learning must be applied. Figure 1.2 shows that individuals must work through awareness, understanding, and action in areas like communications, performance feedback, and selection decisions. Previously, an example was given using the communications item. When an individual has worked through the learning process for many areas of work activity, then she or he will have developed a high level of competency to manage diversity. It should be noted that the items listed in Figure 1.2 are not the only relevant work activities.

Figure 1.3 addresses the organizational level of analysis. In addition to requiring large numbers of individual members to have worked through the model in Figure 1.2, specific conditions must be in place in order for diversity competency to become institutionalized. We can illustrate the use of this figure for organizations by means of the first item. To achieve competency on this item, the organization must recognize that it should be done (awareness), have a good knowledge of why and how it should be done (understanding), and have actually implemented steps to accomplish it (action).

We have found the diversity models to be useful in analyzing the stages of learning and development for individuals and organizations. For example, after an effective two-day workshop on the basics of managing diversity, person A may be at the awareness stage on three of the seven items

Figure 1.2. Diversity Competency Model for Individuals

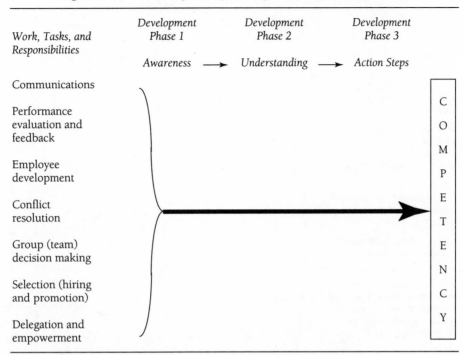

SOURCE: This figure is adapted from one first used by Taylor Cox, Jr., in a presentation to the Human Resource Partnership, University of Michigan, September 1992.

shown in Figure 1.2. The developmental need of such a person is to move to the understanding stage on these three items and to create awareness in other areas. This can be accomplished by a combination of further training, personal study, specific work and nonwork assignments, and personal coaching. Alternatively, person B may have both awareness and understanding in a broad cross-section of work and responsibility areas. This person's developmental need is to translate this new knowledge into specific actions or changes in behavior that can be implemented in his or her daily job performance.

Similarly, an organization's stage of development can be gauged using Figure 1.3. The ability to create a list like the one in this figure requires an awareness of the relevant factors in organizational competency. In many organizations, leaders think that competency to manage diversity already exists when in fact they are nowhere close to achieving it. Their false assumption

Figure 1.3. Diversity Competency Model for Organizations

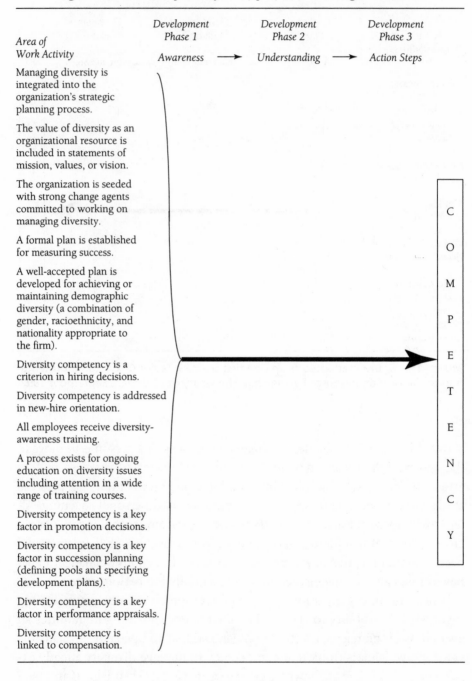

Area of Work Activity	Development Phase 1 Awareness →	Development Phase 2 Understanding →	Development Phase 3 Action Steps
Managing diversity is integrated into the organization's strategic planning process.			
The value of diversity as an organizational resource is included in statements of mission, values, or vision.			
The organization is seeded with strong change agents committed to working on managing diversity.			
A formal plan is established for measuring success.			
A well-accepted plan is developed for achieving or maintaining demographic diversity (a combination of gender, racioethnicity, and nationality appropriate to the firm).			
Diversity competency is a criterion in hiring decisions.			
Diversity competency is addressed in new-hire orientation.			
All employees receive diversity-awareness training.			
A process exists for ongoing education on diversity issues including attention in a wide range of training courses.			
Diversity competency is a key factor in promotion decisions.			
Diversity competency is a key factor in succession planning (defining pools and specifying development plans).			
Diversity competency is a key factor in performance appraisals.			
Diversity competency is linked to compensation.			

COMPETENCY

of readiness is based on a misunderstanding of the requirements of diversity competency that is often manifested as equating diversity competency with vigorous support of affirmative action and equal opportunity.

Once awareness has been created, the developmental need of the organization is for the knowledge that will help it to achieve the stated condition. For example, using item 3 of Figure 1.3, one common way to achieve change agent "seeding" is by forming diversity-change teams, such as steering committees or action teams, composed of representatives from various functions of the organization who invest heavily in accelerating their rate of learning about diversity and then actively take their knowledge back into the various parts of the organization that they represent. When used in this way, the models are potential tools for assessment and developmental planning.

LINKING THE DEFINITION OF DIVERSITY COMPETENCY TO THE CONTENT OF THE BOOK

In concluding this chapter, we want to address how our definition of diversity competency is related to the organization of the book. As mentioned in the preface, the organization of the book is loosely patterned into three main sections that coordinate with those of the theory book, *Cultural Diversity in Organizations* (Cox, 1993). Within each chapter, the content is intended to take you more or less sequentially through the three-step process of awareness, understanding, and action. Of course, there is a limit to how much "action" can be built into a book, so the third phase of the learning model often consists of an exercise that asks you to create a plan for action or to say how the knowledge gained in the readings and other material can be translated into behavior. Thus, each chapter typically ends with one or more activities that require the application of knowledge. We can illustrate the organization of the book with an example from Chapter Two. The introduction and Reading 2.1, "Distinguishing Managing Diversity from Affirmative Action," should raise your awareness that managing diversity is different from the more commonly understood concepts of equal opportunity and affirmative action. Activity 2.1 and Reading 2.2 are intended to deepen your understanding of the terms *diversity* and *managing diversity*, and Activity 2.2, which asks you to actually create a definition of diversity for a fictitious organization, allows you to actually *do* something that applies what you have learned.

The three phases of the learning model overlap with one another, and many of the items included here seem to simultaneously address more than one dimension. In recognition of this fact, we have not attempted to label each item as relating to awareness, understanding, or action; rather, we hope that working through the materials as a set will help you to fulfill all three requirements of developing competency.

Foundations for Competency

This first part of the book addresses two fundamental questions: (1) what is diversity? and (2) why and how are diversity and its management linked to organizational performance? We believe that a proper understanding of the answers to these two questions is critical to further learning and development about the topic of diversity in organizations. We therefore devote Part One of the book to helping to create this understanding.

The questions of what diversity is and why managing it is relevant to organizational effectiveness are addressed through a combination of short readings and exercises. In addition, we have included a short list of suggested films that can be used to promote learning on the two questions of focus.

After completing Part One, you should be able to: (1) explain to others how managing diversity is different from the traditional practice of equal opportunity and affirmative action, (2) understand why developing competency to manage diversity is critical for organizational survival and success as we approach the twenty-first century, and (3) assist your organization in creating a working definition of diversity and in designing initial awareness training for managing diversity.

2

The Meaning of Diversity

Today the term *diversity* is alternately reviled and revered, depending upon one's experience and interpretation of what the term means. For many, the term is a synonym for affirmative action or for groups that are protected from discrimination under U.S. civil rights legislation. However, we are among many scholars and consultants on the topic who present a much broader view of diversity. As noted in Chapter One, we define the term *diversity* as a mix of people of different socially relevant group identities working or living together in a defined social system. Although this definition fits demographic categories such as national origin, gender, race, and age that are covered under the U.S. civil rights laws, it also includes other group affiliations such as occupational specialization and organizational level.

We also find that the term *diversity* is often confused with organizational responses to this characteristic, such as *valuing diversity* and *managing diversity*. Valuing diversity is a philosophy about how diversity affects organizational outcomes that holds that the presence of diversity represents a distinct organizational resource that, properly leveraged, can bring a competitive advantage against organizations that either are culturally homogeneous or fail to successfully utilize their diversity. As previously noted, managing diversity consists of taking proactive steps to create and sustain an organizational climate in which the potential for diversity-related dynamics to hinder performance is minimized and the potential for diversity to enhance performance is maximized. Thus, managing diversity is about improving organizational performance by optimally utilizing every member's abilities and by leveraging diversity as an organizational resource.

The logic of the connections between diversity and organizational performance suggested in these definitions will be made clear through completion of the work outlined in Chapter Three, but first we present several learning vehicles designed to help solidify our understanding of the concept of diversity itself.

RAISING AWARENESS

We begin with an issue that members of organizations often struggle with when it comes to defining *managing diversity*, namely, differentiating it from the traditional work on equal opportunity by employers in the United States. Competency to manage diversity requires people to be clear about how these two domains of work compare. Reading 2.1 is intended to address this need. This reading can be used for personal study and as a basis for discussion for team learning.

Reading 2.1
DISTINGUISHING MANAGING DIVERSITY FROM AFFIRMATIVE ACTION

TAYLOR COX, JR.

One of the most difficult distinctions to get across in learning about diversity is the one between the term *managing diversity* and two more familiar terms, *equal employment opportunity* (EEO) and *affirmative action* (AA). For many people, these three concepts are synonymous, but there is ample reason to conclude that they are really quite distinct. One of the reasons for the confusion about the terms is the way they are treated in the media, as illustrated by the following excerpt from a recent article in *Business Week* magazine: "Call it affirmative action. Or minority outreach. Or perhaps you prefer 'managing diversity,' the newest, politically well-scrubbed name for policies aimed at bringing minorities into the business mainstream through preferential hiring and promotion" ("Race in the Workplace," *Business Week,* July 8, 1991).

The language featured in this article takes the term *managing diversity,* which is comprehensive in the types of human group identities it addresses and in the type of organizational activity it encompasses, and reduces it to only one dimension of difference (race) and only one organizational activity (AA). This choice of language was made despite the fact that even a casual referencing of the available literature of the time on managing diversity for practitioner audiences would have revealed the much broader definition that was commonly used by experts in the field (for example, Thomas, 1990; Copeland, 1988; Cox & Blake, 1991; Loden & Rosener, 1991).

The *Business Week* article further reduces AA, which was defined in the executive order that created it as "systematic steps to ensure that past discrimination is remedied and that further discrimination does not occur" (Werther & Davis, 1993, p. 105), to two actions: preferential hiring and promotion of minorities. A further reading of the article shows that even the attention paid to racioethnic minorities is further restricted to one group, Blacks. Finally, the message that managing diversity is merely a new name for AA is further reinforced in the article with the following statement: "To get past the emotional charge carried by affirmative action, some employers have embraced a new catch-phrase: managing diversity" (p. 58).

What is the effect of this use of language (which I would say represents a distortion of the established meaning of the concepts) on subsequent work on the topic of diversity? If diversity is defined as a new version of AA, then the ideological and motivational obstacles that have plagued AA in both research and practice will also be applied to diversity. For example, Kluegel and Smith (1988) have suggested that these obstacles include self-interest and belief in the "dominant ideology." *Self-interest* refers to the notion that people will tend to resist actions or policies that they think will result in a decline in their personal circumstances and support those that they think will have a positive impact on their personal circumstances. *Collective self-interest* refers to motivations based on how a policy or action is expected to affect a group with which one identifies.

The *dominant ideology* is a set of beliefs about human economic accomplishment that are ingrained in Euro-Western culture, namely, (1) that everyone has an opportunity to succeed economically; (2) that personal, not situational, attributes determine economic success and failure; and (3) that inequality of economic outcomes is justified because those outcomes inevitably represent inequality of effort or contribution. To a large extent the dominant ideology is the belief that social systems, like employing organizations, operate as meritocracies. When one believes that a meritocracy is in place, it seems logical for interventionist strategies related to diversity to be treated as a synonym for AA and for the same objections to automatically be applied to the newer work.

To adopt the language used by *Business Week* in the referenced article is to encourage a narrow agenda for research and practice focused on AA plans for Blacks. Although the study of AA plans for Blacks is important and legitimate, this language use is likely to unnecessarily constrain attention paid to the topic by scholars and management practitioners.

In order to counter the kind of distortion and misunderstanding in the meaning of terms that is indicated in the above quotation, we must be clearer in our writing and training work about the interrelationships and distinctions between EEO, AA, and *managing diversity*. EEO is a goal, AA is a tool or technology, and managing diversity is a process. Another distinction is that EEO and AA are both tied closely to legislation that addresses only a limited number of specific group identities such as gender, race, age, physical ability, and veteran status. Managing diversity, by contrast, is driven primarily by business trends and the quest of organizations to maximize economic performance and the fulfillment of their organizational mission. (See Reading 3.2, "Linkages Between Managing Diversity and Organizational Performance.")

When we compare the type of work being done today in organizations under the label of managing diversity (or some similar name), we discover that there are numerous other differences between this work and what has been traditionally done in organizations under the labels of EEO and AA. Table 2.1 summarizes the main differences.

TABLE 2.1. How Does Managing and Valuing Diversity (MVD) Differ from Traditional EEO and AA Practices?

	EEO and AA	MVD
Emphasizes postentry treatment issues such as the ability to realize one's full potential	No	Yes
Recognizes and emphasizes the impact of culture differences between groups on employee experiences	No	Yes
Recognizes the need for change in the organizational culture	No	Yes
Emphasizes the business's economic reasons for having and managing diversity	No	Yes
Approaches diversity as an opportunity more than as a problem to be solved	No	Yes
Acknowledges a broad range of group identities and identity effects on employment	No	Yes
Recognizes that managing diversity is a competency	No	Yes

Of all the differences indicated on Table 2.1, perhaps the three most important are:

1. The focus on an economic performance motive and the related treatment of diversity as an organizational resource
2. The change in the scope of the group identities addressed
3. The attention to organizational culture and the need for cultural change in order to manage diversity

Although legal and moral motives are still strong factors in organizational change work on diversity, the motive that is by far the most prominently cited in organizations active in this area is to improve organizational performance on the traditional goals of revenue growth, profitability, and maximization of resource utilization in pursuit of the organizational mission. This is a drastic change from AA work in the past.

Similarly, although the goal of equal opportunity is still central in managing-diversity work, attention is now being given to group identities that are not covered by civil rights legislation, such as sexual orientation and work specialization.

Finally, managing-diversity work, for the first time, places great emphasis on various intercultural dynamics, involving the culture of the organization, its various subunits, and the members who work in them. The attention paid to providing access to jobs for people who were traditionally discriminated against has been joined by attention to creation of an organizational culture in which people of different cultural backgrounds can work well together and where all can contribute to the goals of the organization and achieve to their full potential.

Although the viewpoint expressed in the *Business Week* article continues to be prevalent, a careful look at the work that is actually taking place in organizations today indicates that managing diversity is fundamentally different from the traditional EEO and AA programs in the past. The goal of equal opportunity remains central, and properly implemented AA continues to be a major tool in accomplishing that goal. But managing diversity is an ongoing process of organizational change and development directed toward creating a culture that meets the requirements of today's more complex and cosmopolitan workforce and marketplace.

Suggestions for the Use of Reading 2.1

This reading is included to provide information, provoke thought, and prompt discussion about the true meaning of managing diversity. It should be emphasized that the reading does not minimize the importance of AA and equal opportunity initiatives. We recommend consideration of the following discussion questions:

1. Why does the kind of distortion of meaning noted in the *Business Week* article occur? How much impact do you think this has on public opinion?

2. Many people who believe that the work on diversity is broader than AA and EEO will make the statement: "This is not about gender and race." Evaluate this statement. Is it a good or accurate way to express a valuing-diversity ideology? Why or why not?

3. What can organizations do to maintain the value placed in the past on AA and equal opportunity hiring and promotion efforts without reinforcing the view that they are the same thing as managing diversity?

CREATING UNDERSTANDING

We find that failure to create the proper understanding of how managing diversity relates to AA is a barrier to change in many companies. Another frequent barrier is illustrated by the experience of the former president of the Educational Testing Service (ETS), Gregory Anrig. He noted that whereas previous annual ETS conferences had roughly a 50-50 split on gender among attendees, the 1991 conference, whose theme was "gender equity," was composed of 70 percent women. His comment about this is telling: "If sex equity is viewed as a women's issue alone, we have a bigger problem than we thought" (*America,* November 23, 1991, p. 380). This quotation captures perfectly the barrier to change that is created when people view managing diversity and its goals as an activity that excludes them. We have found Activity 2.1 to be helpful in addressing this barrier.

Activity 2.1
MANAGING WORKPLACE DIVERSITY: WHOSE AGENDA?

You will recall that our definition of managing diversity refers to creating a certain "pro-diversity" organizational climate. The question occurs: Whose responsibility is it to do this? This exercise is designed to address this question.

Objectives
1. To achieve a better understanding of the meaning of diversity as a description of the people in a defined social system or systems
2. To assist in dispelling the myth that managing diversity is relevant only to minorities and women

Procedure
This activity is intended to be used in a facilitated group (six to twenty-five people are preferred but it can work with groups of up to forty-five). The facilitator should ask each person to answer questions 1–6 alone and without discussion with anyone. Then ask for volunteers to share their answers, and lead a discussion of their responses. Suggestions for debriefing follow the exercise.

Using gender as an exemplary dimension of diversity, respond to the following questions.

1. Who has gender identity?
   a. Women
   b. Men
   c. Both women and men
   d. Neither women nor men
   Explain your answer:

2. When research indicates that gender affects work experiences in an organization, in most cases this means that gender makes a difference for:
   a. Women but not men
   b. Men but not women
   c. Both women and men

d. Women or men depending on the specific research
Explain your answer:

3. To whom does the phrase "different gender" apply in the typical work setting?
   a. Women
   b. Men
   c. Both women and men
   d. Neither women nor men
   Explain your answer:

4. If all the White males in power positions (or all members of the dominant cultural group, however they are defined) were suddenly free of prejudices, stereotypes, and every other insensitivity to difference, would there still be a need for employee development work on managing and valuing diversity?
   a. Yes
   b. No
   Explain your answer:

5. When performance barriers related to gender are present, or perceived to be present, in an organization, addressing them should primarily be the concern of:
   a. Men
   b. Women
   c. It depends on which gender is experiencing the barriers
   Explain your answer:

6. When work groups that have traditionally been predominantly male become more gender-diverse, it often affects employee commitment (including such things as absence rates and intent to stay) among:
   a. Women
   b. Men
   c. Both women and men
   Explain your answer:

Suggestions for the Use of Activity 2.1

Many people initially respond from the point of view that only women have gender identity or are affected by gender issues and dynamics. Sometimes it is useful to ask, for example, how many answered "a" to question 1. However, when they are confronted with these specific questions, most people will immediately see that we all have gender and that any gender issues in a work group necessarily have an effect on both men and women. It then becomes clear that addressing gender-related barriers to organizational performance is everyone's business. Question 4 makes the important point that it is not just members of the dominant social-cultural group who need to learn how to manage diversity in work groups. This exercise can be followed by Reading 2.2, which further illustrates the point that even when we focus our attention on the core identities of gender and race, the effects of diversity in work groups are not limited to women and racioethnic minorities. Note also that according to the particular research of Reading 2.2, the answer to item 6 in Activity 2.1 is "c" (both women and men), although the specific effects differ with men becoming less attached and women more attached.

Reading 2.2
IS WHAT'S GOOD FOR THE GOOSE
ALSO GOOD FOR THE GANDER?
On Being White and Male in a Diverse Workforce

ELLEN A. FAGENSON

The number of women and minorities in the workforce continues to increase dramatically—matched, perhaps, only by the ink devoted to them in the press. Much has been written about the benefits organizations will gain from a more diverse labor force: better decision making and a boost in creativity. While hard to believe, almost no attention has been paid to the impact this change is having on whites and men. How do they feel about this workforce trend? Do they think of it as a blessing or a bane to their existence?

Authors Anne Tsui and Terri Egan, both of the University of California at Irvine, and Charles O'Reilly III, of the University of California at Berkeley, looked into this matter. While the authors were most interested in white men's reaction to diversity, they also were interested in diversity's effect on individuals' attachment to their organizations in general.

The study took place at a state agency and two Fortune 100 companies. The authors surveyed 151 groups comprised of 1,705 supervisory and non-supervisory workers employed in the lowest operating units of their firms. Employees indicated their sex, age, race, level of education, and tenure in the organization on a confidential questionnaire. To gain a sense of employees' attachment to their firms, survey respondents were asked to report the number of times they had been absent during the past year, their intentions to stay with the company, and the extent of their commitment to the firm.

After controlling for factors that could unintentionally affect individuals' attachment to their firms, the authors found that working with individuals

Source: This reading is taken from *The Academy of Management Executive,* vol. 7, no. 4, 1993, pp. 80–81. Used by permission of the publisher. The original research on which this research translation is based is taken from "Being Different: Relational Demography and Organizational Attachment," by Anne Tsui, Terri Egan, and Charles O'Reilly III, *Administrative Science Quarterly, 37,* 1992, 549–579.

who differed in age, sex, or race negatively affected employees' attachment to their organizations. The greater the diversity, the more detached they were. Working in a unit with individuals who differed in education and company tenure had no effect on individuals' attachment to their firms.

Differences in race were found to have the greatest impact. The more minorities in a unit, the less commitment to their companies was expressed by whites. Whites working in units with no minorities were the most attached to their organizations. Interestingly, minorities' attitudes toward their companies were not influenced by the number of whites in their work units.

Employees' attachment to their companies was also greatly affected by the proportion of men and women in their work units. The more women there were, the more men indicated detachment from their organizations. Women had the opposite reaction. The greater the number of men on their teams, the more committed they were to the organization.

The authors offered some explanations for these unexpected findings. Women and minorities are less powerful and lower in social status than men and whites. Consequently, for men and whites, working in a diverse environment might equate to working in a lower-status environment. Alternatively, white men may be forced to curb their language and behavior in a diverse workplace. "Off-color" remarks and locker room antics may, at the very least, not be tolerated in a coed or racially mixed group. At worst, they may be construed as sexual harassment or discriminatory behavior.

Contact among people with different backgrounds is supposed to lead to better opinions about one another and a more committed workforce—not the opposite, as this study shows. The findings of this study contradict what many predicted would happen when men and women, white and minorities, joined together in the workplace. The authors do not recommend that managers cater to any of the groups in the study. Rather, they simply ask that managers realize that workforce diversity may create a mixture of responses, depending upon which people are being asked to expand their horizons.

Suggestions for the Use of Reading 2.2

This short reading raises some very provocative issues. An important discussion question is: Why do White men, as a group, show lower attendance and less intention to stay in situations with increased representation of women and racioethnic minorities? It is important to note that this research addresses situations that have "unmanaged" diversity. This is useful to keep in mind to avoid interpreting the research to mean that changing the demographics in the workforce inevitably means simply trading the work happiness of one group for that of another. The dissatisfaction that sometimes occurs in the gender or racial majority group when demographics are changing is another reason for proactively managing diversity.

TAKING ACTION

We hope that the previous material has given you a better understanding of the meaning of diversity and why managing diversity is relevant to you. We now want to shift from the cognitive or thinking level to the behavioral, "doing" level of learning. Activity 2.2 addresses one of the first and most critical tasks people face when they become involved in organizational change efforts for managing diversity, namely, creating an operational definition of diversity for use in their organization.

●●●

Activity 2.2
DEFINING DIVERSITY

Objectives
1. To promote additional discussion about the meaning of diversity
2. To provide experience with the task of defining diversity

Procedure
Assume that you are a member of an organizational change team working on diversity at XYZ Company. Thus far four approaches to defining the term *diversity* have been proposed:

1. *Diversity* means any difference between people.

2. *Diversity* means differences related to social or cultural groups. We define such groups broadly to include gender, race, class, education, religion, sexual orientation, physical and mental ability, nationality, ethnicity, work department, job level, and age, among other differences.

3. *Diversity* means differences related to social or cultural groups; although there are many dimensions for defining these groups, we will focus our initial efforts on _____ . (Include a short list of group identities thought to have the highest impact in this specific organization.)

4. Diversity means differences of gender and race or ethnic group.

After reading these definitions and the following data on the XYZ Company, proceed to the tasks listed below.

Data on the XYZ Company
- It is a consumer-products firm.
- It has over twenty thousand employees worldwide.
- The initial focus of its change effort is the United States and Europe.
- The firm has 40 percent women and 60 percent men.
- The firm is 70 percent white, 15 percent Latino, 10 percent African American, and 5 percent Asian; the percentage of gays and lesbians is unknown; and the percentage of people with disabilities is unknown but is thought to be less than 1 percent.

- The breakdown of U.S.-based employees on national origin is 95 percent American and 5 percent people from other countries.
- The global workforce distribution is 80 percent American and 20 percent European.
- Internal data on specific diversity issues are unavailable at this time.

The first set of tasks is for people working alone and not as part of a group. The second set of tasks is for groups.

Tasks for Individuals

1. Working alone, determine which definition you personally favor for adoption or how you would proceed to determine your preferred definition. Create your own definition if you don't like those in the list above.

2. Make a list of the pros and cons of the various approaches, and then use it to write a short explanation of why you favor the definition chosen in step 1. This could be in the form of a memo to your supervisor. The memo could then be given to your supervisor (or some other knowledgeable person) for feedback.

Tasks for Groups

1. Working alone, determine which definition you personally favor for adoption or how you would proceed to determine your preferred definition. Create your own definition if you don't like those in the list above.

2. Working in groups with an assigned facilitator, discuss the pros and cons of the various approaches favored by members of your group. Try to arrive at a consensus definition to present to the senior management team of XYZ as the definition to be adopted during the first phase of the change process in your organization. Please note that even if you have an easy consensus on a definition in your discussion team, it will still be useful to discuss the pros and cons. For example, many teams immediately favor the first definition but run into trouble later when it is necessary to operationalize this definition.

Suggestions for the Use of Activity 2.2

Defining the term *diversity* sounds simple, but most groups find that it is difficult to do in practice. The specification of pros and cons comes easily; for example, a narrow definition may lead to members of certain groups' feeling that they are being left out, too much breadth can make the work hard to operationalize, backlash may occur if there is too much focus on gender and race, and so on. What is more difficult is to weigh these competing concerns and produce a result that is acceptable to all members of the team. The activity provides an opportunity for you to consider your own concerns about defining diversity as well as to prepare yourself for responding to the concerns and preferences of others in your organization.

This is a very realistic exercise. Many change teams are asked to do exactly what is requested here. If the activity is used with a group, the facilitator's main job is to bring out the pros and cons and to help the group think through the implications of each choice.

3
●●●

Managing Diversity
as a Business Strategy

The rationale for managing diversity includes moral and ethical reasons such as fairness and upholding the dignity of every person. It also encompasses legal reasons such as honoring civil rights laws, which are well established in the United States and becoming more common in other places around the world (for example, there is now an equal opportunity law for gender in Japan and laws making sexual harassment illegal in at least eight European countries). These motives rightly focus attention on the responsibility of employers to operate within the moral and legal norms of their environments. Despite these important motives, we find that in many organizations the rationale that gets the greatest positive response is that managing diversity is necessary in order to leverage an important, but underutilized, resource.

Accordingly, this chapter focuses on developing competency by understanding how managing diversity can be used as a business strategy in much the same way that competencies such as Total Quality Management, reengineering, and other such broad-scale efforts have been used.

The chapter contains two readings. Reading 3.1 provides an overview of the relationship between diversity and organizational performance. This "awareness-raising" reading is followed by a longer one (Reading 3.2), which explains in more depth some of the linkages that are outlined in the first reading. Reading 3.2 is intended to take you to the understanding level of the competency model. The chapter concludes with an activity that asks you to apply the ideas and insights gained from the readings to create a presentation that explains how and why managing diversity should be a central part of the business strategy of organizations.

RAISING AWARENESS

Reading 3.2 seeks to create awareness by making specific the logic for the claim that effectiveness in managing diversity is critical for organizations that wish to maximize their performance.

Reading 3.1
EFFECTS OF DIVERSITY ON
ORGANIZATIONAL EFFECTIVENESS
A Conceptual Framework

TAYLOR COX, JR.

The Interactional Model of Cultural Diversity (IMCD), developed by Cox (1993), is shown in Figure 3.1. This model brings together learnings from a wide spectrum of previous work in psychology (for example, Mischel, 1977; Triandis, 1976; Wong-Rieger & Quintana, 1987), sociology (Kanter, 1977; Rice, 1969; Tajfel, 1978), anthropology (Asante & Asante, 1985; Berry, 1983; Hall, 1976), and organizational behavior (Alderfer & Smith, 1982; Ashforth & Mael, 1989; Bell, 1990; Chatman, 1989; Cox & Nkomo, 1990, 1992; Jones, 1986; Nkomo, 1992; Pettigrew & Martin, 1987; Tung, 1988a, 1988b). The framework suggests that a variety of phenomena related to differences in the group identities of workers combine to create potent effects on their career experiences, and that diversity also has direct effects on certain performance measures or work outcomes.

Specifically, the model in Figure 3.1 posits that four individual-level factors (personal identity structures, prejudice, stereotyping, and personality type), three intergroup factors (cultural differences, ethnocentrism, and intergroup conflict), and four organizational-context factors (organizational culture and acculturation processes, structural integration, informal integration, and human resource systems, which may contain institutional bias) collectively define the diversity climate of an organization.

The diversity climate may influence individual career experiences and outcomes in organizations in two ways. First, the climate can affect how people *feel* about their work and their employer. Thus, in many organizations, employee morale and satisfaction are related to identity groups such as gender, racioethnicity, and so on. Second, the actual *achievement* of individuals as measured by such things as job performance ratings may be related to group identities in some organizations. These individual outcomes, in turn, have an impact on a series of first-order organizational-effectiveness measures such as work quality, productivity, absenteeism, and turnover. For

Figure 3.1. Interactional Model of Cultural Diversity

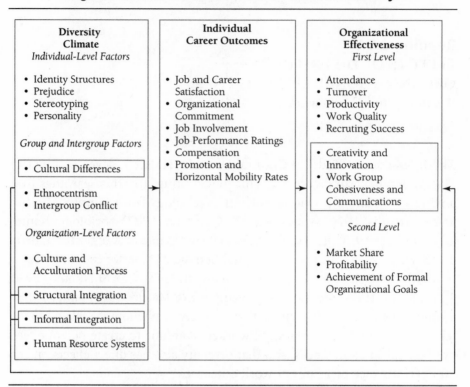

Source: Adapted with permission from Figure 1.1 of Taylor Cox, Jr., *Cultural Diversity in Organizations* (San Francisco: Berrett-Koehler, 1993), p. 7.

profit-making organizations, these first-order measures ultimately translate into second-order results such as profitability and market share. In nonprofit organizations, individual contribution is still crucial in determining the extent to which organizational goals will be achieved.

In addition to these indirect effects of the diversity climate, certain aspects of the diversity climate are thought to directly affect organizational performance. Specifically, the amount of diversity in both the formal and informal structures of organizations will affect factors such as creativity, problem solving, and intraorganizational communication.

Cox (1993) argues that the basic relationships depicted in the IMCD are relevant across many dimensions of group identification. As one example, diversity based on gender, race, and nationality, when it is properly lever-aged, will add value to problem solving, creativity, and innovation in work groups in much the same way that diversity of work function or organiza-tional tenure does. In a second example, factors such as prejudice, stereo-typing, miscommunication, and intergroup conflict, which have been observed to lead to differences in career outcomes based on differences in gender, race, or nationality, will *sometimes* operate in a similar manner based on other differences such as work specialization or organizational level (Cox & Finley, 1995).

Suggestions for the Use of Reading 3.1

This brief reading gives an overview of the theoretical framework contained in the theory book, *Cultural Diversity in Organizations* (Cox, 1993). You will recall that the current book is an extension of the earlier work. We suggest that the theory book be used, if possible, as a source of more specifics on the framework shown here in Figure 3.1. However, if this is not possible, the definitions given below will assist you in understanding it.

Diversity-Climate Terms

Acculturation: the process of resolving differences of culture (see Chapter Eight).

Culture: the values, norms, and ways of thinking that distinguish one group of people from another (see Chapters Seven and Eight).

Ethnocentrism: the tendency to view members of one's own group as the center of the universe, to interpret other social groups (out-groups) from the perspective of one's own group, and to evaluate the beliefs, behaviors, and values of one's own group somewhat more positively than those of out-groups.

Human resource systems: all systems that govern the employment of peo-ple, such as recruiting, training and development, promotion, and com-pensation. The design of these systems tends to institutionalize certain cultural values and norms.

Identity structure: the mix of group identities that are present in the orga-nization and the strength of an individual's association with specific iden-tities (for example, although all people have a gender identity, they vary greatly in the extent to which this identity is important to them in their own self-definition).

Informal integration: the effect of diversity (for example, differences in group identity) on informal networks for socialization and communication and on informal processes of development and sponsorship (see Chapter Nine).

Intergroup conflict: a form of interpersonal conflict that has social (group-based) and not just personal dynamics.

Personality: people's predispositions to respond to diversity in a certain way (for example, people differ in their propensity to trust others and in their tolerance of ambiguous situations).

Prejudice and stereotyping: see Chapters Five and Six.

Structural integration: the level of culture-group heterogeneity in the membership and the power elite of organizations; also, the power dynamics among people of different identity groups.

CREATING UNDERSTANDING

Study and discussion of the relationships shown in Figure 3.1 should provide a basic logic for the reasons that managing diversity has an impact on organizational behavior and performance. These relationships are addressed in more depth in Reading 3.2.

Reading 3.2
LINKAGES BETWEEN MANAGING DIVERSITY AND ORGANIZATIONAL PERFORMANCE

TAYLOR COX, JR.

During the last six years, my colleagues and I have assisted more than twenty organizations with organizational change work related to managing diversity. During these experiences, the most frequently asked question has been: Why is managing diversity relevant to our organizational success? My answer to this question, sometimes referred to as "the business case" for managing diversity, is the subject of this reading. My experience is that in most companies there is little chance of getting a genuine commitment by senior management to change their efforts concerning diversity unless they are convinced that investing in managing diversity is potentially a significant contributor to organizational performance.

Managing Diversity as an Economic Performance Issue

In profit-making organizations, performance is optimized by maximizing the difference between revenues and costs. This same goal exists in many nonprofit organizations, except that the result is called surplus instead of profits. The question, therefore, is: How is workforce diversity and its management related to revenues, costs, or both? Let's begin by considering revenues. First, I will put forth the premise that effective marketing strategies, problem solving, creativity, and innovation are each important factors in revenue enhancement. If you can accept this premise, then the research on the effect of work-team diversity on these processes should be of great interest.

Effective Marketing Strategy

An important consequence of the rising globalization of business is that consumer markets are increasingly composed of people from diverse nationality,

---

Source: This reading is adapted from Chapters Two and Three of Taylor Cox, Jr., *Cultural Diversity in Organizations* (San Francisco: Berrett-Koehler, 1993). Certain material is reprinted here by permission of the publisher.

racioethnic, and gender groups. An automobile manufacturer in Japan cannot afford to ignore the fact that nearly half of all new-car buyers in the United States are now women. This is true regardless of the gender composition of car buyers in Japan. Likewise, no reasonable person in the consumer-goods industry can afford to ignore the fact that roughly a quarter of the world's population is Chinese and immigration in the United States from mostly Asian and Latin American countries is occurring at the rate of more than a million people per year. In the United States, Asians, Blacks, and Hispanics now collectively represent nearly $500 billion annually in consumer spending. Because research on consumer behavior has consistently shown that sociocultural identities affect buying behavior, marketing success will depend, to some degree, on the ability of companies to understand and respond effectively to the cultural nuances of the diverse marketplace.

Selling goods and services in the increasingly diverse marketplace should be facilitated by a well-utilized, diverse workforce in several ways. First, there is a public relations value in being identified as managing diversity well. Just as people, especially those who identify with a nonmajority culture, may prefer to work for companies that are recognized for valuing diversity, they may also prefer to buy from such organizations. This line of thinking is supported by a recent study of stock-price responses to publicity that reflected either positively or negatively on a firm's ability to manage diversity. The authors found that announcements of awards for exemplary efforts resulted in significant positive changes in stock prices while announcements of discrimination suits resulted in significant negative changes in stock prices. They concluded that "high quality affirmative action programs contribute to sustaining a competitive advantage and are valued in the marketplace" (Wright, Ferris, Hiller, & Kroll, 1995, p. 283).

A second reason is that marketing efforts may gain from the insights of employees from various cultural backgrounds who can assist organizations in understanding cultural effects on buying decisions and in mapping strategies to respond to them. Gannett Co., Avon Products, CIGNA Corporation, and Levi Strauss and Company are among the organizations that have been proactive in taking advantage of this benefit of diversity (Cox & Blake, 1991; Business Week, August 1, 1994, pp. 46–52; HR Magazine, February 1994, pp. 79–86).

Problem Solving

Revenue increases related to diversity in work groups can also occur through improved problem solving and decision making. Diverse groups have a broader and richer base of experience from which to approach a problem. In addition, critical analysis in decision-making groups is enhanced by member diversity (Nemeth, 1985). In a series of research studies, Charlene Nemeth found that the level of critical analysis of decision issues and alternatives was higher in groups that were subjected to minority views than in those that were not. The presence of minority views improved the quality of the decision-making process regardless of whether or not the minority view ultimately prevailed. Among the specific differences in problem-solving processes she found were: (1) a larger number of alternatives that were considered and (2) a more thorough examination of the assumptions and implications of alternative scenarios. Although Nemeth was studying the effects of minority opinions and not group identity per se, the fact that members of minority identity often hold different worldviews from majority-group members makes this research relevant to diversity as it is typically defined in managing-diversity work.

The prospective benefits of diversity in problem solving do not necessarily happen by simply mixing people together who are culturally different. Some research also suggests that the effect of diversity on work outcomes depends greatly on the extent to which the diversity is proactively managed. In one of the classic studies of this type, Harry Triandis and his colleagues compared the problem-solving scores of homogeneous groups with those of two types of more diverse groups: diverse with training and diverse without training. They found that the diverse groups that were not trained in the existence and implications of their differences actually produced lower problem-solving scores than the homogeneous groups, whereas the diverse groups that were trained produced scores that averaged six times higher than the homogeneous groups (Triandis, Hall, & Ewen, 1965). A similar result was found in more recent research on ethnically and nationally diverse groups as reported by researcher Nancy Adler of McGill University (1986, p. 111), who summarizes her analysis of the research this way: "Highly productive and less productive [diverse] teams differ in how they manage their diversity. . . . When well managed, diversity becomes a productive resource to the team. When ignored, diversity causes process problems that diminish the team's productivity."

Creativity and Innovation

Creativity and innovation are useful for enhancement of virtually all organizational activities. Sales promotion techniques, advertising, product design, and quality improvement are examples of organizational activities for which creativity and innovation are especially vital. Therefore, evidence suggesting that diversity in work teams promotes creativity and innovation is highly relevant to the goal of increasing organizational revenue.

In her book *The Change Masters* (1983), Rosabeth Moss Kanter notes that highly innovative companies have done a better job of eradicating racism, sexism, and classism; tend to have workforces that are more race-and gender-diverse, and take deliberate steps to create heterogeneous work teams with the objective of bringing in different points of view to bear on problems. A second example is found in research on educational institutions that shows that the most innovative schools are also the most tolerant of diversity (Siegel & Kaemmerer, 1978).

The research on the role of diversity in creativity and innovation has addressed a variety of different dimensions of difference. In one of the more recent studies, my colleagues and I tested the proposition that racioethnically diverse teams would outperform all-Anglo teams in a creativity task. The quantity and quality of the ideas generated during a brainstorming task from diverse groups of Asians, Blacks, Anglos, and Hispanics were compared to the ideas generated by homogeneous groups of Anglos. No significant differences were found in the quantity of ideas, but the ideas produced by the ethnically diverse groups were rated an average of 11 percent higher than those of the homogeneous groups on both feasibility of implementation and overall effectiveness. Our study was particularly relevant to the impact of diversity on marketing success because the task that the groups performed, increasing tourism in the United States, was directly related to marketing (McLeod, Lobel, & Cox, 1996).

Diversity and Organizational Costs

While the evidence is mounting that diversity, when it is effectively managed, can potentially enhance revenues, the relationship between managing diversity and organizational costs is even clearer. This relationship is a two-edged sword. On the one hand, the advantages of diversity for problem solving and creativity can help organizations to make better decisions, develop better technologies, and improve processes, all of which should lead to higher quality and lower costs. On the other hand, when organizations have a low capacity to manage diversity, increasing diversity in work teams can lead to higher cost structures. The reasons for this often-overlooked aspect of workforce diversity are summarized below. The linkages between managing diversity and organizational costs are as follows:

- Employee absenteeism and turnover
- Barriers to contribution due to unresolved intergroup dynamics
- Harassment behavior
- Discrimination suits
- Reduced efficiency of communications

Employee Absenteeism and Turnover

Research on work groups that have diversity but have done nothing to proactively manage it has often shown that employee absenteeism, employee turnover, or both are higher for members of gender or racial minority groups, and that both of these cost factors tend to increase when the composition of work groups is changing toward more diversity. For example, in one study of two Fortune 100 companies, researchers found that working with individuals who differ in age, sex, or race negatively affected employees' attachment to their organization. Attachment was measured by absence rates, intention to stay with the employer, and expressed level of commitment to the organization. One of the interesting aspects of this study is that these effects were specifically found among White men as opposed to women or non-White men (for a brief review of this study, see Reading 2.2.). Research also indicates that managing-diversity actions such as providing more flexible work schedules and child care support can significantly reduce both absenteeism and turnover in diverse work groups (see Cox & Blake, 1991).

This research indicates that *organizations that are more diverse than competitors but fail to effectively manage diversity could be at a cost disadvantage compared to those that either are less diverse or manage it better.*

Intergroup Barriers to Contribution

When organizations that are culturally homogeneous become more diverse, a variety of intergroup dynamics will become potential obstacles to people working together as a team. The most obvious of these barriers are sexism and racism or other forms of identity-based prejudice and discrimination. Too often, managers limit their attention in this area to the possibility of discrimination in hiring and promotion, ignoring a wide range of other effects. For example, my own research from consulting in companies indicates that a significant percentage of employees (as high as 50 percent or more) believe that gender and race affect a person's ability to be accepted by peers and subordinates in leadership roles, that oversensitivity to minority status among women and non-White men sometimes leads to incorrect perceptions about adverse effects, and that a large percentage of women (as high as 75 percent in some companies) are resentful of what they believe to be gender discrimination in compensation administration (a claim that is sometimes supported by real data and sometimes not).

A major role of managers is to remove obstacles to performance, and discrimination is one such obstacle. Managers need to acquire a more thorough and sophisticated understanding of these effects in order to be competent to supervise diverse work groups.

Many other intergroup dynamics can lower productivity and thus increase costs in diverse groups. One of the most prevalent is lack of cooperation and poor communication among people of different work specializations and organizational levels. For example, from his study of scientists and engineers in a Fortune 500 company, John Barnett concludes that engineers tended to dominate the culture and that scientists were viewed as being members of an out-group or, at the very least, as being from a different culture. He further states not only that the two groups were different, but also that these unmanaged differences created work-related barriers between them (Barnett, 1994). When these intergroup dynamics are not well understood and managed, they will tend to lower productivity and thus increase costs.

Harassment Behavior

In a recent class at the University of Michigan, I asked my students to write a biographical essay related to diversity in the workplace. Four of thirty-five students (11 percent) wrote about sexual harassment. Three of the four, including one male, referred to harassment at their former places of work that had contributed to, or led directly to, their resignations. How does this behavior affect the cost structures of organizations? In a recent study by the federal government, researchers estimated the cost of sexual harassment alone (harassment related to factors such as age, racioethnicity, and sexual orientation also occurs) to be $133 million per year, as a result of harassment-related turnover, absenteeism, and lost productivity. Studies in private sector firms suggest that the typical Fortune 500 firm experiences a cost of about $6 million (Sandroff, 1988). The cost for smaller firms may be proportionately larger because they are less likely to have formal training and other prevention processes.

Discrimination Suits

Another cost factor related to how well a firm manages diversity is the avoidance of successful lawsuits based on alleged violations of civil rights laws. Consider these examples. In 1988, Honda Motor Co. settled a discrimination complaint by Blacks and women in its U.S. operations: cost, $6 million. In 1991, a jury found in favor of a woman suing Texaco for sex discrimination: cost, $20 million. In 1997, the same company settled a much-publicized racial discrimination suit for more than $176 million. In 1992, Shoney's agreed to compensate victims of racial discrimination among employees: cost, $105 million.

These examples all deal with alleged gender and race discrimination, but alleged age bias is also generating a significant number of lawsuits (*Wall Street Journal*, June 13, 1994, p. A-1). Although some legal costs associated with discrimination complaints are inevitable in a diverse society that has strong legal protections against such practices, investing in education, systems analysis, and other organizational efforts aimed toward reducing any factual basis for complaints seems more than prudent.

Reduced Efficiency of Communications

One final way that the failure to manage cultural diversity well can accelerate costs is in slower or less effective communications. A female supervisor raises a concern with her older, male colleague and instead of the support, empathy, and listening that she is seeking, she gets a terse lecture on how she should handle the situation. An Asian man reports that he experiences the communication norms in team meetings as outright rudeness, and as a result he withdraws into silence. A manager of chemists reports that cross-functional cooperation between his group and the engineers in the company is suffering because they "just don't speak the same language." A Black, female participant in a recent workshop reported how offended she was that her Japanese coworker would not make eye contact with her in meetings (not realizing that this was a sign of respect). These are familiar examples of how intergroup differences can contribute to communication breakdowns. Research indicates that members of different cultural groups often have significant differences in language and in styles of communication (Tannen, 1994; Kochman, 1981; Hall, 1976). When diversity in work groups is not well managed, these differences present added barriers to understanding and make building trust and rapport more difficult.

Conclusion

The presence of diversity in organizations can make certain aspects of group functioning more problematic. Misunderstandings may increase, conflict and anxiety may rise, and members may feel less comfortable with membership in the group. These effects may combine to make decision making more difficult and time-consuming. In certain respects, then, culturally diverse work groups are more difficult to manage effectively than culturally homogeneous ones. Moreover, diversity inevitably introduces the task of eliminating the human tendency toward in-group bias in interpersonal relations in organizations, as well as the tendency for such biases to become institutionalized in organizations with a history of dominance by one identity group over an extended period of time. At the same time, there is considerable evidence that diversity holds the potential to be a significant value-added resource in organizational performance if its benefits can be fully realized by skillful management.

Thus, the challenge for leaders of organizations with diverse workforces is to manage in such a way as to maximize the potential benefits of diversity while minimizing its potential disadvantages. As suggested above, the performance payoff for meeting the challenge can be substantial.

TAKING ACTION

We have found that understanding the business reasons for managing diversity, as addressed in Readings 3.1 and 3.2, is a major help in overcoming resistance to change efforts. We also have found that resistance to launching organizational change efforts related to diversity often occurs because these efforts are viewed as just another isolated initiative in a seemingly endless succession of "hot" intervention strategies for making organizations more competitive. We believe that this form of resistance is based on very legitimate concerns, especially insofar as they focus on the need to integrate various intervention strategies and to ensure that they all are linked to the overall business strategy of the organization.

Activity 3.1 has been designed to help you to prepare to respond to these concerns. This activity allows you to move to the third stage of the competency model by applying knowledge gained from the readings to create a presentation that shows how managing diversity can be used as a business strategy.

Activity 3.1
LINKAGES BETWEEN MANAGING DIVERSITY AND OTHER STRATEGIC PROCESSES AND BUSINESS TRENDS

Objectives
1. To understand how and why managing diversity is an integral part of other key strategic initiatives
2. To understand why managing diversity is a reasonable approach for responding effectively to a number of major trends affecting organizations
3. To aid in developing competency in aligning managing diversity with other strategic issues of organizations

Procedure
If you are working with a group, either task 1 or task 2 may be used. If not, then task 3 is suggested. Study Figure 3.2 and then do either task 1, 2, or 3.

Task 1
Divide the group into teams of four to five people each and have each team work up a rationale as to why diversity is an integral part of one of the other key processes or business issues shown in Figure 3.2. Each team should prepare a presentation that could be given as part of a workshop on "the business case" for managing diversity.

Task 2
Ask the full group to identify ways in which diversity might be related to the processes and critical competitive issues shown in Figure 3.2. If an expert facilitator is present, he or she will add to the responses and give feedback on the presentations. If not, assign someone the role of facilitator and have this person record the team's work output.

Task 3
If you are working alone, imagine that you have been asked to prepare a presentation for senior management on how and why managing diversity is linked to each of the four key processes and business trends shown in Figure 3.2. When your presentation is completed, find one or more people for a "dry run" presentation. Get feedback from this audience and refine your presentation accordingly.

Figure 3.2. Business Trends That Make
Managing Diversity an Economic Imperative

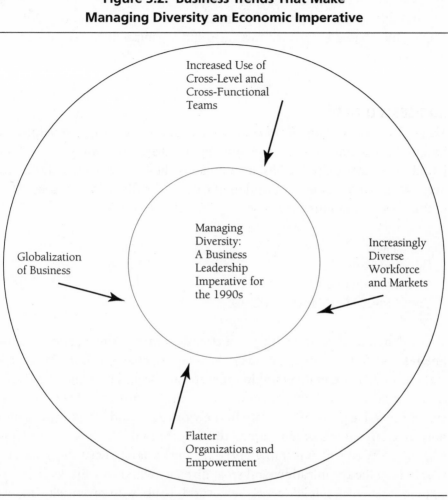

Increased Use of
Cross-Level and
Cross-Functional
Teams

Globalization
of Business

Managing
Diversity:
A Business
Leadership
Imperative for
the 1990s

Increasingly
Diverse
Workforce
and Markets

Flatter
Organizations and
Empowerment

Suggestions for the Use of Activity 3.1

Experienced teachers and trainers will not have trouble processing this activity. The goal is to have people think through and make explicit the ways
in which managing diversity and other change processes are interdependent.
The area that usually gives the most trouble is that of flatter organizations and
empowerment. One way to link this with managing diversity is to understand
that without slack in human resources, every member must be fully utilized.
The absence of slack means that productivity losses related to a failure to effectively manage diversity may threaten organizational survival. Another point

to make here is that empowerment cannot be accomplished until issues of cultural difference and power dynamics related to group identity (for example, those based on gender, race, age, and organizational level) are taken into account.

SUGGESTED FILMS

Many films are available from commercial vendors that may be helpful in facilitating learning on the topics presented in Part One. Two that we have found to be particularly helpful in addressing these issues will be discussed here. We provide a brief description of each of the films, followed by a list of discussion questions they raise.

The Land of "O"s
Goodmeasure, Inc.
One Memorial Drive
Cambridge, Massachusetts 02142

This video links diversity with productivity, competitiveness, and bottom-line results. Today's organizations must adapt to changing conditions, including an increase in diversity, in order to survive and function effectively. Learning how to deal with diversity helps in this process. The video discusses several aspects of diversity in the workplace and offers insight into how diversity allows organizations to compete to be the best. It explains what diversity is, why it is important to the organization, what steps one can take to help the organization, and what diversity will do for individuals, including White males. It addresses "real-world" issues with practicality, and its solution-oriented approach shows how to take a diverse workforce and leverage its inherent differences to the advantage of both the organization and the individual. Additionally, it illustrates that merely having representative numbers of people of different cultures in an organization does not mean that diversity is being effectively managed.

Discussion Questions

1. Why is it important to an organization to have a diverse workforce?
2. Is it important to be concerned about where people of diverse backgrounds are placed in the organization? If so, why? If not, why not?

3. Is there more to managing diversity than measuring the amount of diversity among employees, customers, suppliers, and others?

4. With the decrease in management positions, is it realistic to expect an organization and the people in it to invest in the effective management of diversity? Why or why not?

The Cost of Intolerance
Bureau of National Affairs, Inc.
9439 Key West Avenue
Rockville, Maryland 20850-3396
800-233-6067

This film offers a series of real-life vignettes in which insensitivity to diversity issues by customer contact personnel leads to lost sales. The publisher of the film confirms that each vignette is based on something that actually happened to one of its clients, and most of the vignettes give an actual dollar amount of lost sales that resulted directly from customers being offended by incompetence related to diversity. A variety of group identities are illustrated. A limitation of the film is that it may be perceived as irrelevant by firms that do not interact directly with the end users of their products, because all of the cases involve service companies. On the other hand, the concept of "customer" is now widely understood to include people throughout the chain of distribution and even people internal to a firm; thus this objection is readily overcome with most audiences.

Discussion Questions

1. Who are the people affected by the lack of tolerance for and skill at managing diversity?

2. How is the organization affected?

3. Are real costs associated with the inability to manage diversity effectively? If so, what are they?

4. In your opinion, who is responsible for the effective management of diversity?

5. In your opinion, who should be held accountable for the lack of effective management of diversity?

Developing Individual Competency

The model for competency set forth in Chapter One consisted of working through a three-stage process of awareness, understanding, and action on a continuous basis. This part of the book contains aids for using the process at the individual level. It begins with a chapter on understanding group identities. Because the identification of people with social-cultural groups is a core concept in our approach to diversity, Chapter Four will serve as a foundation for the remaining three chapters in Part Two. Chapters Five through Seven will then address three pervasive and powerful phenomena that are associated with group identification: stereotyping, prejudice, and cultural differences.

Throughout Part Two, we will address various task dimensions that were included in Figure 1.2. For example, Case 4.1 and Activity 7.2 deal, respectively, with performance feedback and communications. In addition, Chapters Five through Seven each conclude with an activity that asks participants to apply learnings from that chapter to the full list of work tasks shown in Figure 1.2. Within each chapter, we have attempted to reinforce our definition of diversity competency by designing the material to move sequentially from building awareness to creating understanding and, finally, to more action-oriented activities.

After completing Part Two, you should feel more competent to:

1. Identify situations in your own work experience in which stereotyping, prejudice, or cultural differences may be affecting events, decisions, or work-related problems and their solutions

2. Identify ways in which you can change your behavior in order to apply your awareness and understanding of stereotyping, prejudice, and cultural differences

3. Assist your organization in designing and implementing educational programs that address stereotyping, prejudice, and cultural differences as common phenomena in culturally diverse social systems

4

● ● ●

Understanding Group Identities

We begin Part Two with learning about group identity in order to set the groundwork for the other topics to be addressed in this part. It should be noted that although our treatment of the term *group identity* is loosely based on work from the field of social psychology on social identity theory (SIT) (Tajfel, 1978; Turner & Giles, 1981; Abrams & Hogg, 1990), we wish to employ a slightly different interpretation of the concept here. Whereas classic SIT limits group identification to personal choice by individuals about the extent to which they define themselves in terms of various social-cultural categories, we also include categories to which people are ascribed by others. For example, the fact that a man may not place importance on gender in his self-definition does not mean that gender is an unimportant group affiliation in his life experiences. As long as other people define him as a man, and if gender has significant effects in the social systems in which he functions, this group "identity" becomes highly relevant.

Although in other contexts, separate terms may be useful to distinguish self-identification from ascription by others, for our purposes we prefer to simplify this into the single term *group identity,* defined as follows: "A group identity is a personal affiliation with a group with which one shares certain social or cultural characteristics in common." As noted in Chapter One, such identities include the high-profile, lifelong, and well-researched characteristics of gender, racioethnicity, and nationality as well as other identities

51

about which we know far less to date, such as sexual orientation, occupational specialization, organizational level, and religion.

RAISING AWARENESS

The existence of group identities, along with their tendency to have a large influence on interactions between people, leads to a variety of behaviors and phenomena that are important for workers in diverse work groups to understand. Three such phenomena—stereotyping, prejudice, and cultural differences—will be addressed in the chapters that follow. First, however, we offer a series of learning aids on the core concept of group identity. The first two of these aids, Activities 4.1 and 4.2, are designed to raise awareness about the meaning and relevance of group identity in the life experiences of all people.

● ● ●

Activity 4.1
GROUP IDENTITY IN THE SELF-CONCEPT
The Pie Chart Exercise, Part One

The self-concept of an individual is only partly defined by group affiliations. Recognizing this, in this exercise, we are concerned only with the part of your self-definition that is related to your affiliation with groups.

Objectives

1. To increase awareness of your own cultural background and how it compares to those of your coworkers

2. To raise awareness of the importance of group identity by seeing how it applies to each of us

Procedure

Working individually, on a blank sheet of paper, create a pie chart to identify group affiliations that have some importance in your self-concept (your definition of who you are). Examples might include "Ph.D.," "woman," "Jew," "Christian," "Asian," "secretary," "sorority member," "Caucasian," and "American." Indicate the approximate importance of each group affiliation by the size of the slice of the pie that it is given.

Suggestions for the Use of Activity 4.1

The following suggestions should be used by facilitators working with a group:

1. Do the pie chart exercise to create a group identity profile on paper for each person.

2. If time permits, collect the pie charts and (with names omitted) post them around the room. Then have the group view the various charts. If time or space does not permit this, have a number of volunteers share their drawings with the group.

3. One of the universal results of this exercise is a recognition of the vast differences between people (even people who are similar in many ways) in

the extent to which group identities are salient in their self-concept and in which specific identities are viewed as important.

4. Note which identities appear most frequently and tend to have the larger slices in the group. This is an indication of the relative importance of various identities in the life experiences of the members of this group at this point in time.

5. The following learning insights can be highlighted:

   a. We all have group identities that are important to us and that have some influence on what we think and do.

   b. Because certain identities are relatively unimportant to us, we may overlook them in others. Also, because certain identities are important to us, we may erroneously assume that they are important to (and recognized by) other people.

The following questions may be used by individuals who are either doing the exercise alone or working with a group:

1. What did I learn?
2. What surprised me the most?
3. What gave me concern or bothered me a little?
4. Was this activity comfortable to do? If not, why not?

Activity 4.2
THE PIE CHART EXERCISE, PART TWO

We have found that Activity 4.1 works well as an introduction to awareness training for diversity. If you have time and want a follow-up to that exercise, try this one, which has been effective for us. It consists of asking people to think through the work-related implications of the differences illustrated in the pie charts. One way to get at this is to ask people to answer the following questions after they have completed their charts:

1. Because I am _____ (a major group identity according to your pie chart), I have a tendency to _____ _____ in relationships with other people who are

_____ .

2. Because I am _____, other people who are _____ have a tendency to _____ in their interactions with me.

After these questions have been answered, have people pair off and share their respective pie charts and answers to the follow-up questions.

CREATING UNDERSTANDING
When they are used together, Activities 4.1 and 4.2 can provide powerful insights into the relevance of group identities, even for people who previously thought that their lives were unaffected by group affiliations. In order to take this learning a step further and deepen understanding about group identity, we suggest the use of Activities 4.3, 4.4, and 4.5 along with Reading 4.1.

Activity 4.3
UNDERSTANDING DIFFERENCES
The Backgrounds Exercise

Objectives

1. To increase awareness of your own cultural background and how it compares to those of your coworkers

2. To learn a technique for team building with diverse work groups that explicitly addresses differences

Procedure

1. Working individually, list three events, activities, or circumstances of your childhood that had a significant impact on how you view the world. We are especially interested in experiences that you think might make you different from others with whom you work, such as the type of family structure you had, the values emphasized by your parents, your socioeconomic level, the type of leisure activities you participated in, the racioethnic diversity or homogeneity of your neighborhood, and your specific experiences with race, gender, nationality, or some other intergroup situation.

2. Write down the effect or effects these events have (or had in the past) on how you view the world?

3. Pair up with someone else whom you do not know well and share one another's results from the first two tasks.

4. Discuss how the differences in backgrounds between the two of you (especially if you didn't know they existed) could potentially affect your interactions at work or how you might approach a decision or work function differently.

If this activity is done in a group setting, the facilitator will ask for volunteers to share some examples of what was learned. If not, tasks 1 and 2 can still be done as listed above. Task 3 should be skipped and task 4 should be changed to creation of a document that lists the effects instead of a discussion.

Suggestions for the Use of Activity 4.3

A nearly infinite number of background differences and implications can result from this activity. For example, a man who spent his early childhood years in a very traditional family in which the father was totally responsible for earning a living and the mother managed the home might, without proper development later on, have difficulty relating to women as professional peers in high-level leadership roles. A woman who grew up in relative affluence may have no understanding of the dynamics of consumer behavior among poor people to whom a particular product may need to be marketed. A person who was never exposed to racial discrimination may have a difficult time accepting the need for a race-based affirmative action plan in his or her organization. The intent of Activity 4.3 is to have you think through and make explicit the practical, work-related implications of differences in background. This activity will help you to see that group identity differences are relevant to work.

Activity 4.4
THE HISTORICAL EVENTS EXERCISE

An additional understanding of group-identity differences can be obtained by focusing people on their varying interpretations of history. This activity must be done in a group setting and requires that someone act as facilitator. It can be done in large groups and requires no more than twenty to thirty minutes in its most abbreviated form.

Objectives

1. To illustrate how group-identity differences influence cognitive processes like memory and values (for example, definitions of what is or is not important)

2. To illustrate the tendency of formal records of world and national history to be biased toward certain cultural interpretations

Procedure

Have all members write down the three events in world history that are of the greatest importance to them. When this is finished, there are a variety of ways of processing this information:

1. Have pairs exchange and discuss lists.
2. Have volunteers share their lists in the full group.
3. Collect the lists and organize them by diversity dimensions such as age, gender, and nationality.

At some point, create a list on easel paper or a blackboard to give everyone an idea of the variety of responses. After everyone has a sense of the events noted by members of the group, lead them in a discussion, using the following suggested questions:

1. Why is there so much variance in the lists, and to what extent is it related to group-identity differences such as gender, age, racioethnicity, and nationality?

2. Which items received the greatest attention in history courses taken through formal education? (If relevant, note differences in educational systems across various countries represented in the group.) How does this list of events emphasized in formal education correspond to the lists of various members of the group? What implications can be drawn from the data on inclusion versus exclusion of "important" historical events.

3. How relevant are these historical events to contemporary interpersonal and intergroup relationships? To the extent that they are relevant, what effects do they have?

Suggestions for the Use of Activity 4.4

This activity works best in a group that is diverse on at least one of the following dimensions: age, gender, racioethnicity, or nationality. Of course, the learning potential is maximized when there is diversity in all four of these core identities. In that event, the exercise can be quite revealing.

One of the learnings from this exercise is that group identities *do* affect the worldviews of people. For example, people who were alive during the Great Depression of the 1930s will often list this and talk about how it has led them to avoid risk. Many people who were in their youth at the time of World War II were influenced by that war, but in a very different way from those who were in their late teens and early twenties during the Vietnam era. African Americans invariably list U.S. slavery, whereas most people in the United States who come from some other ethnic background will not list it. Another learning is that contemporary intergroup relationships should be understood in the context of the historical background pertinent to the groups involved. This insight applies to identity configurations beyond the four core identities mentioned here. An example is union-versus-management identifications.

Differences of Cognitive Style

In this chapter, we are focusing on understanding group identities. Although the extent to which people of different cognitive styles represent different "cultural" groups is arguable, it is clear that people do differ on cognitive styles (that is, in the way they obtain, process, and respond to information). Research has also shown that people of different educational specializations (for example, marketing people versus accountants) tend to have different cognitive styles. It therefore seems reasonable to expect that *unmanaged* differences in cognitive styles may make it more difficult for people to work together well and to achieve consensus. Likewise, it seems reasonable to predict that, if these differences are well managed, diversity of cognitive styles can add value to problem solving and the creative processes of organizations as discussed in Reading 3.2.

An analytical tool that we have found helpful in this area is the one offered by David Whetten and Kim Cameron in their popular book, *Developing Management Skills* (Whetten & Cameron, 1991). Excerpts from their segment on cognitive styles are included here as a basis for personal learning in this area.

Activity 4.5
UNDERSTANDING COGNITIVE STYLE

Objectives
1. To investigate the ways you think about information you encounter
2. To learn about others' ways of thinking and how they may differ from yours, and to think through some implications of these differences

Procedure
Complete the cognitive-style instrument shown in Exhibit 4.1. In responding to the instrument, you should put yourself in the position of someone who must gather and evaluate information. There are no right or wrong answers, and one alternative is just as good as another. Try to indicate the ways you do or *would* respond, not the ways you think you *should* respond.

Each scenario has three pairs of alternatives. For each pair, select the alternative that comes closest to the way you would respond. Answer each item. If you are not sure, make your best guess. When you have finished answering all the questions, use the scoring key that follows the questionnaire as a basis for comparing your score with others. Do not refer to the scoring key until after you have answered all the questions.

EXHIBIT 4.1. The Cognitive Style Instrument

Suppose you are a scientist in NASA whose job it is to gather information about the moons of Saturn. Which of the following would you be more interested in investigating?

1. a. How the moons are similar to one another
   b. How the moons differ from one another

2. a. How the whole system of moons operates
   b. The characteristics of each moon

3. a. How Saturn and its moons differ from Earth and its moon
   b. How Saturn and its moons are similar to Earth and its moon

Suppose you are the chief executive of a company and have asked the division heads to make presentations at the end of the year. Which of the following would be more appealing to you?

EXHIBIT 4.1. The Cognitive Style Instrument, cont'd.

4. a. A presentation analyzing the details of the data
   b. A presentation focused on the overall perspective

5. a. A presentation showing how each division contributed to the company as a whole
   b. A presentation showing the unique contributions of each division

6. a. Details of how each division performed
   b. General summaries of performance data

Suppose you are visiting an Asian country and you are writing home to tell about your trip. Which of the following would be most typical of the letter you would write?

7. a. A detailed description of people and events
   b. General impressions and feelings

8. a. A focus on the similarities between our culture and theirs
   b. A focus on the uniqueness of their culture

9. a. Overall, general impressions of the experience
   b. Separate, unique impressions of parts of the experience

Suppose that you are attending a concert featuring a famous symphony orchestra. Which of the following would you be most likely to do?

10. a. Listen for the parts of individual instruments
    b. Listen for the harmony of all the instruments together

11. a. Pay attention to the overall mood associated with the music
    b. Pay attention to the separate feelings associated with different parts of the music

12. a. Focus on the overall style of the conductor
    b. Focus on how the conductor interprets different parts of the score

Suppose you are considering taking a job with a certain organization. Which of the following would you be more likely to do in deciding whether or not to take the job?

13. a. Systematically collect information on the organization
    b. Rely on personal intuition or inspiration

14. a. Primarily consider the fit between you and the job
    b. Primarily consider the politics needed to succeed in the organization

15. a. Be methodical in collecting data and making a choice
    b. Mainly consider personal instincts and gut feelings

EXHIBIT 4.1. The Cognitive Style Instrument, cont'd.

Suppose you inherit some money and decide to invest it. You learn of a new high-technology firm that has just issued stock. Which of the following would you be most likely to do in making your decision to purchase the firm's stock?

16. a. Invest on a hunch
    b. Invest only after a systematic investigation of the firm

17. a. Be somewhat impulsive in deciding to invest
    b. Follow a preset pattern in making your decision

18. a. Rationally justify your decision to invest in this firm and not another
    b. Find it difficult to rationally justify your decision to invest in this firm and not another

Suppose you are being interviewed on television and you are asked the following questions. Which alternative would you be most likely to select?

19. How are you more likely to cook?
    a. With a recipe
    b. Without a recipe

20. How would you predict the Super Bowl winner next year?
    a. After systematically researching the personnel and records of the teams
    b. On a hunch or by intuition

21. Which games do you prefer?
    a. Games of chance (like Bingo)
    b. Games of skill (like chess, checkers, or Scrabble)

Suppose you are a manager and need to hire an executive assistant. Which of the following would you be most likely to do in the process?

22. a. Interview each applicant using a set outline of questions
    b. Concentrate on your personal feelings and instincts about each applicant

23. a. Primarily consider the personality fit between you and the candidates
    b. Consider the match between the precise job requirements and the candidates' capabilities

24. a. Rely on factual and historical data on each candidate in making a choice
    b. Rely on feelings and impressions in making a choice

EXHIBIT 4.1. The Cognitive Style Instrument, cont'd.

Scoring Key

To determine your score on the two dimensions of cognitive style, circle the items below that you checked on this instrument. Then count up the number of circled items and put your scores in the spaces below.

Gathering Information		Evaluating Information	
1a	1b	13a	13b
2a	2b	14b	14a
3b	3a	15a	15b
4b	4a	16b	16a
5a	5b	17b	17a
6b	6a	18a	18b
7b	7a	19a	19b
8a	8b	20a	20b
9a	9b	21b	21a
10b	10a	22a	22b
11a	11b	23b	23a
12a	12b	24a	24b
Intuitive Score	Sensing Score	Thinking Score	Feeling Score
_____	_____	_____	_____

SOURCE: From David A. Whetten and Kim S. Cameron, *Developing Management Skills,* 2nd edition (New York: HarperCollins, 1991), pp. 44–45. Copyright © 1991 by HarperCollins Publishers, Inc. Reprinted with permission of Addison-Wesley Educational Publishers, Inc.

Suggestions for the Use of Activity 4.5

In addition to providing personal feedback to participants, data from this exercise may be used as a basis for discussions on the implications of style differences. It also can be used to organize pretested people in same-identity groups and then ask them to answer questions designed to illustrate the behavioral manifestations of the style differences. Such questions include the following:

1. How do you like to receive feedback?
2. What type of communication works best for you?
3. What type of decision process makes you frustrated?

Reading 4.1 is recommended as a follow-up to this activity. This reading will increase your knowledge of the meaning of cognitive style and its implications for work-related behavior and outcomes.

• • •

Reading 4.1
COGNITIVE STYLE

DAVID A. WHETTEN AND KIM S. CAMERON

Cognitive style consists of a large number of cognitive factors that relate to the way individuals perceive, interpret, and respond to information. There are literally scores of dimensions used in the research literature to define cognitive style (for example, see Eckstrom, French, & Harmon, 1979). In this chapter, however, we discuss the two major dimensions of cognitive style that have appeared in research on management and that have been shown to have particular relevance for and impact on people with decision-making authority. These are the manner in which individuals gather information and the manner in which they evaluate the information they receive.

The basic premise underlying cognitive style is that every individual is faced with an overwhelming amount of information, and only part of it can be given attention and acted upon at any one time. Individuals, therefore, develop strategies for reducing and interpreting the information they receive. No strategy is inherently good or inherently bad, and not everyone adopts an identifiable, consistent set of strategies that become part of his or her cognitive style. However, about 80 percent of individuals do eventually develop, mostly unconsciously, a preferred set of information-processing strategies, and these make up their particular cognitive styles. The Cognitive Style Instrument (Exhibit 4.1) assesses the two core dimensions of your information-processing preferences.

In order for your scores on the Cognitive Style Instrument to be meaningful to you, you must understand the theory upon which the model is based. It is grounded in the work of Jung (1923). Figure 4.1 illustrates the two cognitive dimensions. The *information-gathering* dimension divides an intuitive strategy from a sensing strategy, and the *information-evaluation* dimension separates a thinking strategy from a feeling strategy.

Source: This reading is an excerpted version of a chapter from David A. Whetten and Kim S. Cameron, *Developing Management Skills,* 2nd edition (New York: HarperCollins, 1991), pp. 65–70. Copyright © 1991 by HarperCollins Publishers, Inc. Reprinted with permission of Addison-Wesley Educational Publishers, Inc.

Figure 4.1. Model of Cognitive Style Based on Two Dimensions

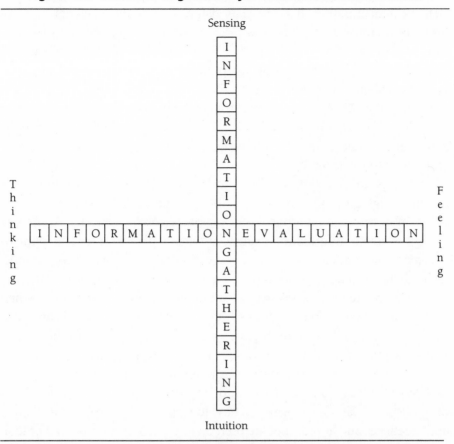

Different strategies for taking in, coding, and storing information (information gathering) develop as a result of certain cognitive filters used by individuals to select the information they pay attention to. An *intuitive strategy* takes a holistic view and emphasizes commonalities and generalizations, that is, the relationships among the various elements of data. Intuitive thinkers often have preconceived notions about what sort of information may be relevant, and they look at the information to find what is consistent with their preconceptions. They tend to be convergent thinkers.

The *sensing strategy* focuses on detail, or on the specific attributes of each element of data, rather than on relationships among the elements. Sensing thinkers are rational and have few preconceptions about what may be relevant, so they insist on a close and thorough examination of the information. They are sensitive to the unique attributes of various parts of the information they encounter, and they tend to be divergent thinkers.

In simplified terms, an intuitive strategy focuses on the whole, a sensing strategy on the parts of the whole. An intuitive strategy looks for commonalities and overall categories, a sensing strategy for uniqueness, detail, and exceptions to the general rule.

The second dimension of Jung's model refers to strategies for interpreting and judging information (information evaluation). These strategies develop from reliance on a particular problem-solving pattern. A *thinking strategy* evaluates information using a systematic plan with specific sequential steps. There is a focus on appropriate methods and logical progressions. Individuals who use a thinking style generally rely on objective data. Attempts are made to fit problems into a known model or framework. When such people defend their solutions, they emphasize the methods and procedures used to solve the problems. Vertinsky (1976) refers to these individuals as members of a "continuous culture," meaning that they operate consistently with existing patterns of thought.

A *feeling strategy,* on the other hand, approaches a problem on the basis of "gut feel," or an internal sense of how to respond. The problem is defined and redefined, and approaches are tried on a trial-and-error basis rather than through a logical procedure. Feeling individuals have a penchant for subjective or impressionistic rather than objective data, and they frequently cannot describe their own problem-solving processes. Problem solutions are often found through using analogies or seeing unusual relationships between the problem and a past experience. Vertinsky (1976) refers to these individuals as members of a "discontinuous culture."

These different strategies have important implications for work behavior. Each has advantages and disadvantages. For example, people high on sensing, because they focus on detail, experience information overload and personal stress more readily than intuitive types when they are faced with a large amount of data. When they encounter too much detail or too much heterogeneity, sensing-style people become overloaded, because each detail receives attention.

Intuitive thinkers, on the other hand, who focus on the relationships between elements and the whole, handle additions of detail relatively easily. However, when diversity or ambiguity is encountered in the information, when aberrations from expected relationships occur, or when preformed categories don't fit, intuitive individuals are likely to have more difficulty processing the information than sensing individuals. Encountering exceptions or the absence of a clear set of relationships among elements is particularly problematic for intuitive individuals. Sensing individuals are likely to handle these situations more easily because of their tendency to do fine-grained analyses of problems.

People with the thinking style are less likely to be effective when encountering problems requiring creativity and discontinuous thinking, or when encountering highly ambiguous problems that have only partial information available. When no apparent system exists for solving a problem, these individuals are likely to have more difficulty than feeling individuals.

On the other hand, when one program or system will solve a variety of problems, that is, when the information suggests a straightforward, computational solution, feeling individuals are less effective because of their tendency to try new approaches, to redefine problems, and to reinvent the solution over and over without following past programs. This generally leads to inefficient problem solving or even to solving the wrong problem. Thinking individuals have less difficulty in such situations.

Research on these cognitive dimensions has found that no matter what type of problem they face, most individuals use their preferred cognitive style to approach it. They prefer, and even seek, decision situations and problem types that are consistent with their own cognitive style (for example, individuals scoring high on thinking prefer problems with a step-by-step method of solution). In one study, individuals who were more thinking than feeling implemented more computer-based systems and rational procedures for decision making. Individuals in another study defined identical problems differently depending on their different cognitive styles. Another study found that differences in cognitive style led to significantly different decision-making processes in individuals (see Henderson & Nutt, 1980; Mulkowsky & Freeman, 1979).

Students with different cognitive styles have also been found to approach learning differently, and different kinds of educational experiences hold meaning for different types of people. For example, individuals who emphasize intuitive strategies tend to do better in conceptual courses and learn more easily through reading and through discussing general relationships. Exams with one right answer may be easier for them than for those who emphasize sensing. Individuals who emphasize sensing strategies tend to do better in factual courses or courses in which attention to detail and dissimilarity is important. Critical and analytical learning activities, such as debates, facilitate their learning, and exams emphasizing implications and applications may be easiest for these individuals.

Individuals who emphasize a thinking strategy do best in courses, such as mathematics, that take an orderly, step-by-step approach to the subject, courses in which what is learned builds on, and follows directly from, what was learned earlier. On the other hand, feeling individuals do best in courses requiring creativity and idea generation. Learning activities such as sculpting, in which the student must rely on a personal sense of what is appropriate, are likely to be preferred by these individuals.

In short, knowing our own cognitive style can prove advantageous to us in numerous situations, such as selecting career options, selecting appropriate business environments and job assignments, and selecting teams of complementary members to solve problems. It also is useful in helping students to capitalize on academic strengths and enhance study skills. Table 4.1 summarizes some personal characteristics associated with each of these major cognitive orientations.

TABLE 4.1. Characteristics of Cognitive Styles

Information Gathering

Intuitive Types	Sensing Types
Like solving new problems.	Dislike new problems unless there are standard ways to solve them.
Dislike doing the same thing over and over again.	Like an established routine.
Enjoy learning a new skill more than using it.	Enjoy using skills already learned more than learning new ones.
Work in bursts of energy powered by enthusiasm, with slack periods in between.	Work more steadily, with realistic idea of how long it will take.

TABLE 4.1. Characteristics of Cognitive Styles, cont'd.

Information Gathering, cont'd.

Feeling Types	*Thinking Types*
Jump to conclusions frequently.	Must usually work all the way through to reach a conclusion.
Are patient with complicated situations.	Are impatient when the details are complicated.
Are impatient with routine details.	Are patient with routine details.
Follow inspirations, good or bad.	Rarely trust inspirations and don't usually feel inspired.
Often tend to make errors of fact.	Seldom make errors of fact.
Dislike taking time for precision.	Tend to be good at precise work.

Information Evaluation

Feeling Types	*Thinking Types*
Tend to be very aware of other people and their feelings.	Are relatively unemotional and uninterested in people's feelings.
Enjoy pleasing people, even in unimportant things.	May hurt people's feelings without knowing it.
Like harmony. Efficiency may be badly disturbed by office feuds.	Like analysis and putting things into logical order. Can get along without harmony.
Often let decision be influenced by their own or other people's personal likes and wishes.	Tend to decide impersonally, sometimes ignoring people's wishes.
Need occasional praise.	Need to be treated fairly.
Dislike telling people unpleasant things.	Are able to reprimand people or fire them when necessary.
Relate well to most people.	Tend to relate well only to other thinking types.
Tend to be sympathetic.	May seem hard-hearted.

SOURCE: From David A. Whetten and Kim S. Cameron, *Developing Management Skills,* 2nd edition (New York: HarperCollins, 1991), p. 69. Copyright © 1991 by HarperCollins Publishers, Inc. Reprinted with permission of Addison-Wesley Educational Publishers, Inc.

In order to fully capitalize on the strengths of your own cognitive style, it is important that you also be aware of your orientation toward change. This is important because, as the environment in which we operate continues to become more chaotic, more temporary, more complex, and more overloaded with information, your ability to process information is at least partly constrained by your fundamental attitude about change.

Suggestions for the Use of Reading 4.1

As previously noted, the main objective for including this reading is to add depth of understanding on the implications of differences in cognitive styles for work-related behavior. The reading gives many specific examples of this. Through study and discussion of the information contained in the reading, you should increase your own self-awareness as well as your ability to interact successfully with people who are different in group situations. Among other things, the reading may be used as a springboard for discussion of ways in which leaders can adapt their approach to supervision for people with different known styles of thinking and to identify ways to prepare people for working effectively with others of a different cognitive style.

As a final tool for creating understanding, we have included two personal essays. These essays are intended to accomplish several things. First, they illustrate the use of dialogue groups as a team development technique for diverse groups. This technique, as applied to managing diversity, has been extensively used in companies like Digital Equipment Corporation (see Walker & Hanson, 1992, for details). Second, the essays give additional perspectives on how increased self-awareness and understanding of others leads to a greater sense of personal competency. Third, they can be used either as common input for group discussions or as learning aids for people who are using this book for individual study.

Reading 4.2
REFLECTIONS ABOUT DIALOGUE GROUPS
ADDRESSING DIVERSITY

This reading is a combination of two essays written by students in an MBA class on diversity in organizations. As part of the coursework, students worked in small groups that were as diverse on gender, race, and nationality as the composition of the class would allow. These essays are reflections on the small-group discussions that they had throughout the term and are included here with permission of the students. The essays are included here because we think that they are interesting and revealing and raise useful discussion issues.

Essay 1

I think the most educational part of the diversity sessions for me was hearing from my group members and understanding their different "diversity experiences." As part of the majority group, I admit I have been ignorant of the fact that there are real differences between groups and that not everyone has the same values, beliefs, motivational drivers, and so on that I have. I had never realized or even thought about the fact that many of the laws and policies that are in place today have been created by members of my group. This in turn has led to many advantages for people in my group.

At certain times during the sessions, I felt uncomfortable because of the color of my skin (white) and my gender (male). I felt as though I was personally being blamed for the way members of minority groups have been discriminated against (even though these feelings were probably unfounded). I was even intimidated about speaking my mind for fear of voicing an unpopular point of view. My small-group sessions were a very positive and valuable learning experience. The experience was particularly valuable because of the diverse racial and gender makeup of the group. Group members were able to enlighten each other about their individual experiences that directly related to the groups with which they identified. In a small-group setting our discussions were much more personal and in-depth.

Essay 2

I enjoyed looking into my own feelings about diversity. I have had the experience of being a "token" and have gained insights into the feelings of people who have often been tokens. I also have learned to listen cross-culturally to differences in communication style such as different word choices, metaphors, slang terms, and inflections. My core group represented three racial groups. I was the only Anglo-American. Throughout the sessions, I had strong feelings of being a token. This was a relatively new experience for me. I have been in situations where the people were from many races and have been in situations where I was the only woman, but I don't recall a time when I was the only White person.

I have learned something about myself and have a new appreciation of those people of color who are the "firsts." One reaction I had was that I cannot speak for all White people. A common practice in the business world is to look to the "token" to answer questions concerning his or her entire race. Another reaction to my "tokenism" was that I could not be blamed for all the negative attitudes and actions of people of my identity group. In one discussion, I mentioned that I felt bad about how some White people acted, but my core-group members reminded me that I was not personally responsible for all White people's actions.

Suggestions for the Use of Reading 4.2

Following is a sample of discussion points that the readings raise:

1. Why is it uncomfortable to be the only person of a visible identity group within a diverse group? What are the implications or behavioral manifestations of this discomfort?

2. What are the implications of always or never being the only member of an identity group?

3. How useful is the tool illustrated by these essays (a dialogue group focusing on diversity) for the development of diversity competency? What are the pros and cons of this tool?

TAKING ACTION

We conclude Chapter Four with two cases that offer an opportunity to apply some of the insights gained from the previous material to analyzing and then developing a plan of response for a pair of real-life situations in which differences of group identity play a major role.

Case 4.1
ADVICE GONE AWRY

A White, male line manager confided that he was sometimes reluctant to give unfavorable performance feedback to non-White subordinates. The corporate human resource development person coached the line manager on the importance of providing such feedback. Following a presentation by an African American, male subordinate, the manager talked with him about how he thought it came across. The manager mentioned that he thought the speaker's style was intimidating. The subordinate responded by saying that he felt that this reaction was a response to his race, not his style. Both people became upset and their relationship was severely strained by the incident. The manager then went back (with clear annoyance) to the corporate human resource development person and said, "You told me to give him feedback, so I did and look what happened!"

What would you do now?

Suggestions for the Use of Case 4.1

This case is based on an incident that was told to one of us by a middle manager from a large oil company during a roundtable of human resource executives. It is included here because it illustrates the effect of group identity on one of the tasks of the diversity competency model (performance feedback). It also allows us to plan some specific actions and thus completes the awareness-understanding-action learning cycle.

The scenario itself is similar to a number of others that we've heard. A thorough discussion of the incident should address (1) how and why group identities may be affecting this situation, (2) advice for working with each of the parties to resolve the conflict, and (3) whether or not the human resource professional should handle similar incidents differently in the future. In addition, the broader issue of giving effective performance feedback in cross-race supervisor-subordinate dyads should be discussed. Many managers have some difficulty in this area. Thus, the larger question of what can be done to "manage" the dynamics of racial diversity in performance feedback meetings should be included in the analysis of the case.

●●●

Case 4.2
THE O. J. SIMPSON TRIAL

One of the authors of this book found an example of differences in racial perspectives close to home. On the day the O. J. Simpson murder trial verdict was announced (the not-guilty verdict), my son reported the following reaction in his multiracial school: "Many of the White kids were crying and upset that he was found not guilty while most of the Black kids were jubilant. In my predominantly White class there was near-silence, while next door, in a predominantly Black class, wild yells of celebration broke out. It was amazing to see the starkly different reactions based on the racial makeup of the classes."

This is typical of what occurred in many settings around the country. Analyze the differences in reaction using the following questions as a guide:

1. Why did reactions differ by race group?
2. What are the implications of the case for justice in the courts?
3. Are there any parallels or transferable learnings from this situation to the employment arena? If so, what are they?
4. Given the insights gained, do you have any suggestions for changes in the criminal justice system in the United States?

Suggestions for the Use of Case 4.2

This case could have been used for learning on several topics in the book. It is used here because it so easily uncovers the effects of group identification on perspectives of world events in mixed-race groups. In all-White groups (or at least groups without Hispanic, Native American, or African American members), this case may not produce a useful learning experience.

We suggest that you give some thought to the questions in advance and then work in either same-race groups or mixed-race groups to develop consensus answers to the three questions. In the former case, the results should be discussed in a mixed-race setting. If no group is available to work with you, give the case to an acquaintance of a different race and ask him or her to prepare answers that can then be compared to yours and discussed.

We think that one of the most important points to be brought out from the reactions to the case is that African Americans found it much more believable that White police officers might plant evidence to incriminate a Black man than did White Americans. Another issue has to do with whether or not the case says anything about ethnocentric behavior by African Americans (for example, to what extent was Simpson's acquittal in the criminal trial a function of the predominantly African American jury "looking out for one of their own"?).

It is not difficult to link the issues in this case to organizational issues like hiring and promotion decisions and the perception of bias in specific cases where, perhaps, none really exists.

5

Stereotyping

In Chapter Four we learned about the core concept of group identity, on which much of the rest of the material in this book is based. In Chapters Five through Seven, we consider three of the most important cognitive processes and behavioral phenomena that result from diversity in group identities in a given social setting. The first such phenomenon, stereotyping, will be addressed in this chapter.

Stereotyping is a mental process in which the individual is viewed as a member of a group and the information that we have stored in our minds about the group is ascribed to the individual. As will be shown later, there are important differences between stereotyping and valuing cultural differences. Because stereotyping is applicable and potent across a broad spectrum of group identities in organizations, we view learning about it as being crucial for developing competency to manage diversity.

In the remainder of Chapter Five, we have organized a variety of readings and other developmental aids to facilitate learning about stereotyping both as a cognitive or mental process and in its behavioral manifestations, all in the context of culturally diverse organizations.

RAISING AWARENESS

One way to clarify and embellish the definition of a key term is to compare it with and distinguish it from other terms or concepts with which it may sometimes be confused. Accordingly, Reading 5.1 addresses the differences between stereotyping, which we believe is a barrier to diversity competency, and valuing cultural diversity, which we believe facilitates diversity competency.

● ● ●

Reading 5.1
DISTINGUISHING VALUING DIVERSITY
FROM STEREOTYPING

TAYLOR COX, JR.

When organizations undertake change efforts to manage diversity, many people are troubled by what they perceive as reinforcement of existing stereotypes. This especially comes up during training sessions devoted to diversity. Why, these people reason, should we spend time learning and discussing issues related to group identification when this "forces" us to think about people in categories? Isn't this exactly the kind of thing we want to avoid? These are legitimate questions that deserve a carefully considered response.

In responding, I believe that we first have to acknowledge that some of what we do to enhance personal and organizational effectiveness for managing diversity does run a risk of reinforcing stereotyping. Certainly this is not a desirable or intended outcome, but it can happen when, for example, exercises that are designed to teach us about cultural traditions different from our own are not done skillfully. While acknowledging up front that this risk is there, we should not let it block our efforts to promote education about intergroup differences. This brings us to the second point to be made here, namely, that understanding differences and stereotyping are not the same. In fact, as shown in Table 5.1, they can be distinguished in three specific ways.

First, stereotypes are often based on folklore, media portrayals, and other highly unreliable sources of information. In contrast, educational work dealing with group-identity characteristics should always be based on systematic research of real differences. Second, while most stereotypes contain negative connotations, valuing-diversity work suggests that most differences that are culturally based should be viewed as potentially positive or, at worst, as neutral. For example, to observe that, compared to Euro-Anglo males, Chinese and Japanese males are typically more reserved and less aggressive in their behavior does not necessarily imply that they are either inferior or superior to Euro-Anglo males. It simply says that, as a group, they tend to be different on these behavioral dimensions.

Third, and most important of all, stereotyping by definition tends to ignore intragroup differences whereas valuing-diversity work does not. In stereo-

TABLE 5.1. Difference Between Stereotyping and Attention to Cultural Differences in Managing and Valuing Difference (MCD) at Work

Stereotyping	MCD
1. Frequently is based on false assumptions and anecdotal evidence, or even on impressions without any direct experience with a group	1. Is based on cultural differences that have been verified by empirical research on actual intergroup differences
2. Ascribes negative traits to members of a group	2. Views cultural differences as positive or neutral
3. Involves the assumption that characteristics thought to be common in a cultural group apply to *every* member	3. Is based on the concept of greater probability
Example: Suzuko Akoi is an Asian; therefore, she is not aggressive by White, male American standards.	*Example:* As a group, Asians tend to be less aggressive than White, male Americans.

typing, one assumes that an individual has certain characteristics simply because she or he is a member of some social-cultural group. For example, we may assume that since Jane is an accountant and most accountants have a penchant for details, Jane must have a penchant for details. By contrast, in learning about valuing diversity, the emphasis is on knowing that, as a group, accountants think differently from, say, marketing people. We do not assume that every accountant is the same. What we are really saying is that the distribution of the trait "penchant for details" looks different for accountants than it does for marketing and sales employees. This knowledge alerts us to important information that may allow us to interact more effectively with the "typical" accountant. At the same time, we have to be alert to the possibility that a given individual may or may not have this characteristic. The fact that individuals may differ from the norms of the identity groups of which they are members should not prevent us from learning about diversity in the workforce. If it did, many other common behaviors in business, including insurance underwriting practices, advertising, and niche marketing, would be equally inappropriate.

Now let us return to the concern that learning about diversity is "forcing" people to think in categories. The fact is that a great deal of evidence exists to show that nearly everyone already thinks in categories (Brewer, 1995; Tajfel & Wilkes, 1963). Educational work on diversity merely makes explicit, and gives focused attention to, thought processes that occur in you and me every day. The hope is that some of these thought processes can be altered by such explicit attention. For example, perhaps unfounded and distorted impressions of certain identity groups can be replaced with knowledge of factual distinctions from systematic research, and we can learn to recognize differences without also judging them as inferior or superior.

Suggestions for the Use of Reading 5.1

This reading addresses one of the most common objections to educational programs focusing on intergroup differences. The ability to respond effectively to this kind of criticism is one of the requirements of diversity competency. In using this reading as a discussion tool, the following questions may be useful:

1. Do you find the distinctions given in the reading convincing? Why or why not?

2. Do you agree that the risk of inadvertently reinforcing stereotyping in some people during education on diversity is outweighed by the potential value of this education? Why or why not?

3. What steps can be taken in training on diversity to minimize the risk cited in question 2?

CREATING UNDERSTANDING

Reading 5.1 was designed to increase our awareness of stereotyping and to distinguish it from acknowledging and valuing diversity. Activities 5.1 and 5.2 have been assembled to extend the learning process regarding stereotyping. This material should deepen your knowledge of the phenomenon of stereotyping. One of the ways in which stereotypes affect behavior is through our perceptual processes. Activity 5.1 is designed to help illustrate the connections between group identity, perception, and cognitive processes such as memory and association.

Activity 5.1
COGNITION, PERCEPTION, AND GROUP IDENTITY

Note: This activity is intended to be used in a facilitated group. If you are not working in a group, you may want to read through the activity to gain insights on your own. If you are working in a group, only the facilitator should read the objectives and procedure for doing the activity in advance. All that participants should be told in advance is that the activity addresses processes of perception and memory and relates to group identification.

Objectives

1. To show that all people have stored information filed in their minds that is tied to specific labels

2. To illustrate how the connections between labels and their associated cognitive processes can often lead to perceptual distortions, an ingredient of stereotyping

Procedure

The exercise works best in groups of twenty-five or fewer people. Divide the full group into two smaller groups that have as close to equal numbers as possible. All participants will need a blank sheet of paper and a pencil. You will also need two sheets of blank transparency paper.

Organize the two groups into two human chains so that each person within a chain can hand off her or his work to the next person in the chain, and so on. Give a copy of the drawing labeled "horse" to the lead person in the first chain, and a copy of the drawing labeled "dog" to the lead person in the other chain. You will note that the drawings are identical except for their labels. *There is to be no discussion whatsoever among group members.* Separate the two groups physically so that they cannot see what the other group is doing.

Each person in the chain has the task of reproducing the drawing given to him or her by the previous person in the chain. The original drawing stays with the lead person. The lead person reproduces the drawing and passes it to the second person in the chain. Each person creates a drawing in the same way and passes it on to the next person in the chain, until the last person

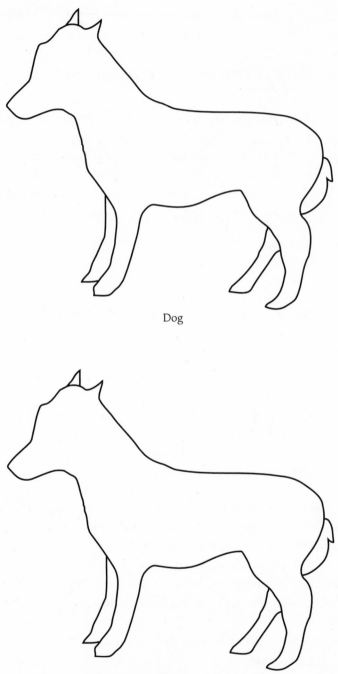

Dog

Horse

has received a drawing. The last person in the chain puts his or her drawing on the blank transparency paper so that it can be projected on an overhead projector.

When both groups have finished, show them the original drawing and the two final "reproductions" created by the human chains.

Suggestions for the Use of Activity 5.1

What typically happens, of course, is that the label influences what is drawn, so that even though the original drawings are identical, the final reproductions reflect stored information about the animal named on the label. The horse gets a mane and hooves, the dog has a collar, and so on.

The activity is fun, but it also illustrates the power of labels and their tendency to affect what we see. In our minds, labels, such as the names of identity groups, are connected to stored information that we have come to associate with those groups. Because we *expect* to see these stored characteristics when a member of a particular group appears, we have a tendency to ascribe those characteristics to the individual whether they are actually present or not.

One difficulty that can occur in the activity is that if the chains are long (more than six or seven people), there can be a considerable time lapse between the first reproduction and the final draft of the drawing. Since those who have completed their drawing are not allowed to talk to the others, it may be useful to plan some parallel activity for them (for example, to make a list of all the information they have stored in their minds about dogs or horses). If the activity works as planned, it is easy to make connections between it and perceptual processes involving labels for people. Activity 5.2 makes these connections more explicitly. *The activity is intended for facilitated groups and only the facilitator should read the objectives and procedure in advance.*

— ●●● —

Activity 5.2
THE STEREOTYPING EXERCISE

Objectives

1. To give visibility and *current-day reality* to the stereotypes that people may have about different groups of people

2. To illustrate the pervasiveness of stereotypes and some of the characteristics of stereotyping

Procedure

This activity works best with a group of no more than around thirty-five people. The following supplies will be needed: Post-it Notes, masking tape, and lots of newsprint or flip-chart paper. Depending on the length of the discussion you allow, the activity could take as little as forty-five minutes or as much as three hours.

1. Present a list of identity groups to be addressed in the exercise (see the suggestions in Exhibit 5.1). It often works best if the groups are defined based on the salient identities in the group you are working with.

2. Ask the participants to identify stereotypes that they have heard about these groups of people, writing each word or phrase on a separate Post-it Note. They should stick the completed notes on the newsprint labeled for the particular identity group. Put the sheets of newsprint up on the walls of the room. It is not necessary (or recommended) to identify who wrote any specific adjective.

3. Have the group look at the data on the labeled sheets after they all have posted their notes.

4. Identify the percentage of potentially positive or enhancing adjectives versus negative or deleterious ones.

EXHIBIT 5.1. Possible Identity Groups

1. White women.
2. Native Americans.
3. Asians (or more specific groups such as Japanese, Filipinos, or Koreans).
4. Arab Americans.
5. Black Americans (African, Caribbean, and so on).
6. Hispanic Americans (Latinos, Mexican Americans, Puerto Ricans, and so on).
7. Jewish Americans.
8. Anglo men.
9. Gays, lesbians, and bisexuals.
10. People who are differently abled (physically or mentally challenged).
11. People who have different socioeconomic statuses (low, middle, or high).
12. People who have different educational levels (college degree, Ivy League, and so on).
13. People who belong to different age groups (for example, young [under thirty] and old [over sixty]).
14. Members of specific nationalities (for example, French men or Italian women).
15. Others. Depending on the composition of the group and the specific organizational culture, the list could include categories like single or married people, Southerners or Northerners, overweight people, attractive or unattractive people, hourly or salaried workers, executives, doctors, workers in line or staff positions, workers in different work functions (for example, engineers or accountants), people with urban or suburban residences, or expatriates or repatriates.

Suggestions for the Use of Activity 5.2

As noted earlier in this chapter, stereotyping is a perceptual and cognitive process in which specific behavioral traits are ascribed to individuals on the basis of their apparent membership in a group (Cox, 1993; Taylor, Fiske, Etcoff, & Ruderman, 1978). Stereotyping has cognitive, affective, and behavioral dimensions.

This activity identifies stereotypes that are prevalent in the social system of the group. They represent things members of the group have heard about different groups or cultures through folklore, the media (such as television, films, or newspapers), their communities, their families, their friends, and so on. The information garnered from this activity can provide a basis for discussion of potential solutions to manage, counteract, or remedy the potentially deleterious effects that stereotyping (often unconsciously) can have on organizational effectiveness and human happiness.

It is helpful to secure volunteers from among the participants and ask them to read the adjectives on the Post-it Notes from the sheets to all of the participants. Then request that the participants come to some "approximate" agreement on which of the stereotypes are positive, negative, or neutral. This will provide a basis for computing the percentages and a comparison of the extent to which the stereotypes are negative for each identity group. There may be some disagreement about which adjectives are actually positive and which are negative. For example, the adjective *emotional* could be viewed as effective or ineffective depending on the situation or one's point of view. You could discuss how the average person in this society might generally respond to that adjective. Generally the lists for racioethnic minorities (especially African Americans, Hispanic Americans, and Native Americans) will be the most negative, with positive traits at only around 15 percent.

This exercise can make some people uncomfortable, to the point where they may say that they don't want to participate. Also, occasionally, people may get angry and say that they were tricked into giving negative stereotypes. The full spectrum of responses, however, usually shows a significant number of positive stereotypes; thus the complaint is rarely supported by the data. For most people, the exercise demonstrates how much work still needs to be done if stereotyping is to be eliminated.

Steps that can be taken to reduce stereotyping and its effects include:

- Self-reflection
- Formal education and training
- Seeking and checking information from members of other identity groups in order to distinguish real intergroup differences from folklore and myths
- Requesting feedback from people about the group's use of stereotypes
- Challenging other people about their assumptions and statements when they appear to be based on stereotypes

TAKING ACTION

The material in the previous two sections of this chapter should have given you a better understanding of stereotyping. In order to complete the learning process, these insights need to be applied to situations that require developing a plan of action. Activity 5.2 was used to illustrate general principles about stereotyping in diverse groups. We now want to provide a vehicle for additional work in this area that is more oriented toward planning action for change. Activities 5.3 and 5.4 have been prepared to aid you in this process. In addition, we will focus attention on a specific dimension of diversity.

In Chapter Three, we noted that increasing work in teams is one of the major business trends that makes managing diversity a leadership imperative. These teams tend to be composed of people from different organizational departments or work specializations. Because we view this trend as one of the most pervasive in organizations today, we have selected cross-functional differences as the point of focus in Activity 5.3. If you are working with a group in which this point of focus is not workable, such as a university class, the activity can be used by substituting another dimension of diversity—such as area of concentration or discipline—for work function.

● ● ●

Activity 5.3
STEREOTYPING AS A BARRIER TO TEAMWORK

Objectives

1. To identify stereotypes that may be hindering effective work relationships for members of cross-functional teams

2. To identify steps that can be taken to reduce stereotypes and their effects on effective work relationships

Procedure

This activity is designed for use with facilitated groups that can be split into no more than four subgroups. It works best with two subgroups (for example, line versus staff units, home office versus field operations, marketing versus manufacturing, or technical versus nontechnical).

Task 1

1. Organize the full group into two to four smaller groups based on work function.

2. Working in their subgroups, the participants should make a list of terms or phrases that describe the other group or groups. If more than two groups are involved, a separate sheet should be done for each of the other groups.

3. If time permits, the participants should make a second list of terms or phrases that they think the other groups will use in describing members of their group.

Task 2

Reconfigure the groups so that they are mixed on work function. Working in these groups, the participants should discuss and try to come to consensus on answers to the following questions:

1. Are the perceptions accurate?
2. Where and how did these perceptions originate?
3. Do these perceptions affect organizational effectiveness? If so, how?
4. What can be done to eliminate these barriers to organizational effectiveness?

Suggestions for the Use of Activity 5.3

We recommend that the responses of the group be recorded on easel paper and that the members be provided with a summary of the responses for follow-up after the session. As a facilitator, you should be prepared to add some input, especially on the fourth question in Task 2. For suggestions on steps to reduce stereotyping, see the list provided in the Suggestions for the Use of Activity 5.2.

We have used a form of this exercise in our consulting work and it has produced good results in surfacing barriers to teamwork and providing a basis for problem solving. It can take anywhere from one to three hours, depending on the extent of any significant problems in cross-functional relations in the work group and how much energy the group has to work on the issues that are identified.

As a summary to Chapter Five, we suggest Activity 5.4, which requires you to apply your understanding of stereotyping to the full range of work tasks that were listed in the diversity competency model.

Activity 5.4
APPLYING STEREOTYPING INFORMATION TO THE
DIVERSITY COMPETENCY MODEL FOR INDIVIDUALS

Objectives
1. To identify specific ways in which stereotyping can affect the performance of various work tasks and responsibilities

2. To identify steps that can be taken to minimize the potential for stereotyping to become a barrier to the effective performance of work tasks and responsibilities

Procedure
The diversity competency model for individuals given in Chapter One specified seven task areas where diversity in work groups is known to have an impact. For your convenience, the model is reproduced as Figure 5.1.

Task 1
Working alone or in a group as directed by a learning facilitator, create a list of one to three ways in which stereotypes may have an effect on the performance of one or more (depending on how you wish to use the activity) of the task areas shown in Figure 5.1.

Task 2
Identify one to three actions that you could take, possibly with the support of others and your organization's leadership, to reduce the probability that stereotypes will be a factor in the performance of these tasks.

Figure 5.1. Diversity Competency Model for Individuals

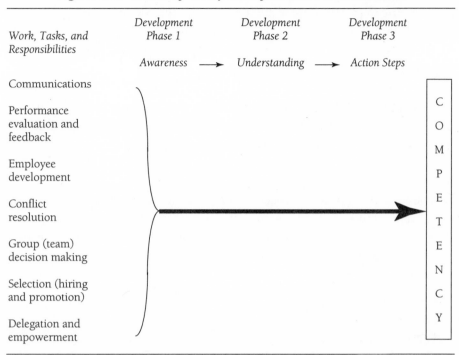

SOURCE: This figure is adapted from one first used by Taylor Cox, Jr., in a presentation to the Human Resource Partnership, University of Michigan, September 1992.

Suggestions for the Use of Activity 5.4

Individuals can work through the two tasks alone and then request that they be reviewed with comments by colleagues whom they trust and who are more knowledgeable than they are on diversity issues. If you are a facilitator working with a group, you may want to have each group work on a separate task area and assign part or all of the seven task areas. You may also want to modify the task areas to better fit the group you are working with. For example, you may want to substitute coaching and counseling for delegation.

The steps to defeat stereotyping that were given in the "Suggestions for the Use of Activity 5.2" may also be useful here. However, push the group to go beyond this. One way to defeat stereotyping in the development area is to monitor staffing decisions to determine if there is a pattern of assigning people of certain identity groups to certain job areas regardless of their previous specialization. For example, some research suggests that racioethnic minority managers tend to be "tracked" into jobs in specific staff areas such as human relations, urban affairs, and public relations even if their formal training is in other areas such as engineering or accounting (Collins, 1989). If internal research of this type is conducted on an ongoing basis, such patterns can be detected and corrected before they become barriers to the optimal utilization of the organization's resources.

One caution we would like to raise about this activity is to try to maintain awareness of the distinction between stereotyping and prejudice in doing the tasks. You can head off problems here by reinforcing the definition of stereotyping when the tasks are assigned.

SUGGESTED FILMS

Several films in Copeland-Griggs Productions' Managing Diversity series address stereotyping. For details on their offerings, contact Lewis Griggs, 302 Twenty-Third Avenue, San Francisco, California 94121. In addition, we have had especially good success with the film featuring Jane Elliott's work, *A Class Divided*.

> *A Class Divided*
> PBS Video
> 1320 Braddock Place
> Alexandria, Virginia 22314-1698
> 800-344-3337

This film is about a third-grade teacher in Iowa, Jane Elliott, who devised an exercise that would help her students to understand some of the problems that stereotyping and prejudice induce in people and that encouraged them to fight against bigotry. The first use of the exercise came the day after the assassination of Martin Luther King, Jr. It worked well. Two years later, the Pubic Broadcasting System came into Elliott's classroom and videotaped the session. Fourteen years later, the third-grade class had a reunion to discuss their views on that experience and what it meant to them, then and now. The reunion is also shown in the film, which includes a segment of the exercise being done with personnel employed in the Iowa prison system.

Discussion Questions

1. How was the third-grade class divided?
2. What makes this film so effective in demonstrating the power of labels? Do the conditions in effect here have any application in "normal" educational and work settings?

3. In what way does the video make a moral and performance-based case for addressing issues on diversity?

4. Should this technique be used in organizational training? Why or why not?

The Color of Fear
Stir Fry Productions
470 Third Street
Oakland California 94607
510-419-3930

The Color of Fear is a film about the pain and anguish that racism has caused in the lives of eight American men of Asian, European, Latino, and African descent. Out of their confrontations and struggle to understand and trust each other emerges an emotional and insightful portrayal into the type of dialogue many of us believe is needed in order to improve race relations in the United States. It addresses racism between the dominant, primarily White culture and the nondominant culture composed primarily of people of color. The second part of the video addresses the biases between minority groups (for example, between Asians and Blacks or between Blacks and Latinos). A drawback of the film is the inclusion of strong profanity that may offend some viewers. However, a version edited to remove profanity is available.

Discussion Questions

1. What are some of the major issues brought up by the men of color in the video?

2. What are some of the major issues brought up by the White men in the video?

3. Do you think that the men of color are hurt, angry, or indifferent? Why?

4. Do you think that the White men are hurt, angry, or indifferent? Why?

5. Do you think that viewing this film has added to your understanding of some of the issues in racioethnic diversity? Identify two important learnings that you gained from the film.

6. Do you think that you could engage in this type of dialogue with others from different backgrounds? Why or why not?

7. Do you see some corollaries with other types of diversity such as age or work specialization? If so, which types?

6

Prejudice and Discrimination

In the previous chapter we learned about stereotyping, one of the most universal phenomena associated with diversity. In this chapter, we want to consider another set of phenomena, prejudice and discrimination.

Although it is closely related to the term *stereotyping,* conventional use of the term *prejudice* in organizational parlance refers to *predetermined negative attitudes toward people based on some group identity.* When prejudicial attitudes get translated into behaviors, then *discrimination* occurs. Because prejudice and discrimination are applicable to a variety of group identities in organizations, and because they can be particularly damaging to interpersonal relationships, we will address them here in some detail. We begin with several readings designed to raise awareness about the nature of prejudice and discrimination and to identify some of the salient issues surrounding these terms.

RAISING AWARENESS

We believe that new information, especially when it is presented in an interesting or compelling way, is highly effective in raising awareness. The readings presented in this first section of the chapter were selected with this in mind. Reading 6.1 is taken from commentaries written by students in an MBA class on diversity one of us recently taught. This short essay gives a cogent account of the awareness-raising process concerning prejudice and discrimination in the life of one young person. Reading 6.2 presents selected commentaries excerpted from a larger set assembled by Fred Lynch in his 1991 book, *Invisible Victims: White Males and the Crisis of Affirmative Action*. One purpose that we have in including this reading is that it gives a voice to members of an identity group that is often underrepresented in discussions about prejudice: White men. We also believe that addressing the sentiments expressed in these readings is another of the requirements of diversity competency.

Reading 6.1
THE PERSONAL AWAKENING OF A
COLLEGE-EDUCATED WHITE, MALE AMERICAN

I am often naive when it comes to negative, deep-rooted issues such as inequality. I grew up in a very liberal town where my best friends represented many different nationalities, religions, and races. I do remember people who would stereotype. I'm ashamed to admit that some of my older relatives and relatives of my friends would make comments that were degrading to others. I also knew that discrimination and segregation had existed in the past, but I shrugged off the negative comments by my elders as outdated remarks from a previously unjust generation. It wasn't until I went to college and then to work that I became aware of the current state of inequity and the fact that discrimination was alive and well, especially in corporate America. I would hear comments from afar that women *wouldn't* do well in certain positions and I heard comments up close that people of color *couldn't* do well in most professional positions.

I had assumed that other people were raised in a relatively open and accepting environment, had many role models from their own culture, and were free to pursue whatever opportunities they wanted without obstruction. It wasn't until I went out into the world of higher education and the world of work that I became aware of the realities of present-day inequalities and the difficult experiences of hostile environments for those who do not fit in the in-group. It has become clearer to me that the poor management of diversity within the workplace has a negative impact on the productivity of both the minority and majority populations. I want to develop some useful skills that will make a better experience for all of us.

Suggestions for the Use of Reading 6.1
This reading contains reactions that we have observed in many people who participate in some kind of formal education on diversity for the first time. Perhaps the most important insight to be gained from the reading is that low

awareness of the continued presence of gender-and race-based prejudice and discrimination is a significant barrier to developmental attention toward diversity competency in the U.S. population. The "shrugging off" of awareness is also a major barrier to change. You might ask yourself, "To what extent am I guilty of naïveté, ignorance, or indifference when it comes to the existence of prejudice or discrimination in organizations?" We suggest that this reading be used for personal insight and as a basis for group discussion of these and other points raised in the essay.

● ● ●

Reading 6.2
INVISIBLE VICTIMS: INDIVIDUAL REACTIONS

FREDERICK R. LYNCH

The previous chapter [in the Lynch book] illustrated the collective compli-
cations wrought by race-and gender-conscious policies in organizational settings. As stated, no one knows how widespread reverse discrimination has
been. One telephone survey of white males suggests a one-out-of-ten figure
(interview with Gordon Black Associates consulting firm, September 1984).
Also largely unknown is how individual white males responded to actual
encounters with reverse discrimination. As William Beer has pointed out in
his review of sociological literature on affirmative action, there is only one
small-scale, laboratory, social scientific study of the reactions of white males
to reverse discrimination situations.

Stephen Johnson tested reverse discrimination reactions of thirty-two white
undergraduate students in a university laboratory setting. Each of the subjects was asked to solve a puzzle. The subjects were told that their responses
would be judged against that of a competitor, who was actually nonexistent.
Half of the subjects were told they had lost to the competitor because the latter's solution of the puzzle was better. The other half were told after solving
the puzzle that the competitor had been assigned a bonus score based on the
other's economic deprivation. Half of the subjects were told the competitor
was black; the other half were told their competition was white.

Attitude measurements taken before and after the experiment indicated
that the subjects who were told they had lost because of the "economic deprivation" factor showed more aggression and perceived injustice toward
black competitors than whites. On the other hand, "When the S's loss
resulted from the other's superior performance . . . the white S's were less

aggressive toward the black other than toward the white other" (Johnson, 1980, p. 15). In other words, the subjects perceived reverse discrimination when told they had lost in competition to a black person because the experimenter had added an arbitrary bonus for economic deprivation. No such reaction occurred when they were told they had lost to the competitor's superior performance. While Johnson's study was cast in the classic experimental paradigm, the results, nonetheless, are of limited depth and generality because of the use of student subjects in a laboratory setting at a university.

Attitude surveys on affirmative action also provide an artificial and highly superficial feel for white males' true feelings on affirmative action. As was seen in Chapter 2 [of the Lynch book], attitude surveys on this topic are highly dependent upon the wording of the questions asked respondents. Chapter 8 [of the Lynch book] shows that an atmosphere akin to 1950s McCarthyism has thwarted open criticism of affirmative action. Thus, though attitude surveys are amenable to the quantitative techniques championed by many leading sociologists, affirmative action realities are resistant to count-and-prove approaches. Institutions and individuals are very sensitive and guarded about this issue.

When studying white males' reactions to reverse discrimination, the researcher must deal with the subjects' strong feelings of self-censorship, pride, shame, pain, and blame. . . .White males' reaction to affirmative action is relatively new and neglected psychological terrain. A more flexible, case-study "logic of discovery" must be employed. Affirmative action might be seen as squarely in the "underground" area of inquiry probed by anthropologist Alan Dundes, who has stated: "The oral tradition has no censorship. . . . That's what makes it so valuable to study. It brings you very close to the cutting edge of what people are thinking. . . People will say a lot of things to each other that they won't commit to paper" (*Los Angeles Times,* April 27, 1986). As was seen in Chapter 3 [of the Lynch book], and will be seen further in this chapter, affirmative action decisions are often informally or orally made with only vague (if any) reference to written policies.

Therefore, the two interviewers and I used more flexible "open-ended" interviewing formats (see Appendix 5 [of the Lynch book]) in our case-study approach to reactions of white males to reverse discrimination situations. We especially wanted to elicit the subjects' reactions *in their own words* whenever possible.

Locating Invisible Victims

From late 1984 to the spring of 1986, two researchers and I sought white, male subjects through networks of friends, acquaintances, coworkers, and a few students. We networked our way to thirty-four subjects and interviewed each in depth, utilizing an interview format of open-ended questions. In locating our subjects, we initiated "referral chains" in a manner outlined by Patrick Biernacki (1986, pp. 200–220). The first contact in a network of six schoolteachers was obtained from a newspaper report on affirmative action preferences in teacher assignments. One of the research assistants worked in a large state bureaucracy—thus, he began a referral chain into that organization. Some subjects were acquaintances or acquaintances of acquaintances who, in turn, suggested others they knew who had confronted reverse discrimination situations. Three individuals who had taken legal action in the courts were obtained from newspaper accounts.

In selecting subjects, we tried to determine to the best of our abilities that the only or primary reason for a subject's losing a job or promotion was race or gender. We eliminated two cases after the interviews were concluded because it could not be clearly determined whether affirmative action was the key factor in a job loss. We also tried to obtain a balance of white-collar and blue-collar employees and private and public employees, though corporate employees were ultimately underrepresented. Approximately one-third of the interviews were conducted by telephone.

Direct interview data were supplemented with subsequent informal interview data with students and others who heard about the project—usually after the formal interviewing had been completed. Interviews with primary subjects were also supplemented with background interviews of ten affirmative action or personnel officers, about half of whom worked for major corporations. More recently, I was able to supplement directly gathered data with accounts of reverse discrimination published in newspapers (May & Houston, 1985) and in political scientist Stanley Greenberg's studies of disaffected white Democrats (1985).

Attempts to sample respondents randomly simply made no sense. Reverse discrimination has not been a randomly distributed phenomenon. My research in this area has led me to believe that reverse discrimination has occurred primarily in public sector employment in states with large minority populations or liberal political traditions. (That affirmative action has operated very strongly in the public sector is suggested by the following statistic: "Fully half of all black managers and professionals are government work-ers" [*The New Republic,* February 6, 1989, p. 18]). Corporations that are gov-ernment contractors have also been subjected to affirmative action reviews by the Office of Federal Contract Compliance. Such reviews have led to somewhat greater gains for minorities (Leonard, 1984a, 1984b) and, hence, may have led to more reverse discrimination situations than in nonmoni-tored corporations (Jencks, 1985).

The interviewers and I sought subjects who were "reasonably sure" that they'd been excluded from a job or a promotion because of their race or gen-der. Approximately one-third of the subjects were interviewed by telephone. Most interviews lasted approximately ninety minutes, though some ran as long as three hours. We promised the subjects full confidentiality. Therefore, in this study all names of individuals are pseudonyms, and no employer is identified by name. In the cases of some of the subjects, I was able to obtain some degree of external validation of their accounts through accounts of others familiar with the case or through statistics on changes in the race and gender composition of workforces. In most subjects' cases, however, I went no further than the individual accounts of reverse discrimination.

It might be argued that the study would have been a stronger one if my interviewers and I had been able to obtain greater external confirmation of subjects' accounts. Yet in terms of the study's focus on the subjects' social psychological reactions, external validation was not of utmost importance. Following the old dictum of the symbolic interactionist perspective in soci-ology: if the subjects perceived the situation as real, then their responses to it were real.

The search for corroborating evidence would have immediately compro-mised the confidentiality of the subjects. Even if this had not been the case, there would have been the time-consuming and logistical problem of locat-ing former employers or administrators and trying to confirm the experience of a single employee that might have occurred several years before. Further-more, it seemed ludicrous to assume that corporate or government officials would readily admit that they had, in fact, openly and deliberately discrimi-nated against a specific white male. The legal implications were obvious.

Social Characteristics of the Subjects
Fourteen of those formally interviewed claimed to have been denied pro-motions primarily or exclusively for reasons having to do with affirmative

action. Eight persons asserted that they had lost jobs for similar reasons, and four persons claimed to have been "ambushed" in the name of affirmative action during job reclassification procedures. The six teachers were caught up in various mandatory teacher transfer programs conducted by the Los Angeles Public School District to provide city-wide racial balance in its teaching force.

Twenty-nine subjects were located and interviewed during 1985 and the spring of 1986. Three pretest subjects, interviewed in 1982, were also included in the total sample, since their responses were comparable to those in the 1985–1986 interviewing period. The average age at time of interview for all subjects was 41.4, with a range of 27 to 58 years of age. However, it should be remembered that most subjects were five to ten years younger when the incidents of reverse discrimination took place, during the 1970s, for the most part. Furthermore, the social characteristics of a distinct subgroup—six teachers and a community college instructor—were somewhat different from the rest. As a group they were older, more liberal (registered Democrats), wealthier, and better educated. Thus, if we factor out this teacher subgroup in terms of age, the median age for the rest of the sample dropped to 38.2.

All the subjects had finished high school, and twenty-two were college graduates, some with graduate degrees. Most were in middle-level white-collar occupations, such as administration or teaching, while others were in sales or crafts occupations (for example, the subgroup of cameramen). One was a truck driver, and one was a law student. Note that these were not necessarily the occupations in which the respondents had experienced discrimination.

Twelve were single or divorced, while the remainder were married. In terms of social origins, it is interesting to observe that few had fathers in high-level professions. Only one was the son of a doctor, and another was the son of a dentist. One had a mother who had been a lawyer. Much more typical was the blue-collar, craftsman, or lower-level white-collar father. Many of the subjects in this study have experienced upward mobility in their occupational history. Some have maintained that direction of movement, while others, through affirmative action or other problems, have lost ground.

Affirmative Action Defined: Classification of Responses

I will use the terms *affirmative action* and *reverse discrimination* somewhat interchangeably throughout this study. By *affirmative action,* I will be referring primarily to those policies which allegedly attempt to remedy past discrimination against minorities and women through the use of numerical quotas and preferential group treatment (that is, "goals and timetables"). I am primarily concerned with minority quotas and somewhat less with quotas for women. Quotas for minorities seem to have had more emotional and political bite than those for women. Until a few years ago, social scientists and proponents of affirmative action tended to ignore or simply dismissed the probability that reverse discrimination against whites might even exist. The same was true of the mass media. Therefore, professional and popular literature simply has had no place for such social realities.

There have been numerous studies of how other groups have reacted to race or sex discrimination. The following list of possible responses can be culled from this literature: acceptance, avoidance, aggression, deviance, negative self-image, increased in-group solidarity, assimilation, denial of membership in the affected group, or the "vicious circle" in which discrimination causes negative behavior among members of the affected group, which, in turn, reinforces stereotypes leading to discrimination (Allport, 1958; Vander Zanden, 1980; Parello, 1985). A problem with such categorization schemes is that classifications are not necessarily mutually exclusive; that is, there can be combinations such as "acceptance-anger," "acceptance-avoidance," or "acceptance with self-hatred." For purposes of classifying white males' responses to discrimination, the categories such as "assimilation" or "denial of membership in the affected group" really made no sense. Instead, I have classified the thirty-two subjects' responses into five categories: (1) Acquiescence, (2) Acquiescence/Anger, (3) Acquiescence/Departure, (4) Defiance/Protest, and (5) Circumvention.

Acquiescence

The men who acquiesced usually did so with a measure of quiet resignation. "There was nothing I could do," was a common refrain. Most felt they had no alternative job opportunity at the time or in the foreseeable future. Nearly all sensed—or were told by superiors or coworkers—that they should keep their mouths shut. One or two felt that setbacks were temporary and expressed optimism that they would get their chance eventually. Such persons usually felt that the goals of affirmative action were worthy and that they were willing to endure the sacrifice.

Bob Allen

Allen (age forty at the time of the interview) was one of those who passively and optimistically acquiesced. He was a supervisor in a personnel department of a large California financial corporation. During the mid–1970s, he and other coworkers began to wryly observe that you "had to wear a skirt to get ahead here." Allen was passed over for promotions on three consecutive occasions. All three individuals promoted over Allen were females, two of whom he felt were much less qualified than he; in fact, he had hired one in an entry-level position only the year before. (Data obtained from this corporation indicate that, during the 1970s, the percentage of female managerial personnel jumped sharply from 8 to 36 percent.) Though there was some grumbling, Allen viewed the situation as temporary and felt he would eventually be promoted. Generally, he favored affirmative action as it is practiced in his corporation, "though I wouldn't want them to go any further." He opposed strict quotas and felt that the only long-run solution was selection by merit. He classified himself as a liberal and continued to vote for liberal Democratic candidates.

Allen's was one of the first interviews conducted for this study, part of an initial pilot sample conducted in 1981. In 1985, he was reinterviewed. He had, indeed, been promoted. He maintained that he was glad he kept silent concerning earlier episodes of reverse discrimination because "it would have been more damaging to my career to have complained rather than maintain silence." He felt that affirmative action pressures at his corporation climaxed in the early 1980s "when there was sort of a revolt among black employees in one division who felt they were being discriminated against. . . . Everyone was accusing everyone else of being racist." The matter was finally settled. Allen worked on labor-force statistics to determine if the corporation was utilizing representative numbers of minorities, a task he found difficult to carry out because the corporation was spread throughout the state but was concentrated in two large urban areas. He said, "We didn't know which statistics to use."

Acquiescence/Anger

This response category contained the largest number of persons who simply felt they could do nothing about a reverse discrimination episode but were nonetheless angry or very angry. The very angry persons often complained to coworkers or friends and sometimes to supervisors. One or two wrote letters to superiors, but no one took the incident to outside agencies such as the courts or the Equal Employment Opportunity Commission (EEOC).

Robert Oakes and George Mann

Robert Oakes (fifty-six at the interview) had been working as a cameraman in a pool used by local television stations during the late 1960s and 1970s. He began to notice that more and more minority (and a few female) apprentice/trainees were being hired on and, eventually, sent out with teams of experienced cameramen. He also observed that, in the wake of the 1965 Watts riots, more and more news assignments were minority-oriented: "I began to wonder if there was any other news in this town besides minority-concerned stuff."

As opposed to a specific jolt or event, Robert Oakes and a fellow cameraman, George Mann, began to notice affirmative action as an unfolding pattern of events, but they didn't think it would affect them. For one thing, the quality of the trainees, they both claimed, was extremely poor. But, in the late 1970s, the stations converted from film equipment to videotape cameras. The stations made all cameramen and apprentices reapply for videotape cameraman credentials. When they did so, the older white male veterans were screened out while the young minority trainees were given the jobs. Robert Oakes recalled:

> The transition from film to tape involved making the veterans apply for their own jobs. You had to get a Number One ticket from the FCC. Guys went through a lot to get those tickets—it cost some of them $700 to do it—and they still couldn't get their old jobs back. They had to try and buy their own jobs and they couldn't do it.

Oakes was angry, in part, because he "saw it coming too late" and was resentful that the union did nothing about it. He also sustained greater financial injuries than did his friend George Mann, who was ten years younger. Mann admitted, "I knew they'd sell us out—the stations and the union . . . and the studios to eliminate the high-seniority people."

Defiance/Protest

Three persons interviewed for this study filed lawsuits against employers on charges of discrimination: Mike Grant, Frank Nunn, and Samuel Gray.

A fourth subject, teacher David Brown, tried to seek redress through his teacher's union (to no avail).

Frank Nunn

By his own admission, forty-six-year-old Frank Nunn has always been a "classic Jewish liberal." He was active in the civil rights movement and suffered a back injury during a police beating, which has hospitalized him twice since that time. He believed in affirmative action and still does, though he admits he still hasn't sorted out his feelings on the matter ("I agree with Justice Powell in the Bakke decision that race can be *a* factor, but not *the* factor.").

While involved in the civil rights movement and other social causes, Nunn obtained bachelor's and master's degrees in social science and, in the 1970s, became actively involved in the administration of a popular black mayor. Because of his background and training in public administration, Nunn obtained a rather high-level job, though he did notice that he was the only white at that level in that particular agency.

The agency for which he worked for two years was not covered by the city civil service system until 1977, when plans were made to convert the agency positions to civil service status. The agency employees had to take the civil service examination and be merged with civil service employees already on the list seeking promotions. Nunn claims to have been at the top of the merged list, but the next six highest scores went to persons already in city government in other agencies. There were eight new positions. Two minority administrators in Nunn's agency were not high enough on the list to retain their positions in the transformed agency unless Nunn was removed from the list.

Therefore, according to Nunn, he was abruptly and without warning fired from his position two weeks before it was to come under civil service rules. By law, his name was automatically removed from the list, and the two minority administrators retained their positions in the "new" agency. (Nunn obtained internal memoranda detailing these intentions, and these documents were the basis of his legal proceedings.)

Nunn filed charges with the EEOC and the Civil Service Board. The latter voted unanimously to restore Frank to two civil service lists and he was offered another job at $8,000 a year less than he had previously earned. But city officials refused to follow through on the other recommendations of the board, and Nunn again filed charges with the EEOC and other federal agencies. He claimed to have been harassed in his new position to such an extent that he was forced to seek psychiatric counseling for the first time in his life. The conflicts on the job compounded problems in his social life, and Nunn wound up taking two short disability leaves and a final long-term disability leave.

Since the EEOC had a huge backlog of cases and since the city was reneging on promises made to him, Nunn filed a reverse discrimination case against the city in 1979. He reached a settlement with the city regarding the job in which he was harassed (after the reverse discrimination event) and he enrolled in law school in another city.

Looking back on the situation in which he eventually suffered reverse discrimination, he admits:

> I should have seen it coming. . . . I was the only white male at that level in the entire agency. There were various slights and slurs that I took because I wanted to work in the administration of a black mayor. So I turned the other cheek and got the . . . slapped out of me. . . . It was a twenty-four-hour-a-day battle. . . . It shot my personal life to h_____.

Nunn lost his reverse discrimination lawsuit against the city in 1986.

Suggestions for the Use of Reading 6.2

The great contrast in themes between this reading and Reading 6.1 is one of the reasons that we have chosen this reading. Although we do not agree with some of the statements in the reading (for example, we do not think that it is appropriate to use the terms *affirmative action* and *reverse discrimination* interchangeably), we do agree that the reactions expressed by these White men are important to efforts to change organizations toward multiculturalism. The reading raises other significant issues as well. The following questions are a mere sample of the many useful ones that could be used for discussion of this reading:

1. Evaluate the three reactions illustrated here. Which ones are useful and appropriate? Why? Is one of them "best" or better than any other?

2. Do you agree that *affirmative action* and *reverse discrimination* are interchangeable terms? Why or why not?

3. What is your reaction to the statement: "I am primarily concerned with minority quotas and somewhat less with quotas for women because quotas for minorities seem to have had more emotional and political bite than the latter" (Lynch, 1991, p. 56)? What effect, if any, do you think this kind of decision has on the affirmative action debate?

CREATING UNDERSTANDING

The previous material in this chapter was designed to increase your awareness of prejudice and discrimination and to present it from more than one point of view. Readings 6.3 and 6.4 have been assembled to extend the learning process further. These longer readings should deepen your knowledge of the phenomena of prejudice and discrimination as well as making the point that their application is not limited to the identities of gender and racioethnicity.

Reading 6.3
ATTITUDES THAT AFFECT EMPLOYMENT OPPORTUNITIES FOR PERSONS WITH DISABILITIES

HENRY MCCARTHY

Even today, when leisure-time interests exert increasing influence in our lives, employment is, for most adults, the primary source of not only income, but also identity and interactions, if not satisfactions. Unfortunately, for most adults with disabilities, employment represents only a yet-to-be-fulfilled hope, a close but inaccessible goal, a daily reminder that they are not among the majority. Survey statistics estimate the employment rate in the disabled population to be 34.5 percent (27.4 percent full-time and 7.1 percent part-time) among men and 19.4 percent (11.9 percent full-time and 7.5 percent part-time) among women (Bowe, 1983). Comparative rates for the general population are 79.7 percent (70.4 percent full-time and 9.3 percent part-time) and 58.6 percent (41.0 percent full-time and 17.6 percent part-time), respectively. Thus persons with disabilities are gainfully employed at a rate one-quarter to two-fifths that of the general working-age population. This inequity in employment is compounded by the fact that many persons with disabilities work in the secondary labor market (Dunn, 1981); thus they experience underemployment in seasonal or low-level jobs, with less pay, security, and promotional opportunities than their skill and motivation warrant.

Although recent, this information is hardly new. Since 1920, a massive public system of vocational rehabilitation (VR) throughout the United States has attempted to remedy this problem by providing assessment, training, support, and placement services to get disabled persons permanently and (preferably) competitively employed. Much of the personal frustration, for both VR professionals and their clients, that the poor employment statistics

Source: This reading is excerpted from Henry McCarthy, "Attitudes That Affect Employment Opportunities for Persons with Disabilities," in Harold E. Yucker (Ed.), *Attitudes Toward Persons with Disabilities* (New York: Springer, 1988), pp. 246–261. Copyright © 1988 by Springer Publishing Co., Inc. Used by permission.

summarize is mirrored in our inadequate understanding of the problem and what we can do to tackle it effectively. Considerable speculation, debate, and research have been carried out for the last two decades for the purpose of identifying, clarifying, and altering factors that contribute to the employment inequity that confronts persons with disabilities. This reading discusses the prominent explanations for employment problems among persons with disabilities and offers a developmental framework for possibly addressing the problems.

Principal Explanations for the Poor Employment Rates of Persons with Disability

Several of the pioneers in the social psychology of disability were students of Kurt Lewin and thus had a strong Gestalt orientation (for example, Barker & Wright, 1954). From the beginnings of rehabilitation theory and research, there was an appreciation of how characteristics of both the individual and the environment interact to shape the definition and outcome of life events in general and goal-directed behavior in particular. At the same time, the emerging practice of rehabilitation was being shaped by physical medicine and vocational education, disciplines that are emphatically more geared to clinical assessment and treatment of individual differences and deficits than to person-environment interaction. These disciplines' change-the-client orientation took hold and became the implicit assumption of rehabilitation programming and philosophy (Berkowitz, 1984; Stubbins, 1982). Since the mid-1960s, however, the various civil rights and consciousness-raising movements have revived consideration of the role of the environment in human affairs, particularly as a perpetrator of social disadvantage. Reflections of this trend are evident in the philosophy of the Independent Living movement (Crewe & Zola, 1983; Frieden, 1980, 1984), in the shift from positivist to social constructionist theories in medical sociology (Szasz, 1961), and in the critical writings of rehabilitation scholars like Finkelstein (1980), Hahn (1984), and Stubbins (1984). Table 6.1 lists the major causes that have been advanced to explain the poor outcomes that persons with disabilities have experienced in the labor market. I have subsumed the common explanations under three principal paradigms that differ in the definition of the source of the problem and the consequent change strategies to be pursued.

**TABLE 6.1. Explanations for Employment Inequities
Experienced by Persons with Disabilities**

Clinical Services Model
  Functional limitations
  Poor motivation to work
  Social-skill deficits
  Job-search-skill deficits

Social Systems Model
  Architectural and worksite inaccessibility
  Lack of accessible and affordable transportation
  Disability income and benefits disincentives
  Tight labor-market conditions and policies
  Prejudice of employers and coworkers

Career Development Model
  Shortsighted perspective (finding a job instead of developing a career)
  Neglected or sheltered work socialization
  Unilateral and isolated approach to vocational programming
  Narrow concept and application of accommodation for employment
  Insufficient self-responsibility for own career activities and outcomes

SOURCE: Henry McCarthy, "Attitudes That Affect Employment Opportunities for Persons with Disabilities," in Harold E. Yucker (Ed.), *Attitudes Toward Persons with Disabilities* (New York: Springer, 1988), pp. 246–261.

Clinical Services Model

Explanations based on this *client-focused* model attribute the problem of unemployment to failings within the individual who has the disability. Thus the person is seen as the source of the problem and as an appropriate target for intervention efforts.

Although this model focuses on the client, only one of its five principal explanations (inadequate work motivation) tends to imply that the person with the disability is responsible. Functional limitations are usually seen as an unavoidable consequence of the disabling condition itself, and the three types of skill deficits (social, occupational, and job-search) are as likely to be blamed on the family or involved professionals as on the individual.

Accordingly, it is worth recognizing that even though the clinical model defines the problem as existing within the person, it often extends responsibility for it to the social environment. *The conclusion that adherents of this clinical ideology draw is a recommendation to increase services and professional specialization to wage a better attack on eliminating the personal deficits of the clients.*

Social Systems Model

Given their sensitivity to the influence of the many facets of society, it is not surprising that the proponents of this model have identified a broader scope of contextual barriers than the personal handicaps that comprise the clinical model. The most concrete of these barriers is the inaccessibility of the environment in general and worksites in particular. Even getting *to* barrier-ridden buildings is difficult or impossible, it is pointed out, because public transportation is largely inaccessible and private transportation options are usually unaffordable. Labor-market constraints exist when there is a lack of jobs due to depressions in local economies or a lack of a compensating federal commitment to a full-employment policy such as Holland and Sweden have (Conte, 1982). Furthermore, our system maintains some explicit regulations that can create significant financial disincentives by inadvertently discouraging qualified clients with several physical handicaps from accepting employment because they would have to relinquish their welfare income or subsidized medical coverage and attendant care.

Although often unexpressed, discriminatory attitudes of people in employment settings have not gone unacknowledged as a major perceived cause of the vocational problems of persons with disabilities. Whether conceived as ignorance, inexperience, or interaction strain, the prejudice of employers and coworkers has been the subject of more research and remediation efforts (Phillips & Smith, 1982; Schroedel & Jacobsen, 1978; Schweitzer & Deely, 1981) than possibly the four other principal systemic barriers combined. Expression of this emphatic attribution to employers' negative attitudes ranges from the pointed to the implied, from scholarly writing (Hahn, 1984; U.S. Commission on Civil Rights, 1983) to bumper stickers declaring that attitudinal barriers are the biggest handicap that persons with disabilities face. Even the adherents of the clinical model operate in ways that reflect, in part, an underlying assumption that employers and coworkers are particularly unaccepting of this minority. For example, prolonged tenures in sheltered workshops and in other capacity-building re-habilitation programs are often the consequence of rehabilitation person-nel's underestimation of client competence. However, they may likewise be misguided by exaggeration of community employers' discriminatory prac-tices, believed to be counteracted by making persons with disabilities over-compensate just so they can compete (Rickard, Triandis, & Patterson, 1963). Explanations and implications of this strong belief in the existence of nega-tive employer attitudes are discussed in the next section. *Before detailing this specific explanation, it should be noted that the strategy consistent with all of the causes identified by the socioenvironmental model is one of advocacy for social change that will reduce or eliminate the systemic barriers.*

Disability Prejudice as a Proximal and Appealing Cause of Employment Inequity

Negative attitudes toward persons with handicaps in the workplace have be-come somewhat blown out of proportion among employment barriers, due to their immediate plausibility and intervention appeal. That is, the most immediate reason why a person who is in the complex and subjectively evaluated situation of applying for a job gets rejected would appear to be something involved in the judgment of the evaluator. And the most salient stimulus that an unknown applicant presents to an employer-evaluator is the negatively valued disability. The plausibility seems indisputable. Fur-thermore, in a topological analysis, the evaluator stands as a gatekeeper con-trolling entry to employment; therefore, because this is the first encounter as we search backward from the rejection event for explanations, the evalu-ator emerges as the proximal cause. In addition, most people, regardless of how important they believe the other system barriers to be, would be more personally motivated and professionally prepared to attempt to change the attitude of the evaluator than to work for architectural barrier removal, lobby for regulatory revisions in benefits programs, and the like. Not that attitude change is an easy task, but it has a definite appeal that has long captivated the rehabilitation community.

My point is not that negative attitudes toward persons with disabilities in the workplace are negligible, but that there are numerous other issues and agendas that also need to be addressed to improve the employment opportunity structure. We should not be trapped by the proximal and appealing cause.

Data from persons who themselves have handicaps are an important source of perspective on these issues and provide direction for determining needed interventions. In a Louis Harris and Associates (1986) survey, for example, the percentage of respondents whose employers had made some sort of accommodation to enable them to do their jobs was 10 percent greater than the percentage who said that they had encountered job discrimination because of their disabilities (35 percent versus 25 percent). Even the perception of barriers by those from this survey who were not working full-time was telling. The most frequently acknowledged reasons for their unemployment were the handicapping consequences of the disability (78 percent) and the treatment it required (51 percent). Forty-seven percent did believe that employers would not recognize that they are capable of doing a job because of their disability; however, almost as many (40 percent) felt that the lack of available jobs was an important reason why they were not working, 38 percent felt that their inadequate education and lack of marketable skills hindered them, and 28 percent considered the lack of accessible and affordable transportation to be a problem. Among the respondents who reported still facing barriers in their lives, only 1 percent suggested that changing employer attitudes was the most important thing that could be done to help them, and only another 1 percent offered this secondarily as a remedy.

Another survey (McCarthy, 1986) of persons with disabilities asked them why they thought they had not been hired for jobs for which they had applied. The most frequent reasons identified by the respondents, who were in their twenties, were the extent of their (limited) work experience (43 percent), competition from other candidates (23 percent), and the prejudice of employers (14 percent).

In summary, we have to consider seriously how each of several factors can create for persons with disabilities problems comparable to or greater than those stemming from employer prejudice.

Attitudes, Disability, and Employability:
A Career Development Analysis

In order to capture a broader picture of factors that can influence the occupational achievement of persons with handicaps, it is useful to consider not the event of getting a job (or even *the* job of one's dreams), but the long-range, evolving process of career development (Akridge, 1985; Navin &

Myers, 1983; Vandergood, Jacobsen, & Worrall, 1977). The proposed career development perspective consists of three distinct but potentially overlapping phases. The first is the stage of *work socialization,* during which children and young adults are shaped by education and experience, mostly indirect and informal, to value challenge and effort, to accept responsibility and independence, to demonstrate both initiative and teamwork.

The second phase of career development involves intensive *vocational habilitation or rehabilitation.* This is accomplished through a variety of services typically referred to as career education and exploration, vocational evaluation, training (for example, personal adjustment, work adjustment, occupational skill, or work hardening), and job placement.

The third phase of career development concerns *entry, integration, and advancement in employment.*

Even this brief outline of a career development paradigm demonstrates how it offers some advantages in being either more analytical or more comprehensive than the clinical services or social systems models, particularly for investigating potential attitudinal influences.

"Hiring the Handicapped" Versus Human Resources Accommodation and Development

Once the bold slogan for getting persons with disabilities into the economic mainstream, "hiring the handicapped" is now recognized as having strategic and semantic disadvantages. From a career development perspective, it is not sufficient to establish hiring (or getting oneself or one's client hired) as the goal. When coupled with pity or paranoia (about governmental intrusion for lack of compliance with nondiscrimination legislation), such a shortsighted orientation could lead to creating and accepting less-than-desirable, if not downright dysfunctional, matches between job vacancies and applicants (Daniels, 1985; Young, Rosati, & Vandergood, 1986). Instead, initiating employment should be conceived of as merely one significant step in a process that continues to evolve, while several equally important issues, such as satisfactory job performance, career advancement, job satisfaction, skill enhancement, and wellness in the workplace, are pursued.

Part of the agenda of every civil rights group is working to effect positive attitude change by promoting more affirmative terms for its constituency and activities. Much has been written, for example, about sexist terminology in our everyday language and the impact this can have on limiting our images and expectations of women. The disabled community has likewise combined its search for equality with a scrutiny of the terms used to refer to it. Among the preferred terms, *the handicapped* is not included. It homogenizes a group that is truly heterogeneous and should be recognized and treated accordingly. Particularly in the context of employment, the term highlights problems and deficiencies rather than assets. Nor is this just a matter of terminological niceties, for one could easily imagine the consequences of a strict "hire the handicapped" mentality. If hiring is done from a motive based on charity or tokenism, the employee is hardly going to be given the experience, challenge, and consideration—regardless of her or his potential—that it takes to get promoted. Furthermore, if job performance problems (actual or anticipated) are perceived as an inevitable function of disability, they will be unnecessarily tolerated, instead of being investigated and ameliorated. Usually the simplest and cheapest solution to the problem is to accommodate the disability.

Accommodation has become synonymous with the practical solutions to specific problems posed by disability or other special circumstances; but fundamentally, *accommodation is an attitude* that allows for the full expression of human talent. It does so either by removing any barriers (attitudinal, physical, or procedural) that interfere with accomplishing a goal or by providing whatever assistance or support is needed to bring someone to the level where goals can be approached by standard or alternative means. Accordingly, accommodations should be thought of as a right by which to obtain equal opportunity to participate, not as a special privilege. By analogy, accommodation could be said to encompass the concept of a negative right (for example, a guarantee against interference with individual decision making) and a positive right (for example, a guarantee of provision of the resources needed by an individual), as discussed by Scull (1981).

This broader conception of what accommodation means is at the crux of the labor policies of many European, and particularly Scandinavian, countries (Habeck, Galvin, Frey, Chadderdon, & Tate, 1985), as well as the developing movement for "supported work" in the United States (Ellien & Vandergood, 1985; Mank, Rhodes, & Bellamy, 1985). Although almost thirty federal laws prohibit discrimination on the basis of handicap, many of them explicitly or implicitly providing for accommodation (U.S. Commission on Civil Rights, 1983), this principle is incompatible with the spirit of rugged individualism that has pervaded American culture and has been absorbed by its social institutions, including rehabilitation (Stubbins, 1982). Thus the typical attitude toward accommodation connotes something special being done for a few who do not fit in, rather than a benefit that we all enjoy, both directly and indirectly. Adherents of this attitude fail to acknowledge the ample evidence demonstrating the general usefulness and cost-effectiveness of many accommodations. For example, barrier-free buildings qualify for lower insurance rates (Asher & Asher, 1976); they also ease access for workers transporting heavy loads, pregnant women, and many others in addition to persons with permanent mobility limitations.

Findings from a nationwide study of corporate accommodation practices for employees with handicaps clearly indicated that the firms most likely to consider and successfully implement accommodations were those with a philosophy emphasizing the importance of the individual and with a notably low turnover (Berkeley Planning Associates, 1982). Such qualities reflect not merely a policy for personnel management, but a commitment to human resource development. Typically, this approach is also characterized by extra efforts to ensure the safety, wellness, career enhancement, and self-fulfillment of employees. These goals are reflected in corporate support of carpooling, child care, health promotion, recreation, volunteerism, continuing education, flextime and job-sharing options, and assistance and rehabilitation programming for troubled employees and injured workers. By embracing a philosophy of accommodation and pursuing a human resource development strategy (Campbell, 1985), employers will end up screening in, integrating, and promoting many more useful employees with disabilities than by waiting to react to "hire the handicapped" appeals. And that is how it should be.

Passivity Versus Self-Responsibility in Pursuing One's Career Development

Throughout this reading I have discussed socializing agents, employment brokers, and employers in terms of their lack of awareness of, or attention to, the career development process, and particularly their participation in it and how this leads to lost opportunities for enhancing, if not detrimental effects on, the eventual employment of persons with disabilities (see McCarthy, 1988, for a more complete discussion). Only when each group recognizes and fulfills the responsibilities of its role will the employment preparation and integration of this minority be achieved. One of these groups is persons with disabilities. Indeed, they have the ultimate responsibility for securing the extent and quality of experience and assistance needed to accomplish their career goals. Unfortunately, many of the same factors that detract specifically from their vocational success can also have a deleterious effect on their general ability to determine and satisfy their needs. For example, the lack of self-concept as a skillful person and potential worker that characterizes some persons with disabilities could be merely one manifestation of a larger sense of inferiority and learned helplessness. There is extensive literature describing the second-class treatment allotted to persons who have disabilities or other stigmas in our society (for example, Eisenberg, Griggins, & Duval, 1982) and the ways in which the consequences of this mistreatment are exacerbated by its becoming internalized by its very victims.

Neither the deprived situation nor the succumbing reaction, however, is inevitable or, these days, more likely to occur than not. The rippling effects of consciousness-raising efforts and advocacy campaigns have taught many persons with disabilities to take initiative in shaping their lives, to familiarize and assert themselves with the established service systems and the laws protecting their rights. Their energies need to be applied to fulfilling their own responsibilities as well as to making the system accountable. Those who seek change through growth accept the burdens of engaging in self-development activities such as acquiring knowledge and skills, cultivating support systems, and seizing opportunities for enrichment. Recognition is rightly given to the Independent Living movement for effecting an enormous elevation in the levels of consciousness and commitment of persons with disabilities to directing their own destinies. Among its various agendas, however, career development issues have typically been a lower priority than psychosocial peer counseling, transportation, housing, health care benefits, and assistive devices. While all of these concerns contribute to employment prospects, it would be desirable for Independent Living centers to intensify their efforts toward directly maximizing the career development of their patrons.

Conclusions
The thesis of this reading is that, in order to understand how attitudes affect the employability of persons with disabilities, it is necessary to consider more broadly than has traditionally been done both the processes and the participants involved in the employment enterprise. Specifically, it is argued that research and practice have focused exclusively on clients' deficits or em-

ployers' negative attitudes as the cause of underemployment among persons with handicaps. This results in a disproportionate emphasis on or downright restriction of intervention efforts to a single stage and group, rather than the lifelong career development process, which many individuals, groups, and systems influence. We need to acknowledge the impact of, and encourage collaboration among, the constellation of people who shape the work socialization, career education, vocational habilitation and rehabilitation, and equal access to employment, integration, and advancement of persons with disabilities in our society.

Suggestions for the Use of Reading 6.3

This reading provides a conceptual framework for thinking and discussion about factors that affect employment opportunities for persons with disabilities. It also provides some data on the extensiveness of the unemployment or underemployment problem for persons with disabilities. All of this is expected to increase your knowledge about disability as a dimension of diversity in the workplace. Opportunities for discussion abound in the reading. Some questions that we especially like include:

1. Which of the three models explaining employment barriers is the most compelling for you?

2. How do you interpret the author's position that the role of prejudice in the employment problems of persons with disabilities is often exaggerated, in light of the data in the article (for example, 47 percent say that employers do not recognize their employment capabilities and 25 percent say that they have faced job discrimination)?

3. What messages does the reading have for persons who have disabilities themselves?

4. Given the information in the reading, what strategy would you suggest be taken by organizations for increasing the employment opportunities of persons with disabilities?

Reading 6.4
SEXUAL ORIENTATION IN THE WORKPLACE
The Strategic Challenge

CHARLES R. COLBERT III AND JOHN G. WOFFORD

Sexual orientation in the workplace has become a critical issue in human resource management. Employers of all kinds—private corporations, public agencies, and nonprofit organizations—today face the challenge of creating a hospitable and fair work environment for lesbians, bisexuals, and gay men.[1]

Gay people have always been in the workplace. In the past, however, most concealed their sexual orientation, thereby making themselves a largely invisible minority. Now, more are becoming open about their sexuality, displaying photographs of significant others at their work stations, talking about the personal side of their lives to coworkers, and requesting for members of their families health care coverage and other benefits traditionally accorded only to the families of heterosexuals. They are insisting on fairly managed workplaces, with full respect and equal employment entitlement and opportunity.

This reading describes the pattern of discrimination against gays that has existed, the legal mechanisms for challenging it, and the changing climate of opinion that makes it increasingly unacceptable. It notes some of the complexities of the subject, including the relationship of sexual orientation to issues concerning HIV/AIDS in the workplace, and offers concrete suggestions for human resource managers facing the challenges of creating a non-hostile work environment and developing strategies for improvement of workplace conditions and attitudes within a framework of recognized organizational principles. Such strategies should include responsible actions at all levels of the workforce—chief executives, union heads, supervisors, coworkers, and gay men and lesbians themselves.

Source: This reading is excerpted from Charles R. Colbert III and John G. Wofford, "Sexual Orientation in the Workplace: The Strategic Challenge," *Compensation and Benefits Management,* Summer 1993, pp. 1–18. Copyright © 1993 by Panel Publishers, a division of Aspen Publishers, Inc. Used by permission.

The Hostile Work Environment

Approximately 5 percent to 10 percent of the general population is estimated to be gay or lesbian in fundamental sexual orientation (Gonsiorek & Weinrich, 1991). Unlike other minorities whose race, color, surnames, physical handicap, age, or gender may make it obvious that they are members of a legally protected employment category, gay men and lesbians can be identified only by choosing to be open, by being "outed" (having one's sexual orientation revealed by others), or, where protective legislation exists, by filing a claim of discrimination. (Generally, in order for a claim of discrimination to succeed, it must be shown that an employer was aware of an employee's sexual orientation prior to the alleged incidents of discrimination.)

Sexual orientation is one of those basic elements of identity that make gay people part of a minority in a diverse workforce. The other primary elements include race, age, gender, ethnicity, and disability.

In many places and for a long time, gay men and lesbians have faced a hostile work environment—so hostile, indeed, that most have been afraid to be open about their sexual orientation. The extent of hostility is therefore hard to measure; the invisibility of most of the victims makes workplace discrimination more prevalent than most people think.

Despite such invisibility, a number of studies document discrimination in the workplace. A pattern emerges from studies made during the last decade: about one quarter of gay men and lesbians actually have experienced discrimination in the workplace, and about three quarters fear it.[2]

Such discrimination occurs throughout the employment cycle, from hiring to firing and everything in between:

Denial of Recruitment Opportunities

In a 1987 nationwide survey of 200 members of the National Association of Corporate and Professional Recruiters, 51 percent said they screened out job applicants who are homosexual (*Hartford Courant*, November 23, 1987). Such practices are being increasingly challenged in court.

Limits on Promotions

In another nationwide survey in 1987, 66 percent of 351 top executives responded that they would hesitate to promote someone who is homosexual to management committee level (*Wall Street Journal*, March 26, 1987). In one company, a senior professional was offered a transfer and major promotion by headquarters, only to have the division's chief executive raise problems when he discovered the transferring employee had a same-sex partner who would be moving, too.

Limits on Work Assignments

Some employers have limited work assignments available to openly gay employees based on assumed customer expectations or the wishes of other employees. "Our customers don't want to deal with an openly lesbian loan officer" is a typical justification. By analogy to other developments in employment law, employers should not be able to bar gay employees on the basis of assumed objections from clients. Just as the airlines were prohibited from hiring only young, female flight attendants because they claimed that was what customers expected, so employers should not be able to limit their hiring only to employees thought to be "acceptable." In another company a straight man refused to be put on a team for a business trip with a gay colleague, even though both were essential to the purpose of the trip.

Restrictions on Social Opportunities

Social events, business trips, or small talk in the workplace can be big trouble for closeted gay people. They may fear bringing significant others to social functions, such as holiday parties or company picnics. They may also feel restricted in talking about their private lives in the way other employees talk about their dates, or about the health, job accomplishments, or travels of their families.

Physical and Verbal Harassment

A few illustrations in a state with protective legislation against workplace discrimination show the extent of harassment:

- Coworkers in one large Boston-based financial institution were charged with harassing an employee by leaving notes on his desk saying, "Die, fag."
- In an agency of the federal government, a new gay and lesbian support group was targeted by a fellow employee who stood outside the door and said, "They should all be videotaped and then every last one of them shot."
- At a furniture manufacturer's, coworkers threw wood chips at, taunted, and assaulted a gay employee; supervisors later fired the gay man for causing trouble.

Termination of Employment

Employees are often fired because they are perceived to be gay—sometimes with this perception made explicit, but more often with the reason cloaked. Cases include one in which a highly placed manager with eight years of outstanding evaluations was fired "because of the business climate" after other workers were outraged when he circulated a sign-up sheet seeking sponsors for the AIDS Action Committee's annual fund-raising walk and started to wear an earring to work.

A hostile work environment has been the norm in too many workplaces. From recruitment to retention, from limits on assignments to limits on promotions, from taunts to threats to outright violence, gay men and lesbians have been subjected to many indignities for many years. Most stayed in the workplace closet out of fear, shame, guilt, or a combination of these. But dramatically increasing self-esteem is changing these attitudes, radically and quickly. One result is insistence on fair treatment under the law.

The Emerging Legal Context

Legal developments are expanding the rights of gay men and lesbians to be free of hostile work environments and to share fully in the American promise of equal employment opportunity by making it unlawful to consider sexual orientation in employment decisions. But the legal battles, and the political controversies that underlie them, are far from over. Opponents attack these legal developments as "preferential treatment" for gay people; proponents respond that it is a simple matter of fairness and nondiscrimination.

Legal protections of gay people in the workplace have been established by legislation, executive orders, municipal ordinances, employment contracts, and case law applying the general principles of employment law as well as specific constitutional protections. At least seventy-two million Americans are now covered by these requirements—close to 30 percent of the total U.S. population. A summary of legal developments follows.

State Law

States that have enacted protective legislation in the workplace are: Wisconsin (1982); Massachusetts (1989); Hawaii and Connecticut (1991); New Jersey, Vermont, and California (1992); and Minnesota (1993). The District of Columbia (1977) also has enacted protective legislation. In states where more comprehensive protective legislation has not been enacted statewide, at least eight governors have issued executive orders banning discrimination in public employment. The states include Minnesota, New Mexico, New York, Ohio, Oregon, Pennsylvania, Rhode Island, and Washington.

Massachusetts' Lesbian and Gay Civil Rights Act (Massachusetts General Laws Chapter 151B; Chapter 272 sections 92A, 98) has the features typical of the state and municipal laws:

- It adds "sexual orientation" to the list of already protected categories: race, color, religious creed, national origin, sex, age, ancestry, and handicap. It defines sexual orientation as "having an orientation for or being identified as having an orientation for heterosexuality, bisexuality, or homosexuality."
- There are four areas where discrimination on the basis of sexual orientation is illegal—housing, public accommodations, credit, and both public and private employment.
- In the employment area, the new law makes it illegal for employers, labor unions, and employment agencies to refuse to hire or employ, to discharge, or to discriminate against workers in compensation or in other terms, conditions, or privileges of employment on the basis of sexual orientation.
- The remedies for employment discrimination can include hiring or rehiring, promotions, back pay, damages for emotional distress, and attorney's fees.
- Employers with fewer than six employees, either full-or part-time, are exempt from the law.
- Religious organizations are also exempt with respect to positions that promote the principles of the particular religion, as they are generally from many other state nondiscrimination provisions because of constitutional protections of freedom of religion.
- Complaints of antigay discrimination must be filed with the Massachusetts Commission Against Discrimination (MCAD) within six months of the alleged event and may also be the subject of court action. MCAD conducts an investigation, determines whether probable cause exists, and, if it does, pursues a full hearing, resulting in an enforceable order and potential award of damages.

Local Ordinances

At the local level, at least seventy municipalities and counties have enacted legislation protecting gay men and lesbians from discrimination and unfair treatment. In Los Angeles, San Francisco, Detroit, Minneapolis, and Howard County, Maryland, for example, coverage includes the full range of protection: public and private employment, public accommodations, education, real estate and housing, credit and union practices. Other municipalities and counties have enacted ordinances that cover only employment, and at least forty municipalities have issued council or mayoral proclamations banning discrimination in public employment.

Union Contracts

Negotiated contracts may have specific protections against discrimination based upon sexual orientation, along with other protected categories. Unions are increasingly adopting nondiscriminatory policies with respect to sexual orientation, including demands for domestic partnership benefits, and urging local branches to include these in their negotiating agendas. At the federal level, employee groups at several departments, including the Internal Revenue Service, Health and Human Services, and Housing and Urban Development have successfully negotiated protections against discrimination based on sexual orientation for employees covered by collective bargaining.

General Employment Law Principles

Even where no specific state or municipal legislation exists, courts have, in some cases, intervened to protect employees who experience discrimination on the basis of sexual orientation. Typical grounds for such rulings have been wrongful discharge, failure to follow company personnel policies and procedures, breach of a covenant of good faith and fair dealing in employment contracts, failure to provide fair hearings on grievances and complaints, sexual harassment, discriminatory application of company practices, intentional infliction of emotional distress, breach of other general state employment laws, and the right to be free from a hostile work environment.

This is not the place for a detailed analysis of this burgeoning area of the law; there are a number of legal publications and other resources covering that ground. Contradictory case law can be shown on virtually every one of the above conceptual grounds for relief. Establishing a legal basis to challenge allegedly wrongful discharge or to correct a hostile work environment is never easy. Particular fact situations, as complex as in other employment cases, are always crucial. But employment lawyers around the country are finding it an issue they have to face as sexual orientation becomes a more frequently found "key word" in summaries of decided cases.

Constitutional Law

Certain protections in both state and federal constitutions have been invoked to establish a nondiscriminatory work environment. The basic principles of due process, equal protection, right to privacy, and the first amendment guarantees of freedom of speech and assembly may limit the ability of employers to hire and fire at will, particularly where the employer is a governmental entity. Cases at both state and federal levels have not yet created a clear pattern with respect to the applicability of these constitutional protections.

Federal Legislation

At the federal level, a bill has been introduced in every session of Congress since 1975 to add sexual orientation to the categories (race, color, religion, sex, and national origin) protected by Title VII of the Civil Rights Act of 1964. As of December 1992, there were 117 cosponsors in the House and 21 in the Senate who had endorsed the latest version of the Federal Gay and Lesbian Civil Rights Act. This bill would ban discrimination based on sexual orientation in employment, federally assisted programs, housing, and public accommodations.

In this emerging legal context, controversy and change are in the air. With a new tone of leadership from the White House on this issue, both the intensity of controversy and the rate of change are likely to increase.

The Changing Climate of Opinion

When *Fortune* magazine, in December 1991, featured a cover story on being gay in corporate America, the number of letters to the editor was larger than for any *Fortune* article in the previous decade. The ratio of favorable to unfavorable responses was nearly five to one.

Business attitudes are changing, and public opinion polling indicates strong support for nondiscrimination in the workplace, even though only one fifth of Americans are aware they are working with someone who is gay. In a nationwide poll conducted in April 1991, 81 percent of Americans agreed that homosexuals should have equal employment opportunity; only 17 percent disagreed. This was 10 percent higher than the 71 percent figure in 1989. According to a *Newsweek* poll published in connection with a cover story in the fall of 1992 (September 14, 1992), 78 percent of Americans believe that homosexuals should have equal rights in job opportunities, even though only 41 percent found homosexuality "an acceptable alternative lifestyle." Only 20 percent, however, work with someone they know is gay, while 43 percent have a friend or acquaintance who is gay. When the question was narrowed from the general "Should homosexuals have equal rights in job opportunities?" to "Should homosexuals be hired in each of the following occupations?" the percentage of people saying yes were: salespeople, 83 percent; members of the president's cabinet, 64 percent; members of the armed services, 59 percent; doctors, 59 percent; high school teachers, 54 percent; elementary school teachers, 51 percent; and clergy, 48 percent (*Newsweek,* September 14, 1992, p. 36).

Insisting on nondiscriminatory policies that ensure fair treatment, equal opportunity, and equitable compensation and benefits, gay men and lesbians are organizing and becoming more vocal.

Sources of Homophobia

Homosexuality in the abstract is an uncomfortable issue for many to deal with at first—as a result of lack of contact with openly gay people, some moral stance, concern (often unconscious) about one's own sexuality, or the inherent privacy of sex itself. *Homophobia is an irrational fear and hatred of homosexuals and homosexuality based to some extent on misinformation.* Such discomfort leads to fear, stereotypes, rumors, suspicions, and discrimination, the usual attributes of prejudice.

As more homosexuals become visible in the workplace, employers will find themselves dealing with various reactions by heterosexuals. Many will discover that they have been working with homosexuals for a long time but did not know it. The response to such startling information can vary from acceptance to tolerance, curiosity, disappointment, fear, anger, or open hostility, each posing challenges to workplace management. For some, such new awareness offers the opportunity to educate themselves, substituting information for ignorance. For others, harassment can result. Take the case of the store supervisor who wanted to date an employee but had him fired when he rebuffed her advances and she found out that he was gay. In that instance, the termination was challenged in court, and ultimately a settlement was worked out. But such conflicts should not wait for a court to resolve them; intelligent management will expect conflict, take steps to prevent it when possible, and resolve it when it appears.

Moral and Religious Objections

Managers should be prepared to deal with moral objections on the part of some heterosexuals to working with homosexuals. Some hold religious beliefs and moral convictions that homosexual acts are sinful, and that homosexuals should reform their sexual behavior; some extend this belief to feel that they should therefore not have to work closely with homosexuals. However, managers must remember that the workplace is an essentially secular environment; divergent religious or moral convictions on matters relating to private behavior away from the workplace that does no harm to others should not be permitted to affect workplace decisions or relationships. Just as people work side by side with others who may hold different moral beliefs about, and engage in different practices concerning, divorce, abortion, premarital sex, interracial marriage, or the use of alcohol, so people who differ fundamentally on the issue of homosexuality can get along and work together productively. There is no requirement for anyone to change his or her religious beliefs or moral convictions while at work; acceptable behavior, not acceptable belief, is the proper workplace standard.

AIDS and Homosexuality

It is important to differentiate gay and lesbian workplace issues from HIV/AIDS workplace issues. Although more than a majority of AIDS cases in the United States are still gay men, AIDS is now spreading faster among other elements of the population, including women, heterosexuals, and intravenous drug users. There is some overlap in affected groups, but AIDS can and does strike anywhere in the population. Under the law AIDS in the workplace relates to illness and disability; being gay is neither. Employees with AIDS are considered legally to be persons with a disability. With passage of the 1990 Americans with Disabilities Act (ADA), people infected with HIV or those perceived to be HIV-positive are protected from discrimination. Ironically, in some states and localities, gay men and lesbians have more protection against discrimination on the basis of disability than sexual orientation. HIV/AIDS issues require workplace education, as do gay and lesbian issues. They are separate—and only partly related—matters.

Meeting the Challenges

A nonhostile workplace in which gay men and lesbians can have full opportunity to contribute to their own and the organization's livelihood can be achieved by applying traditional organizational and management principles to this new human resource challenge. Here are some suggestions.

Recognize Sexual Orientation as Another Element in Workforce Diversity

The *Workforce 2000* study has recognized that the American workforce is becoming increasingly diverse—racially, ethnically, and educationally (Johnston & Packer, 1987). Valuing this diversity, and managing it creatively, has become a major human resource objective.

Hiding one's sexual orientation at work takes great effort; for some, doing so makes them less than fully productive. Try hiding one's heterosexuality for a week: no mention of husband or wife, no pictures on the desk, no discussion of the weekend dates. (This is the focus of one sensitivity exercise in "Homo-work," which contributes to the theoretical foundation for Blumenfeld's *Homophobia: How We All Pay the Price,* 1992). This exercise illustrates the effort required; lifting this burden increases productivity. "Once I came out at my job I realized how much more energy I had for it," one gay man noted. "The effort I had put into concealing such an important part of myself was available to do a better job, because I could tap into my whole self."

Moreover, with increased public scrutiny of workplace discrimination based on sexual orientation, employers failing to provide a nondiscriminatory environment are likely to be confronted with negative publicity and litigation. Both mainstream and gay and lesbian media are quick to report claims of workplace hostility. Egregious discrimination on the part of companies with national products has led to organized boycotts. And whether successful or not, alleged discrimination in the workplace requires an effort to answer. Morale can suffer. Taking steps to avoid such hostility and the publicity that often accompanies it frees management for more productive tasks.

Provide Equal Compensation for Equal Work

Extending benefits to the partners of gay and lesbian employees has become a cutting-edge issue in both the public and private sectors. A number of unions and employee associations have put this issue on their bargaining agendas with management. They are arguing, along with unorganized gay men and lesbians, that it is a simple matter of workplace equity. Gay and lesbian employees believe that without access to benefits for their partners, they are unfairly receiving less compensation than married heterosexuals performing the same work.

Although no state protective legislation requires employers to grant health care and other benefits to partners of gay or lesbian employees, some employers have voluntarily decided to do so, some for unmarried opposite-sex and same-sex couples, and several for same-sex couples only. The term *domestic partner* usually refers to both unmarried heterosexual and homosexual couples while *spousal equivalent* refers only to same-sex couples (the "equivalent" of spouses because there is no current way for them to be legally married).

Some employers are extending benefits initially in areas where they see fewer potential financial burdens than in the health care area, such as leave related to death or illness of a partner or a partner's children or relatives, relocation assistance, or merchandise discounts. Governor Weld of Massachusetts recently issued an executive order, the first of any state, extending such rights to all management-level public employees.

A growing number of employers are extending health benefits to families and partners of gay employees. In September 1991, the Lotus Development Corporation offered a full range of family benefits to spousal equivalents, attracting national attention as the first major corporation to do so. Partners of homosexual employees receive family benefit coverage equal to that offered spouses of married heterosexual employees, including medical, dental, vision, and hearing coverage and bereavement leave. Lotus requires gay and lesbian couples to certify their long-term commitment and economic status. Management opted for this approach because gay men and lesbians, unlike unmarried heterosexual couples, do not have the option to marry. The University of Chicago, the University of Iowa, and Stanford University have used the same rationale to extend benefits to gay faculty and staff.

A number of employers have extended such benefits not only to gay employees, but to all unmarried employees in committed relationships, whether homosexual or heterosexual. These workplaces now number over thirty in the private sector, including MCA, Inc.; Minnesota Communications Group; Ben & Jerry's Homemade, Inc.; the American Psychological Association; Kaiser Permanente (Northeast Region); Levi Strauss and Company; and New York's *Village Voice* and Montefiore Hospital; and at least seven in the public sector, including the municipal governments of Berkeley, Laguna Beach, San Francisco, Santa Cruz, and West Hollywood, California; Cambridge, Massachusetts; and Seattle, Washington.[3]

Financial concerns over health care costs and inexperience in dealing with nontraditional families require special attention. Existing actuarial data do not indicate a statistically significant difference in the cost of covering homosexual and heterosexual partners; furthermore, committed gay couples are at no greater or lesser risk of catastrophic illness. The average cost of AIDS and two weeks of intensive care for a heart attack are about the same, ranging from $50,000 to $70,000. In comparison, the cost of a kidney transplant or long-term treatment of cancer may run as high as $200,000. Extended hospital care for a premature infant can easily cost $350,000 to $500,000.

Offering full family benefits to domestic partners or to spousal equivalents has not turned out to be a budget buster. Fewer than a dozen employees (out of a total workforce of approximately 3,100) at Lotus have signed up for benefits for spousal equivalents. At the *Village Voice,* where extended benefits to spousal equivalents and domestic partners were first granted in 1982, fewer than 20 employees (out of a total workforce of approximately 220) participate in the extended plan. Small participation rates are also common at Ben & Jerry's Homemade, Inc., in Vermont and Montefiore in New York City. One reason may be that, as a result of an IRS ruling, the value of such benefits is taxed for unmarried couples, but is not taxed for married couples.

While bereavement or leave related to family illness is something generally within the control of private corporations to offer as a management decision, extending health insurance benefits almost invariably involves negotiation with an insurance carrier. Under competitive pressure, some insurance companies are now offering coverage for partners of unmarried employees, and more are likely to follow suit.

Apply the Lessons but Not the Strictures of Affirmative Action

Most state legislation has a specific provision negating any requirement of "affirmative action" with respect to workplace discrimination based on sexual orientation; court-ordered quotas, goals, percentages, timetables, or reporting requirements are therefore not likely remedies for past discrimination against gay men and lesbians. Unlike Hispanics or African Americans, the homosexual minority as such is not considered to be a social underclass or an economically disadvantaged minority, [because] gay people are present in every economic class. Because sexual orientation, like gender, cuts across all minority categories, it is important to note that gay or lesbian Hispanics or African Americans often suffer from double discrimination, and to the extent that affirmative action is in place to benefit the racial or ethnic minority, it will also benefit the gay and lesbian members of that minority.

Given the need to respect the privacy of the gay men and lesbians who choose to keep their sexual orientation invisible, it is not wise for organizations to attempt to quantify in any precise way their gay and lesbian component. To record the demographic information of an unknown population for the purposes of tracking and reporting would be difficult if not impossible. Freedom to be visible, and the organizational leadership to make that freedom real, is the major goal, but not everyone will discard invisibility even in the most tolerant environment.

Self-Support

Assisting the invisible minority in creating a discreet means of self-support is also important. Some companies have named in employee newsletters a contact in human resources whom gay men and lesbians can call to find out ways to participate in an internal support network. Others have begun computer networks, both locally and nationally. Some companies have lunch groups formed by and composed of gay and lesbian employees. At U S West and Levi Strauss, these groups function as social and professional support groups as well as sources of accurate information for the company on lesbian and gay issues and concerns. Such empowerment lessens fear and fosters confidence, because the gay or lesbian employee discovers that he or she is not alone. This self-help approach also enables human resources professionals to take a proactive role in reaching out to the invisible minority. It is also consistent with the way employers have assisted other minority groups to gain a sense of their own empowerment. A strategy that emphasizes leadership only from the top will fail to marshal all available resources.

Critical Mass

It is useful to have a critical mass of openly gay and lesbian employees, because it increases the comfort level, and therefore the productivity, of those who are out and makes it clear to those not yet out that the workplace is a supportive environment with respect to sexual orientation.

Develop Education and Training Programs Early

Counterproductive behavior on the job resulting from homophobia undermines the effectiveness of both heterosexuals and homosexuals. This bottom-line effect on productivity underscores the need to establish internal programs that help make all employees feel more comfortable with the presence of lesbians and gay men in the workforce. This is a challenge for corporate trainers and employee relations representatives, as well as for lawyers seeking compliance with the law and the prevention of illegal and discriminatory behavior.

Educational videos and training materials are available. (Sources for such educational materials may be obtained from the National Gay and Lesbian Task Force, Washington, D.C.) Firm-specific case studies and role-playing exercises can be developed, equipping managers and employees to deal effectively with matters of sexual orientation. Because the basis of discrimination against homosexuals is often based on inaccurate stereotypes, the content of these educational efforts should focus on providing accurate information about homosexuality and gay people. Participation by openly gay employees to coordinate internal programs and to become more visible in the organization reinforces the policy commitment and leadership mandate to effect change. It also enables the human resources department to develop a program that works best and fits with the organizational culture.

Manage the Inevitable Conflict

The charged nature of the issue of homosexuality makes conflict in the workplace inevitable. Because there are still significant societal sanctions—cultural, legal, religious, and familial—against homosexuality, human resource professionals should be prepared to intervene early when conflicts emerge. They need exceptionally strong skills in crisis management, consultation, negotiation, facilitation, and fact finding. Their goal should be to resolve problems internally in a fair and speedy manner. If problems cannot be settled within the organization, mediation may be preferable to arbitration and litigation. The corporate law department and human resource professionals should remember their fiduciary responsibility to protect the business from the threat of legal action.

Provide Leadership for Workplace Equity

Strong leadership at all levels is required. Most organizations have a stated policy of nondiscrimination, and many have added sexual orientation to their own list of protected categories. This self-help approach is particularly useful right now in areas without protective legislation. An unambiguous policy stating that discrimination will not be tolerated sets the right tone and establishes a clear framework for the organizational culture to acknowledge the contributions of gay and lesbian workers.

Top management also needs to set an example and directly instruct line supervisors and division heads to follow it. Managers and supervisors not only need to be concerned about their own behavior, but also about the behavior of those they lead. Eliminating derogatory comments and immediately halting any harassment may be the single easiest and most important step that can be taken to foster respect for lesbians and gay men in the workforce. Because so many gay people are invisible, nobody can be certain whom he or she may offend; furthermore, some heterosexuals have gay children, parents, grandparents, or other members of their extended family about whom they care deeply.

In the illustration of the business trip cited earlier, top management of the company insisted that the straight man and the gay man both go on the trip. The straight man came back enthusiastic about the professional contributions of his colleague, feeling that he had actually been given an opportunity to learn more about what it was like to work closely with an openly gay man. The message is clear: if it is sensitively handled, firmness in applying a nondiscriminatory policy can lead to communication, tolerance, and understanding. The unknown becomes known, fear is lessened, and artificial barriers are broken down. It takes time, and it takes professionals skilled at internal conflicts of this kind.

It sounds easy: treat gay men and lesbians like everyone else and do not discriminate. If employers recruit, assign, compensate, promote, evaluate, and dismiss based on workplace competence, not sexual orientation, there should be few problems. In far too many workplaces, however, the corporate culture must be changed as well. Transforming an indifferent or hostile workplace into one of tolerance and acceptance for lesbians and gay men requires vision and informed advocacy.

Sexual orientation in the workplace is a unique opportunity for human resource professionals to take charge as advocates for change, working both to resolve and prevent conflicts and to ensure compliance with nondiscrimination requirements. Working together, the legal and human resource departments can develop an approach that draws upon an organization's culture and traditional management practices. There is a direct link to the bottom line, improved productivity and quality of work life for all employees.

A varied workforce, including its gay and lesbian component, can be a higher-quality workforce. But enhanced quality and productivity are not achieved automatically. Strong management is required to value differences and turn diversity into an asset. Leadership is needed at all levels—by chief executives, union heads, managers, supervisors, coworkers, and gay men and lesbians themselves.

Notes

1. References to *gay, lesbian,* and *bisexual* are intended to refer to all three types of sexual orientation; sometimes the references are shortened to *homosexual, gay, gay people,* or *gay and lesbian,* but there is no intent to exclude bisexuals from the analysis or from the protections.

2. In a 1987 survey conducted by the Philadelphia Lesbian and Gay Task Force among gay city residents on the subject of employment discrimination, 81 percent of the men and 90 percent of the women said they concealed their sexual orientation at work at least some of the time to avoid discrimination. In this sample of several hundred lesbians and gay men from Pennsylvania, 28 percent of males and 25 percent of females actually experienced employment discrimination, and 71 percent of males and 78 percent of females said they fear it. Surveys in Boston (1983) and New York City (1980) reported similar findings. The Boston Project was a year-long study sponsored by the City of Boston; this survey of more than 1,000 city residents generated a comprehensive list of recommendations and set an agenda for gay and lesbian citizens. The National Gay Task Force's "Employment Discrimination in New York City: A Survey of Gay Men and Women" included more than 300 respondents. In an Alaska sample of 734, 11 percent experienced difficulty getting a job because of sexual orientation, 35 percent noted problems at work because of it, and 8 percent had been fired. Identity, Inc., a nonprofit organization serving the gay and lesbian community, conducted a statewide survey in Alaska. Their report, "One in 10: A Profile of Alaska's Lesbian and Gay Community," was released in 1986. The Philadelphia Gay and Lesbian Task Force conducted a more recent survey in 1991–1992 and had more than 2,000 respondents. In Philadelphia, 25 percent of the men and 31 percent of the women had experienced discrimination on the job or in housing or public accommodations.

3. For an up-to-date status report of employers providing various types of benefits for gay and lesbian couples, see *Partners Magazine for Gay and Lesbian Couples,* Box 9685, Seattle, Washington 98109 (206-784-1519).

Suggestions for the Use of Reading 6.4

This reading is one of the best we've seen at identifying issues and possible organizational responses for the diversity dimension of sexual orientation. The following list of questions might be used for discussion:

1. In what ways is this group identity similar to gender, race, age, nationality, and others? In what ways is it different? What are the implications of the differences for organizational policy or response?

2. Evaluate the content of the reading regarding the tension between religion and support of equal employment opportunity for gays and lesbians. Identify your points of agreement and disagreement. Refer to Case 6.2 for additional input on this issue.

3. Evaluate the suggestions given here for organizational response. Are there additional actions that could be taken?

TAKING ACTION

The material in the previous two sections of this chapter should have given you a better understanding of prejudice and discrimination. In order to complete the learning process, it may be helpful to work through some exercises in which these insights can be applied to analyze work situations and develop a plan of action. Accordingly, Cases 6.1 and 6.2 and Activity 6.1 have been prepared to aid you in this. *Note:* One of the authors of Case 6.1 is the person who received the call and request for assistance described in the case. Following is the record of what happened.

Case 6.1

IS THE PLAINTIFF'S SOCIAL SCIENTIST OFF THE WALL?

MARK CHESLER AND RUBY L. BEALE

I received a telephone call from an attorney representing a large firm. There is an employment discrimination lawsuit against this firm, and the attorney wanted my opinion, advice, and potential assistance. The situation involved a Hispanic supervisor and a White employee. The White employee had been discourteous and nonresponsive to the Hispanic supervisor. The Hispanic supervisor has been known to carry a knife and to talk a lot on the telephone. After repeated episodes of improper behavior, the Hispanic supervisor arranged for the White employee to be transferred. On the day of the transfer, the White employee placed a Mexican plastic figurine in the supervisor's office with a telephone in one hand and a knife pointed at his head in the other hand.

The White employee left for another location in the firm. On that same day, a new plant supervisor arrived. He seemed sympathetic to the Hispanic supervisor (who was subordinate to him) and urged everyone to "let it go." He saw the figurine placement as a "joke," "a stupid prank."

Six months later, the Hispanic supervisor resigned and filed a lawsuit against the firm, claiming a "constructive discharge," and stating that he was forced to resign by this racist act, by the firm's lack of response to it, and by the subsequent nonsupportive climate. In filing the lawsuit, the plaintiff has arranged for a prominent social scientist to appear on his behalf. The social scientist, who has done considerable research and writing in the area of race relations, will testify that the figurine placement was a racist act, and that the firm's lack of response to the act reflects their condoning it, or at least making no attempt to alter a racist atmosphere and environment.

The firm's lawyer has already arranged for a change in venue, so that the case will not be tried in the Hispanic inner-city area but in a predominantly White suburban area. She has done this in order to get a jury she thinks will be more sympathetic to the firm's position.

Source: This case is used by permission of the authors.

The firm's defense lawyer has the following questions for you:

1. Is the plaintiff's social scientist "off the wall"? Was it a racist act? The employee states that he had no intention to be racist, but that he did dislike the supervisor and on the spur of the moment saw the figurine and thought up the prank.

2. Will people in general, or a jury, to be specific, see this as a racist act? Should we undertake a survey of people in the metropolitan area to see what the public would say about whether it was a racist act? What might come out of the survey results?

3. Is the firm responsible? What else could the firm have done except let the incident blow over? How could the firm be responsible for a nonconstructive atmosphere when it cannot do anything about individual employees' attitudes or motivations?

4. Would you testify for the firm?

As you ponder the attorney's questions, your mind races through a list of your own: What do I ask? What should I say? Is this a practical joke, racism, and/or harassment?

What do you think?

Suggestions for the Use of Case 6.1

This incident actually happened in an organization. In using this case, we have heard of similar stories that have taken place in other organizations; thus it brings these issues into the real-world, current-day workforce. It is important to read the case as objectively as possible and decide what you think would be appropriate in this situation. It may also be helpful to take on different perspectives, first as the plaintiff, then as the defending firm, and then just as a third-party observer. See if your ultimate decision and/or strategies change, and why.

The case usually elicits rich conversation about what was done, why it was done, and its ultimate impact on organizational effectiveness and individual well-being. Individuals or groups might be asked to prepare an answer for each of the defense attorney's questions.

Case 6.2
INTERGROUP CONFLICT AT XYZ CORPORATION

You are working on a consulting project for the XYZ Corporation, a medium-sized financial services company located in the southeastern United States. The organization has launched a change initiative on cultural diversity. One consequence of the awareness raising that has occurred is that two new support and advisory groups have formed, the Gay/Lesbian Network and the Christian Employees Network. Some members of the Christian network oppose even the existence of the Gay/Lesbian Network and also oppose its agenda, which is equal employment opportunity for its members. There is increasing tension between the two groups, and the leadership of the organization, including members of the diversity-change team, feel caught in the middle. It seems that any movement to be responsive to the concerns of one group causes problems with the other.

As the consultant working with the company on diversity issues, you have been asked to address the following specific issue: how can we respond to the objection of the Christian network that any recognition of, or attention to, the employment concerns of the Gay/Lesbian Network by the organization is offensive to them because "accommodation" of gays and lesbians goes against their religion (that is, the teachings of the Bible). What steps can be taken to defuse the tensions between these two groups?

Suggestions for the Use of Case 6.2

This case provides a basis for action planning in conflict resolution, one of the task areas shown in the Diversity Competency Model for Individuals (Figure 1.2). The case is loosely based on an actual experience of one of the authors while working on a consulting project some years ago. In the real case situation, the organization continued to recognize both groups and worked with them to have their concerns aired in open forums involving members of both networks. In some of these forums, the debate became quite heated. The company responded to the concerns of the Gay/Lesbian Network with a number of changes, including making this identity factor a point of emphasis in diversity training and changing employment benefits to provide additional benefits to gay and lesbian employees. The reading and discussion points from Reading 6.4 may be helpful here.

The following points may be useful in lowering tensions between the two groups:

1. A distinction can be made between acceptance of a gay or lesbian lifestyle as morally right and support of equal opportunity for all people regardless of sexual orientation.

2. The argument that often arises over whether or not this lifestyle is a choice can usually be defused by simply asking whether this really matters if the issue is equal opportunity employment, consisting of nondiscrimination and sensitivity to all.

3. It should be acknowledged that Christians and others whose religious teaching takes a moral stand on sexual lifestyle should not be put in the position of having to violate their beliefs in order to perform their jobs. (For example, is it fair to ask a Christian employee to endorse the statement that all sexual orientations are equally moral?)

We conclude this chapter with a summary activity similar to the one that ended Chapter Five. The intent is to reinforce the linkages between the content of the chapter and the diversity competency model for individuals that was presented in Figure 1.2. This activity asks participants to apply the knowledge gained from the chapter to the full range of work-task and responsibility areas listed in the diversity model.

Activity 6.1
LINKING LEARNING ON PREJUDICE AND DISCRIMINATION TO THE DIVERSITY COMPETENCY MODEL FOR INDIVIDUALS

Objectives

1. To identify specific ways in which prejudice and discrimination can affect the performance of various work tasks and responsibilities

2. To identify steps that can be taken to minimize the potential for prejudice and discrimination to become barriers to organizational performance

Procedure

Figure 1.2 specified seven task areas where diversity in work groups is known to have an impact. For your convenience, the model is reproduced here as Figure 6.1.

Figure 6.1. Diversity Competency Model for Individuals

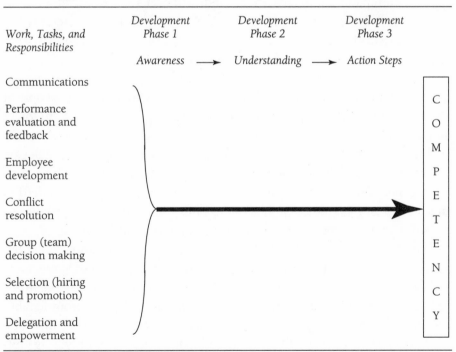

SOURCE: This figure is adapted from one first used by Taylor Cox, Jr., in a presentation to the Human Resource Partnership, University of Michigan, September 1992.

Task 1

Working alone, or in a group as directed by a learning facilitator, create a list of one to three ways in which identity-based prejudice may have an effect on the performance of one or more (depending on how you wish to use the activity) of the task areas shown in Figure 6.1.

Task 2

Identify one to three actions that you could take, possibly with the support of others and your organization's leadership, to reduce the probability that prejudice will be a factor in the performance of these tasks.

Suggestions for the Use of Activity 6.1

Individuals can work through the two tasks alone and then request that they be reviewed with comments by colleagues whom they trust and who are more knowledgeable than they are on diversity issues. If you are facilitating a group, you may want to have each group work on a separate task area and to assign part or all of the seven task areas. You may also want to modify the task areas to fit the group you are working with. For example, you may want to substitute coaching and counseling for delegation.

It will not be difficult for most groups to identify ways in which prejudice might affect the various task areas. Negative attitudes toward people of another racioethnic group may lead to rating members of that group lower on performance appraisals. Prejudice toward people with disabilities could lead to rejecting them as applicants for jobs or to a reluctance to delegate tasks to them. An African American who is prejudiced against Whites may react to any criticism from Whites (however constructively it is intended) as an act of racism. Prejudice on both sides often contributes to poor communications in union-management labor negotiations, and so on.

The steps to defeat these effects must include, but should not be limited to, educational efforts. For example, collection and analysis of specific organizational data is necessary. As an illustration of this, in many organizations gender is a factor in compensation and age is a factor in promotability and performance ratings. In one organization in which we did consulting work, data were uncovered that indicated that employees with young children tended to have lower promotability ratings than employees who did not have young children, even when their job performance ratings were the same (this was true for all workers, but more so for women than for men). These data tended to bolster the perception of many women in the organization that the organization was prejudiced in favor of "career-only" women and against women who had obvious family responsibilities, regardless of their job performance. By conducting internal research of this type on an ongoing basis, such patterns can be detected and corrected before they become barriers to the optimal utilization of the organization's resources.

SUGGESTED FILMS

There are many films that are useful in addressing issues of prejudice and discrimination. *A Class Divided* and *The Color of Fear,* described in Chapter Five, are excellent choices here. An additional film that we have found to be especially powerful is *True Colors.*

> *True Colors*
> ABC Distribution Company
> 825 Seventh Avenue
> New York, New York 10019
> 800-913-3434

This fifteen-minute video illustrates how much difference skin color makes in the everyday life of two men, one White and one Black. The two were equally matched on background in terms of class, age, and education. They were then given the same background information and were sent as testers to a new city to secure a job, housing, and a car and to go shopping. They both kept personal diaries, and the "Primetime Live" television show's camera crew followed them and videotaped many of their interactions with the other people. Significant differences in social and economic realities were illustrated in the interactions of the two men in a variety of settings. Afterward, certain of the prospective employers, apartment managers, car salespeople, and so on were questioned by the "Primetime Live" news commentator as to why different treatment and information were given to the two testers, often within a matter of minutes. Each person denied any difference in treatment, though the empirical evidence and behavior were captured on camera. This video demonstrated the additional burdens that people of a minority race are likely to encounter in everyday situations that are critical and necessary in order for them to live a comfortable life.

Discussion Questions

1. Were the two men in the video treated differently? What were the differences?

2. When the differential treatment was pointed out to the people involved in the interaction, why do you think that they consistently stated that there was no difference in treatment, even after they were told that the interaction had been recorded on tape?

3. How might this type of differential treatment affect the feelings and subsequent behavior of the White man in the video?

4. How might this type of differential treatment affect the feelings and subsequent behavior of the Black man in the video?

7

Cultural Differences

As noted in the Interactional Model of Cultural Diversity presented in Chapter Two, there are multiple dimensions to the intergroup dynamics of diversity. These dynamics include ethnocentrism, intergroup conflict, and cultural differences. Since a treatment of all of these topics is beyond the scope of this book, we have chosen to focus this chapter on learning about cultural differences. This point of focus was chosen because we believe that differences of culture are not only highly significant but also frequently overlooked or poorly understood as factors affecting the quality of work relationships in diverse work groups. We have also observed that when the idea that identity groups have cultural significance is invoked in discussions of diversity, it is often not substantiated with clear examples. We hope to give readers a better understanding of this important topic by offering a variety of readings and activities to promote learning about the content and implications of cultural differences between identity groups based on a variety of diversity dimensions.

As noted in Chapter One, the concept of culture refers to differences in values, behavioral norms, goal priorities, and ways of thinking that distinguish one group of people from other groups. Although the importance of culture to interpersonal and intergroup relations in organizations is easiest to comprehend when it is applied to nationality differences, various scholars have shown that nationality is not the only type of group identification that has cultural significance. In addition to the material presented here, see Chapter Seven of the theory book, *Cultural Diversity in Organizations* (Cox, 1993), for more specifics on this scholarship. By including material on examining cultural differences based on age, work specialization, gender, and racioethnicity, in addition to nationality, we hope to establish that an understanding of cultural dynamics is essential for developing diversity competency.

RAISING AWARENESS

We present here two readings and an activity that we hope will pique your interest in learning more. The first reading describes a widely quoted research study on cross-national cultural differences. When using it, keep in mind that organizations are marketing globally and that culture is a major influence on consumer behavior. In addition, workforces in some countries of the world (the United States in particular) have large representations of immigrants or descendants of immigrants, thus making differences of national culture relevant to understanding the behavior of workers, even within a single country.

Reading 7.1
THE CULTURAL RELATIVITY OF
THE QUALITY OF LIFE CONCEPT

GEERT HOFSTEDE

What people see as the meaning of their lives and the kind of living they consider desirable or undesirable are matters of personal choice. However, personal choices are affected by the cultural environment in which people are brought up. Thus one can expect definitions of the quality of life to be culturally dependent as well. For example, in some cultures the quality of life is strongly associated with the degree of satisfaction of material needs. In others, it is associated with the degree to which people succeed in subduing and reducing their material needs.

One facet of a people's quality of life is their quality of work life. The relative contribution of the quality of work life to the quality of life is, in itself, a matter of personal and cultural choice.

This reading deals primarily with cultural aspects of the quality of *work* life. However, *work* first must be placed in the wider context of total life patterns; that is, the quality of (total) life must be kept in mind. At the level of culture, work and life cannot and should not be separated. "Quality," by definition, is a matter of values. It relates to standards for "good" and "bad." Values depend partly on personal choices, but to a large extent what one considers good or bad is dictated by one's cultural context. In this article, conclusions about the cultural relativity of the quality of life concepts are based on data about the cultural relativity of values.

Value Patterns

A shorthand definition of a value is a broad preference for one state of affairs over others. Culture can be defined as the collective programming of

---

Source: Excerpted from Geert Hofstede, "The Cultural Relativity of the Quality of Life Concept," *Academy of Management Review,* 9(3), 1984, pp. 389–398. Copyright Academy of Management Review, used by permission. An earlier version of this paper was presented at the 20th International Congress of Applied Psychology, Edinburgh, Scotland, 1982.

the mind which distinguishes the members of one category of people from those of another. Elsewhere (Hofstede, 1979, 1980) I have reported on research into national differences in work-related value patterns in forty countries. Later on (Hofstede, 1983), this research was extended to another ten countries and three multicountry regions, so that it now encompasses fifty countries and three regions. Paper-and-pencil answers on thirty-two value questions by matched samples of employees of subsidiaries of the same multinational business corporation in all these countries were used to study the relationship between nationality and mean value scores. In a factor analysis of thirty-two mean scores for each of the forty countries (an ecological factor analysis), three factors together explained 49 percent of the variance in means (Hofstede, 1980). Afterward, several reasons led to the splitting of one of these factors into two parts. Thus four dimensions were created. Together they explained about half of the differences in mean value scores among the forty nations. Each country could be given an index score on each of these four dimensions.

The subsequent phase of the research was devoted to the validation on other populations of the four dimensions. This showed their meaningfulness outside the subsidiaries of this one multinational corporation. About forty other studies were found that compared conceptually related data for between five and forty of the countries involved. These studies produced qualitative outcomes that correlated significantly with one or more of the four dimensions scores (Hofstede, 1980).

The labels chosen for the four dimensions, and their interpretations, are as follows:

1. *Power distance,* as a characteristic of a culture, defines the extent to which the less powerful person in a society accepts inequality in power and considers it as normal. Inequality exists within any culture, but the degree of it that is tolerated varies between one culture and another: "All societies are unequal, but some are more unequal than others" (Hofstede, 1980, p. 136).

2. *Individualism,* as a characteristic of a culture, opposes *collectivism* (the word is used here in an anthropological, not a political, sense). Individualistic cultures assume that individuals look primarily after their own interests and the interests of their immediate family (husband, wife, and children). Collectivistic cultures assume that individuals—through birth and possibly later events—belong to one or more close "in-groups," from which

they cannot detach themselves. The in-group (whether extended family, clan, or organization) protects the interest of its members, but in turn it expects their permanent loyalty. A collectivistic society is tightly integrated; an individualistic society is loosely integrated.

3. *Masculinity*, as a characteristic of a culture, opposes femininity. Masculine cultures use the biological existence of two sexes to define very different social roles of men and women. They expect men to be assertive, ambitious, and competitive; to strive for material success; and to respect whatever is big, strong, and fast. They expect women to serve and to care for the nonmaterial quality of life, for children, and for the weak. Feminine cultures, on the other hand, define relatively overlapping social roles for the sexes, in which neither men nor women need to be ambitious or competitive. Both sexes may go for a different quality of life than material success and may respect whatever is small, weak, and slow. In both masculine and feminine cultures, the dominant values within political and work organizations are those of men. In masculine cultures these political and organizational values stress material success and assertiveness. In feminine cultures they stress other types of quality of life, interpersonal relationships, and concern for the weak.

4. *Uncertainty avoidance,* as a characteristic of a culture, defines the extent to which people within a culture are made nervous by situations that they consider to be unstructured, unclear, or unpredictable, and the extent to which they try to avoid such situations by adopting strict codes of behavior and a belief in absolute truths. Cultures with a strong uncertainty avoidance are active, aggressive, emotional, security-seeking, and intolerant. Cultures with a weak uncertainty avoidance are contemplative, less aggressive, unemotional, accepting of personal risk, and relatively tolerant.

Country scores on the four dimensions have been plotted in Figures 7.1 and 7.2. Figure 7.1 plots power distance against individualism/collectivism (I/C).

Power Distance, Individualism, and the Quality of Life

Although occupational and organizational differences have to be considered, the focus of this article is national differences. Figure 7.1 considers differences on the dimension of power distance and I/C. A society's position on the I/C continuum will have a strong impact on the self-concept of its members and on the way in which they define the quality of their lives (Kanungo, 1982).

Figure 7.1. Power Distance × Individualism/Collectivism Plot for Fifty Countries and Three Regions

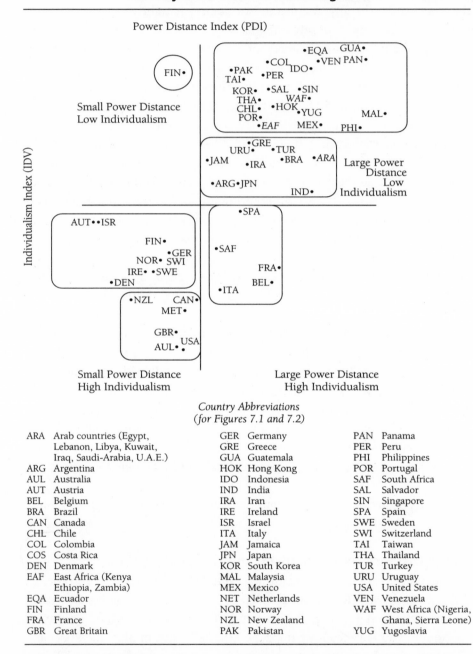

Power Distance Index (PDI)

Individualism Index (IDV)

•EQA GUA•
•VEN PAN•
•COL
•PAK   IDO•
TAI•   •PER
KOR• •SAL •SIN
THA•   *WAF*•
CHL• •HOK
POR•   •YUG   MAL•
•*EAF*   MEX•   PHI•

Small Power Distance
Low Individualism

FIN•

•GRE
URU• •TUR
•JAM   •IRA •BRA •ARA
•ARG•JPN
IND•

Large Power
Distance
Low
Individualism

AUT••ISR

FIN•
•GER
NOR• SWI
IRE• •SWE
•DEN

•SPA

•SAF

FRA•

BEL•

•ITA

•NZL   CAN•
MET•

GBR•
AUL• USA
•

Small Power Distance
High Individualism

Large Power Distance
High Individualism

*Country Abbreviations
(for Figures 7.1 and 7.2)*

ARA	Arab countries (Egypt, Lebanon, Libya, Kuwait, Iraq, Saudi-Arabia, U.A.E.)	GER	Germany	PAN	Panama
		GRE	Greece	PER	Peru
		GUA	Guatemala	PHI	Philippines
ARG	Argentina	HOK	Hong Kong	POR	Portugal
AUL	Australia	IDO	Indonesia	SAF	South Africa
AUT	Austria	IND	India	SAL	Salvador
BEL	Belgium	IRA	Iran	SIN	Singapore
BRA	Brazil	IRE	Ireland	SPA	Spain
CAN	Canada	ISR	Israel	SWE	Sweden
CHL	Chile	ITA	Italy	SWI	Switzerland
COL	Colombia	JAM	Jamaica	TAI	Taiwan
COS	Costa Rica	JPN	Japan	THA	Thailand
DEN	Denmark	KOR	South Korea	TUR	Turkey
EAF	East Africa (Kenya Ethiopia, Zambia)	MAL	Malaysia	URU	Uruguay
		MEX	Mexico	USA	United States
EQA	Ecuador	NET	Netherlands	VEN	Venezuela
FIN	Finland	NOR	Norway	WAF	West Africa (Nigeria, Ghana, Sierra Leone)
FRA	France	NZL	New Zealand	YUG	Yugoslavia
GBR	Great Britain	PAK	Pakistan		

SOURCE: Geert Hofstede, "The Cultural Relativity of the Quality of Life Concept," *Academy of Management Review,* 9(3), 1984, pp. 389–398.

Figure 7.2. Masculinity/Femininity × Uncertainty Avoidance Plot for Fifty Countries and Three Regions

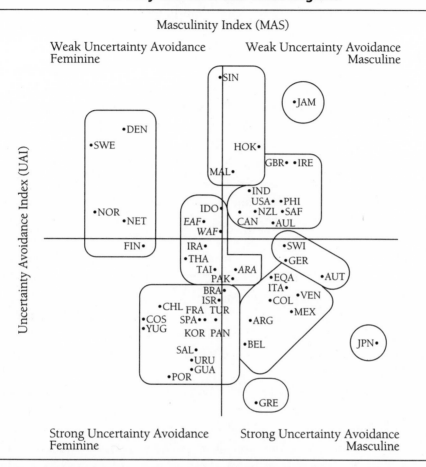

SOURCE: Geert Hofstede, "The Cultural Relativity of the Quality of Life Concept," *Academy of Management Review, 9*(3), 1984, pp. 389–398.

In an individualistic society (lower part of Figure 7.1) a high-quality life means individual success, achievement, self-actualization, and self-respect. The capitalistic economic system prevalent in and originating from these countries is based on enlightened self-interest. However, in a collectivistic society (upper half of Figure 1), a high-quality life is defined much more in family and group terms. Children in collectivistic societies learn to think of themselves as "we" rather than "I." Whoever has success and wealth is supposed to let his or her relatives and friends share in it. The satisfaction of a job well done (by one's own standard) is an individualistic goal. In a collectivistic society, people seek the satisfaction of a job well recognized. Students are less motivated by a need to master their subject and more by a desire to pass their examinations and acquire the status that a degree can provide. Preserving face—that is, preserving the respect of one's reference groups—is the collectivistic alternative to preserving self-respect in individualistic cultures. Avoiding shame in a collectivistic society takes the place of avoiding guilt in an individualistic one. In Southeast Asian cultures, such as Indonesia (upper right-hand corner of Figure 7.1), preserving harmony with one's social environment is a powerful motivator. People would probably define a high-quality life as one in which harmony is achieved and preserved. In many Third World countries, national unity is an important symbol. A criterion for a high-quality job will be the degree to which people can serve their country.

In the individualistic society, job life and private life are sharply set apart, in both time and mind. Not so in the collectivistic society. People accept having the job invade their private life. But they also expect the employer to take account of family problems and allow time to fulfill family duties, which may be many. Most importantly, in individualistic work organizations, the task comes before the relationship. In collectivistic work organizations, the relationship has precedence over the task. This is because a society in which people think of themselves as "we," not "I," also will teach people to distinguish between "us" and "them." Others are classified as belonging to "our" in-group, or not belonging, and the way others are treated depends on their group membership. In order to perform a task together, or to do business together, there must be time to develop a relationship with the other person, allowing him or her to be "adopted" into the in-group. Developing such a relationship will take time—anything from two minutes to two years—but it is an essential precondition for achieving the task.

In medium-power-distance societies such as the United States and Canada, consultation is usually appreciated but not necessarily expected. "Participative leadership" is initiated by the participative leader, not by the rebellious subordinate. Ideal leaders are resourceful "democrats"—that is, individuals with some outstanding characteristics people enjoy. Moderate status differences and privileges for leaders are socially acceptable. However, laws and rules are expected to apply to superiors and subordinates alike.

In large-power-distance societies (to the right of the vertical line in Figure 7.1), subordinates have strong dependence needs. They usually aspire to democracy as an impersonal ideal. Subordinates expect superiors to behave autocratically and not to consult them. They may even be uncomfortable if superiors consult them. The ideal superiors in such a culture are benevolent autocrats or paternalists, "good fathers" on whom subordinates like to depend. Everybody expects superiors to enjoy privileges. Moreover, laws and rules differ for superiors and subordinates. In addition, status symbols are widely used and contribute to the superiors' authority in the eyes of subordinates.

This set of connotations should make it clear that equality, participation, industrial democracy, and leadership mean different things for the quality of work life in societies at different positions on the power distance scale. North Americans are often appalled and uncomfortable at the legally required codetermination procedures in countries such as Sweden or Germany. They suppose a degree of subordinate initiative and basic equality not in the American book.

On the other hand, northern and western Europeans have trouble with the vertical society of nearly all Third World countries. They believe the first thing these Third World countries need is the elimination of their power inequalities. However, after a certain time in those countries they usually adopt "neocolonial" attitudes. This means the northern and western Europeans start behaving toward the native lower classes just as the native ruling class does. Third World citizens in Western countries often initially feel lost. This is because of the lack of dependable superiors to take a personal attitude toward them and give clear orders.

Differences in I/C and power distance affect the feasibility of sociotechnical [organizational] interventions. This is because different societies define the "socio" element in the system quite differently, as should be clear from the previous paragraphs. Should the "system" include family relationships?

What degree of consultation and visible leadership makes people feel comfortable? These are missing considerations in the classical Anglo-American imported sociotechnical approach.

Kanungo (1982) suggests that differences in the cultural environment also affect the appropriateness of research instruments. Instruments developed by and for the North American mind are too often exported indiscriminately to other cultures. These instruments overemphasize items related to North American (individualistic, medium-power-distance) values and lack items related to other cultures' values. As an example, Kanungo uses the emphasis on intrinsic need satisfaction of most instruments for measuring the quality of work life. Even the classification of needs as "intrinsic" and "extrinsic" ceases to make sense in cross-national research (Hofstede, 1980). These instruments need to be redesigned and the entire research paradigm merits redefinition (Morrow, 1983).

Masculinity, Uncertainty Avoidance, and the Quality of Life

Figure 7.2 shows plots of masculinity/femininity versus uncertainty avoidance. These plots denote the prevalent standards in a country for the quality of work life in different ways than Figure 7.1 does. The differences among countries in Figure 7.2 are unrelated to whether the country is wealthy or poor. Both dimensions relate to human motivation. Masculinity in society relates to the desirability of achievement; femininity relates to interpersonal relationships (not, as in the case of collectivism, with relatives and in-group members, but with people in general). Uncertainty avoidance relates to the acceptability in a society of personal risk taking (weak uncertainty avoidance) versus an emphasis on personal security (strong uncertainty avoidance).

The consequence of country differences along these two dimensions is that management conceptions about the motivation of employees, common in North America, do not necessarily apply abroad. For example, with the help of Figure 7.2, Maslow's hierarchy-of-needs theory (1954) can be unmasked as ethnocentric. Empirical evidence of its cultural limitations is found in the classic fourteen-country study by Haire, Ghiselli, and Porter (1966). In this study, managers were asked to rate the importance to them of, and their satisfaction with, the fulfillment of a number of needs. These needs were chosen to represent the five levels of Maslow's hierarchy (specified by Maslow from low to high as: security, social, esteem, autonomy, self-actualization). Although Haire, Ghiselli, and Porter never drew this conclusion from their data, the only nationality group that ordered their need importance almost, and their need satisfaction exactly, in the Maslow order was the U.S. managers. The other nationalities showed more or less deviant patterns. I concluded (Hofstede, 1980) that the ordering of needs in Maslow's hierarchy represents a value choice—Maslow's value choice. This choice was based on his mid-twentieth-century U.S. middle-class values. First, Maslow's hierarchy reflects individualistic values, putting self-actualization and autonomy on top. Values prevalent in collectivistic cultures, such as "harmony" or "family support," do not even appear in the hierarchy. Second, the cultural map of Figure 7.2 suggests that even if just the needs Maslow used in his hierarchy are considered, the needs will have to be ordered differently in different culture areas. Maslow's hierarchical ordering (with self-actualization on top) corresponds to the upper right-hand quadrant of Figure 7.2. In the lower right-hand quadrant (strong uncertainty avoidance and masculinity), a combination of security and assertiveness needs should be placed on top of a need hierarchy. In the upper left-hand quadrant (weak uncertainty avoidance and femininity), social (relationship) needs should be placed on top. In the lower left-hand quadrant (strong uncertainty avoidance and femininity), security and relationship needs should be placed on top.

It is important for managers operating internationally to realize what countries tend to order human needs differently. Moreover, these countries are not necessarily inferior technologically, economically, or in the quality of their management. Some countries may even be superior in some or all of these respects. Japan, a country in which security needs rank very high, has been outperforming the world in recent years. Other East Asian countries follow closely. However, the dominant motivation patterns may affect the type of economic and technological activities at which a country is best. Masculine cultures may have an advantage when it comes to mass production. Feminine cultures may have an advantage when it comes to providing services (such as consulting) and to growing things rather than mass-producing them (as in high-quality agriculture and biochemistry). For example, the leading companies in the world in the field of penicillin and enzymes are in the Netherlands and Denmark. A truly international management should be able to recognize the strengths and the weaknesses in any country's culture pattern, including that of the home culture.

Improving the quality of work life often has been interpreted as offering to people satisfaction of needs higher on their need hierarchy. Thus, it should be recognized that different cultures have different need hierarchies. In the lower half of Figure 7.2, improving the quality of work life probably implies offering more security and possibly more task structure on the job. In the left half of Figure 7.2, improving the quality of work life implies offering opportunities for creating relationships on the job. In this context a difference is noted between the North American and northern European schools of improving the quality of work life (humanization of work, job restructuring). In North America, the dominant objective is to make individual jobs more interesting by providing workers with an increased challenge. This grew out of the earlier "job enlargement" and "job enrichment" movements. In countries such as Sweden and Norway, the dominant objective is to make group work more rewarding by allowing groups to function as self-contained social units (semiautonomous groups) and by fostering cooperation among group members. Humanization of work means "masculinization" in North America, but "feminization" in Sweden (Hofstede, 1980). This shows another aspect of the cultural relativity of the quality of work life.

Farewell to Ethnocentrism
Concern for the quality of life is a worthwhile issue in any culture (Adler, 1983). It is time to bid farewell to ethnocentrism in social science theories in general, and in definitions of the quality of life in particular.

Suggestions for the Use of Reading 7.1
This reading provides a large amount of empirical data on cultural differences. Reading it should alert you to the fact that these differences exist and to the fact that paying attention to culture for marketing and management in a global context is essential for effectiveness. When the reading is assigned as a class or group assignment, the group might be asked to respond to the following questions:

1. Can you identify any additional implications of the cultural differences presented here (beyond those noted in the reading) for marketing and management? For example, what implications would the data have for implementation of an employee empowerment initiative worldwide?

2. The article is now more than ten years old. Are you aware of differences in the countries noted that may update the data presented here?

3. The data are taken from members of the same multinational firm (although some effort was made to validate it with other subjects). What implications does this have for interpretation of the results?

Cultural Differences in the Classroom

Reading 7.2 is another in the essay series taken from an MBA class of one of the authors. The sessions referred to by the author of the essay (who was from Japan) were dialogue groups composed of people of different genders and racioethnic and nationality backgrounds.

Reading 7.2
A PERSONAL PERSPECTIVE ON CULTURAL DIFFERENCES

During these sessions, I had the opportunity to ponder my cultural, ethnic, and racial identity. Because I had no work experience in the United States, the classroom discussions and opinions were of great help to me in understanding the current situation of diversity in the workplace. I will comment on two issues that I faced while in school.

The first issue is the difference in communication style between Asian culture and the Anglo culture. Asians generally have "speech anxiety" or verbal reserve. Most Asians are hesitant to speak out in public or in front of a large audience, even when they are familiar with the subject. People are often considered to have more manners and etiquette if they do not speak out, especially in front of people who are older than they are. Keeping silent in certain situations is regarded as a positive attitude. I was brought up this way, and education and my country's social norms reinforced my behavior and beliefs throughout my adolescent period. This led to much difficulty and anxiety when I first arrived in American classes.

I found out for the first time that most of the classes in the graduate program were conducted by the case method and relied heavily on discussions and debates. This was a culture shock to me that was very difficult to adapt to and overcome. I would have to admit that there were many times when I didn't talk out in class even though I knew the answers to the questions that the professors were asking. Such an atmosphere was very uncomfortable and strange to me at first, though now I have adjusted more to the environment.

The second issue that came up for me was the fact that some of my classmates began to develop negative judgments about Asians' not being able to present their own ideas in front of people. Part of the problem may have come from the language barrier, but this is by no means the sole reason; rather, behind this lies a deep cultural difference in communication behavior and style.

Suggestions for the Use of Reading 7.2

After reading the essay, put yourself in the position of an instructor of a class containing a number of Asian students who shared the experience of this student, and respond to the following questions:

1. What advice would you have for the Asian students?
2. What changes, if any, would be warranted in your own behavior?
3. What, if anything, should be done about the pedagogical techniques used in the class?

We also suggest that you refer to this reading later in the chapter when you are working on Activity 7.4.

Cultural Differences Related to Age

As a final learning device for raising awareness about cultural differences, we propose Activity 7.1, which deals with age cohorts. Around the year 2000 the median age of the population in the United States will be thirty-six, six full years older than at any time in the first 204 years in the history of the nation (Johnston & Packer, 1987). We know of large organizations in which the median age is as high as forty, even though substantial numbers of new college hires continue to be recruited. Generational differences among workers therefore loom large as a dimension of the workforce diversity challenge.

But does age really have much effect on things that influence organizational behavior, like values, decision styles, goal priorities, or attitudes toward affirmative action? Activity 7.1 explores this question.

Activity 7.1
EXPLORING CULTURAL DIFFERENCES: AGE COHORT ANALYSIS

Objectives
1. To raise awareness about the implications of generational gaps among members of organizations
2. To learn specific cultural differences that may be related to age

Procedure
This activity must be done in a group that contains substantial diversity of age. The group will be divided into smaller teams based on the following (approximate) age breakdowns:

1. Those born in 1970 or later
2. Those born between 1945 and 1955
3. Those born before 1940
4. Everybody else

Each team will work on two tasks.

Task 1
With a minimum of discussion, try to come to consensus on a one-line reaction (a comment expressing your feelings or thinking about the issue) to the following work-related issues or topics.

1. Working mothers of young children
2. Working at home
3. Casual dress at work for professionals or managers
4. Dealing with gay or lesbian issues
5. Antiunion actions by management
6. Policies to support dual-career couples
7. Women as senior managers
8. Japanese men or women as senior managers

9. Blacks or Mexican Americans as senior managers

10. Supervisors as coaches and counselors

11. Electronic mail

12. Rapid changes in computer technology

Examples:

1. Working mothers of young children: "They're better off staying at home."

5. Antiunion actions by management: "They are misguided at best and illegal at worst."

6. Policies to support dual-career couples: "This sounds like a personal problem."

Task 2

What world or national conditions, events, or cultural norms that occurred or were prevalent when you were growing up may have influenced your views about the items listed in Task 1? List them.

Suggestions for the Use of Activity 7.1

Although people can and do change over time, this exercise illustrates that different age cohorts, in general, may have somewhat different values, goal priorities, and attitudes that are shaped partly by the world events and prominent norms that existed during their formative years. At the very least, differences between the views that are dominant in our national and local culture today and those that were dominant when we were first forming our worldviews can create some ambivalence about issues that require our attention as working adults. Therefore, the success of this activity depends greatly on the breadth of age in the group and on the willingness of the participants to give honest responses to the items.

In addition to the learning that takes place within groups in the activity, it may be helpful to look at responses between groups to see if the position statements vary in predictable ways. In addition, it may be insightful to look at the extent to which the fourth, mixed-age team had more difficulty than the others coming to consensus on the items discussed. Perhaps the greater variance in age may have added some additional diversity-related barriers to consensus. Learning about age-related cultural differences will give us a better understanding of the people we work with and may facilitate cooperation and communication in our increasingly age-diverse work groups.

CREATING UNDERSTANDING

We now continue the learning process with Activity 7.2 and Case 7.1, which are designed to extend your knowledge of cultural differences and their effects in the workplace.

Cultural Differences in Communication Styles

Reading 7.1 shows how culture may differ for people of different nationalities, but how would you respond to the question: Are men and women members of different cultural groups? Certainly most of us would accept that there are some differences between men and women, but we tend to think of people from the same country as sharing a culture, especially if they are of the same racioethnic group. A growing body of research, however, suggests that gender is indeed a group identity with cultural as well as social meaning (see, for example, Tannen, 1995; Glass, 1992; Gray, 1992; Helgesen, 1990). It should be noted that not all scholars who have written on gender share this conclusion. For example, Cynthia Fuchs Epstein (1988) argues in her book, *Deceptive Distinctions,* that what are taken for intercultural differences are really effects produced by a "social order" that is biased in favor of men.

In Activity 7.2, we want to look at communication styles using gender as the dimension of diversity. This activity is based largely on the work of Lillian Glass (1992) and Deborah Tannen (1990, 1995).

Activity 7.2
EXPLORING CULTURAL DIFFERENCES:
FOCUS ON CROSS-GENDER COMMUNICATIONS

Although this exercise is based on gender research, the learnings are applicable to all communications in organizations where the parties differ in communication-style preferences along the dimensions addressed here.

Objectives

1. To identify some research-based differences in communication styles between men and women

2. To learn how differences in communication styles can affect interpersonal effectiveness and other work experiences of individuals

Procedure

1. Working alone, complete the Communications Quiz in Exhibit 7.1.

2. Grade yourself by determining the number of "correct" answers, using the answers shown on page 167. It should be stressed that these are backed by systematic research, not just anecdotal evidence.

3. If possible, organize the group into gender-diverse teams, and then discuss the following questions:

a. What implications do these differences have for cross-gender or cross-style work relationships? In other words, how could differences between parties to a work relationship along the lines outlined here affect the quality of the work relationship and the ability of the parties to achieve peak performance?

b. Have members of the team observed situations in this organization where one or more of these differences or other insensitivities occurred in communications? Take some time to share thoughts on this topic.

EXHIBIT 7.1. Communications Quiz

Indicate by circling either "T" or "F" whether each of the following statements is true or false. Respond with your best judgment based on the question alone; no additional information or qualifying data are available.

1. At business meetings, coworkers are more likely to listen to men than they are to women.   T   F

2. Men use more eye contact and exhibit more friendliness in communication than women.   T   F

3. Women tend to give more praise than men.   T   F

4. In conversation, men interrupt women more often than women interrupt men.   T   F

5. In conversation, men tend to discriminate in interrupting; they are more likely to interrupt a woman than a man.   T   F

6. Women use direct orders more than men in communication.   T   F

7. Men ask for assistance less often than women do.   T   F

8. Through nonverbal communication, women make themselves less confrontational than men.   T   F

9. Men tend to explain things in greater detail than women when discussing an incident.   T   F

10. Women speak more than men in mixed-sex groups.   T   F

SOURCE: Reprinted by permission of Penguin Putnam Inc. from *He Says, She Says* by Lillian Glass, Ph.D. Copyright © 1992.

Suggestions for the Use of Activity 7.2

We have found that this activity works well to reveal differences in communication style that, in general, differentiate men from women (at least in the United States). It should be emphasized that styles do vary within gender groups, but the activity highlights normative differences based on gender-identity group.

The following steps are suggested for use by facilitators for debriefing groups, based on time availability:

1. Have individuals indicate how well they did on the "test" (scores will vary but 100 percent is rare).

2. Get the mixed-gender teams to report on their responses to the discussion questions.

3. Go over the implications for practice shown in Exhibit 7.2.

Answers:

1. True
2. False
3. True
4. True
5. True
6. False
7. True
8. True
9. False
10. False

EXHIBIT 7.2. Communication Style Differences: Some Implications for Practice

1. In meetings (especially in diverse groups), all participants (and especially the chair) should be sensitive to: (a) air time distribution, (b) interruptions, and (c) the willingness to acknowledge the contributions of members by reacting to their ideas, building on them, and so on.

2. Aggressive participants should be more sensitive in allowing others to have their say.

3. Differences in eye contact, or other nonverbal communication differences such as the amount of smiling, should not automatically be interpreted as implying a lack of interest, friendliness, or confidence.

4. A lack of questions should not be interpreted as understanding or agreement. People should be asked directly for both their ideas and their reactions to yours. Questions should be invited. Ask for questions outside of group settings as well as during the meetings.

5. Body posture (or things like the firmness of a handshake) should not be used as a sign of character strength or weakness.

6. Respond to requests for assistance or questions with support and information, not a judgment of incompetence or a directive about what to do.

EXHIBIT 7.2. Communication Style Differences:
Some Implications for Practice, cont'd.

---

7. Allow more time to understand, when necessary, as an accommodation to difference (for example, plan a longer time for meetings at which a person with a speech deficiency or language barrier will be presenting).

8. Assist and support members of identity groups who have not traditionally held power in the organization. This should not be done by the statement: "I think what Beth is trying to say is . . ." A better statement is: "I agree with Beth," or "What John says makes a lot of sense."

9. Avoid the trap of confusing oral communication-dominance behaviors with intelligence, creativity, or problem-solving ability. Recognize multiple methods of communication. Give more attention to the listening aspect of communications in rating overall communication effectiveness.

10. Help others to increase their self-awareness by calling to their attention times when their communication style is insensitive to you or someone else.

Activities 7.1 and 7.2 addressed cultural differences among different age cohorts and gender groups, respectively. Both of these activities demonstrated that culture can vary within nationality groups. Another way in which this occurs is by differences of language. It is estimated that thirty million people in the United States speak a language other than English at home. Case 7.1, based on a real experience of one of the authors, illustrates how differences of language among employees can lead to problems if they are not properly managed in the workplace.

Case 7.1
ENGLISH ONLY, PLEASE

Today I received a call from a reporter for the *Detroit Metro Times*. A financial services firm (a credit union) is battling a union grievance filed on behalf of some Spanish-speaking workers in protest of a company policy that essentially prohibits workers from speaking languages other than English on company premises during working hours, even if the conversations are social and not work-related. Following are some concerns of the company:

- Some White employees complain that not knowing what people are saying when they work in such close proximity makes them uncomfortable and fuels suspicions that the workers are talking about them.
- Such language use will increase interethnic tensions that already exist in the work group.
- All workers should be using every opportunity to develop English skills in order to better serve the predominantly English-speaking customer base.

The Spanish-speaking workers contend that the company's position is essentially racist and a denial of their civil rights, as well as being culturally insensitive.

Suggestions for the Use of Case 7.1

At the time of this writing, the ultimate disposition of the case is not known. My response to the reporter, based on the information available (all of which is included in this short case), was that the issues illustrated here occur frequently today, that a number of companies have taken the approach of not only accepting the use of multiple languages but proactively teaching second languages other than English to employees, and that the company's position is inconsistent with a goal of promoting multiculturalism.

Among the questions for discussion are these:

1. Evaluate the concerns of the company. Do you agree with their position and rationale? Why or why not? If not, what should the policy of the company be?

2. Have you observed situations where differences of language were at issue in your work experiences?

3. Should a national policy on language use in schools be established? If so, what should the policy say?

TAKING ACTION

If you have completed all of the previous readings and activities in this chapter, you should have a better understanding of cultural differences than before you started the book. Some opportunities for action planning were incorporated into these materials. In order to further solidify the action step of our diversity competency model, three additional items are included in this final section to provide vehicles for translating the insights gained into implications for behavioral or organizational change. Case 7.2 returns us to the national-origin dimension of diversity, while Activity 7.3 illustrates the applicability of cultural differences to the group identity of work specialization. Finally, Activity 7.4 is the promised summary activity that requires you to link the content of the chapter to organizational behavior more comprehensively through the diversity competency model of Chapter One.

Case 7.2
FEELING FOREIGN: MANAGING
THE GLOBAL ASSIGNMENT

MAURA A. BELLIVEAU AND CAROLINA B. GOMEZ

American companies are globalizing their operations. This is not news to anyone who reads *The Wall Street Journal* or any other business publication. What *is* news? That American companies are questioning the viability of using expatriate managers as a vehicle for enhancing their firm's international perspective. An estimated 41 percent of major U.S. multinational corporations report that they intend to reduce the number of overseas assignments for their U.S. staff (Boyacigiller, 1995). American companies are learning that expatriate assignments are enormously costly and while these costs are immediate and readily identifiable, the benefits of having expatriate managers overseas—and back in the home office—may only emerge over time.

Expatriate Managers

An expatriate manager is defined as an individual who performs management tasks in a country other than his or her native land. Most expatriate managers are selected for foreign assignments on the basis of their technical expertise. In many firms, a global placement is part of the career path for high-potential employees, and the repatriation of these individuals is seen as a means to increase the firm's ability to succeed in global markets.

Unfortunately, firms are learning that success in global assignments requires more than technical expertise and the other characteristics that put an employee on the fast track in the United States. An average American expatriate assignment is only two to three years in duration versus an average of five years for Japanese and European placements. Nevertheless, studies estimate that anywhere from 20 to 50 percent (Mendenhall, Dunbar, & Oddou, 1987) of all Americans placed in expatriate assignments fail, more than half because of difficulties experienced by the expatriate manager's family (Solomon, 1994).

Expatriate Failure: The Causes and Consequences

Expatriate failure is defined as the inability of an expatriate to perform effectively in a foreign country and, hence, the need for the employee to be fired or recalled home (Tung, 1987). Studies estimate the cost to be on average $100,000 per returning employee (Black, Mendenhall, & Oddou, 1991). Some firms estimate the cost of failure as close to $250,000 when losses from unrealized business are calculated (Mendenhall, Dunbar, & Oddou, 1987). Failure costs can include preassignment site visits, moving and travel, training, and expenses related to replacement (Solomon, 1994).

The statistics describing failure rates are only one source of concern for firms. According to one study using both self-reports and managers' assessments, nine out of ten American expatriates placed in Japan were significantly less productive there than they were in the United States (Seward, 1975, as cited in Tung, 1987). Strikingly, 30 to 50 percent of American expatriates stay in their positions but are viewed to be ineffective or only marginally effective by their firms (Black, Mendenhall, & Oddou, 1991).

Research has identified the primary reasons why an American expatriate manager fails:

- Inability of his or her spouse to adjust
- Other family-related problems
- His or her inability to adapt to a different physical or cultural environment
- His or her personality or emotional immaturity
- His or her inability to cope with the responsibilities posed by overseas work
- His or her lack of technical competence
- His or her lack of motivation to work overseas
- The short duration of American expatriate assignments
- Overemphasis on technical competence over other attributes
- Lack of training (Tung, 1987)
- Lack of management support and mentorship of the expatriate in the new site (Oddou, 1991)

Summary

Given these problems, it is not surprising that U.S. firms are reevaluating the use of expatriate assignments in managerial development and strategy formulation. However, firms are grappling with this challenge just as they seek to expand their global operations. According to a recent survey, 60 percent of CEOs polled expect their firm to enter new international markets within the next year (Oddou, 1991). The question becomes how to rapidly expand a firm's operations globally without using expatriate managers.

Should firms send American managers overseas, rather than drawing from the managerial talent in host nations? Can American firms better manage expatriate assignments? Do global assignments contribute to a manager's development, professionally and personally? Are there general "people management" lessons to be learned from the experiences of expatriate managers? Can American expatriate managers be successfully repatriated? Finally, what do the experiences of Americans abroad teach us about the management of diversity in the United States?

These are among the questions considered in this case. To illustrate the challenges and rewards of global assignments and repatriation, three Fuqua School of Business alumni who are—or were—assigned overseas agreed to describe their experiences from a professional and personal perspective.

The Personal Stories: An Introduction

John Grabino and Chuck Wagner, both of whom graduated from Fuqua in the 1980s, work for the same American investment banking firm. John has spent his entire tenure with the firm in its London office. Chuck began his career in New York, spent more than three years in London, and is now back in New York. Finally, James Stephens, a more recent Fuqua alumnus, currently works in the German operation of a large American packaged goods company. We begin with his story.

James Stephens

While still a Fuqua student, James Stephens knew that he wanted to pursue a career in international management. Having an Austrian mother and a British father, James held dual citizenship (the United States and the United Kingdom) and had spent time in Europe from an early age, visiting family, working, and studying abroad. To take advantage of his German-language skills, he targeted his search for internship opportunities in Switzerland and Germany. James was interested in marketing and packaged goods companies, and so his first-year internship with Premium Products in Germany was ideal. After he completed this summer internship, the German operation presented him with a full-time offer as a marketing assistant and the opportunity to continue working overseas.

James accepted the offer and became a local employee of the German Premium Products organization. As such, James was never considered to be an expatriate manager. Despite his familiarity with Germany and his own expectation that he would not experience culture shock, James did find that the move required a major adjustment.

His first manager, a Norwegian, was attuned to James's development as a manager in the Premium Products system, but she was not particularly sensitive to his situation as an American relocating to a new culture. As he described:

> She was focusing on where my strengths were, where my areas of improvement were . . . but in terms of being sensitive to some of the difficulties of moving to a foreign country, I would say not. I think her attitude was, "You are just like anyone else and you need to deal with this just like any other person whether coming out of a German university or an American university."

James suggests that his situation was unique in that, although he faced many of the same adjustment challenges as an expatriate manager, he was not seen as an expatriate: "I think I kind of fell through the cracks a little bit: on one hand, I was coming from a different country; on the other hand, I wasn't coming as an expatriate."

Despite these challenges, James was working for an American company and one with a very strong corporate culture. James described the culture as one that "travels well, which creates a fair environment—open to people of all nationalities." The German organization, one of the largest Premium Products' operations outside of the United States, was composed of managers from many different nations.

James discovered early on that there were forms of diversity in addition to nationality that critically affected his work life: differences in age, education, experience with Americans, English-language skills, and openness to others. James found that he worked in "two worlds": one inside the management group and one outside its boundaries. Inside the management group, James interacted with other product managers who had general management responsibilities. Many of these product managers were German, but all possessed excellent English skills, and most were very familiar with American culture, many having spent time studying in the United States. Within this group, James observed that people tended to be better educated, younger, and more open-minded.

Outside the management group, James interacted with people in staff and support departments such as marketing research, product development, design, and advertising. Here, he found people to have much more diverse backgrounds. While most of these people had better-than-average English skills and some exposure to American management practices, they did not necessarily understand or value such practices.

James found that the potential for cultural misunderstanding was greatest when he dealt with people outside the management group—support staff members whose work was critical to James's success as an assistant product manager. Reflecting on his personal style as a manager, he noted:

> I have an account management background. . . . For me there [is] heavy emphasis on relationships, communication, on networking. . . . This is more or less how I got my work done: by forging relationships, by forging a mutual understanding and communicating clearly. I would describe myself as an enthusiastic person, somebody with a lot of initiative, somebody with leadership skills, and I think in some departments, particularly outside the management group, . . . what I would consider as enthusiasm and initiative, I think was coming across as pushiness, being overbearing and inflexible. . . . [Germans] tend to see Americans as being very "in your face," . . . very direct, blunt, where Germans tend to be a little more reserved, not coming quite to the point. I think this was contributing to some of the difficulties I was having in trying to lead projects with some of these staff departments.

This difficulty came to a head when James was preparing to qualify a new product for a Europe-wide launch. The key marketing research contact was in Rome, and James was based in Frankfurt. In James's view, the project was not getting sufficient attention from the marketing research staff person in Rome, and worse, it seemed to be going in the wrong direction. James had taken on the project at a point when he felt it required an injection of leadership. His attempts to rectify the problems he saw seemed instead to exacerbate them:

> What I perceived to be leadership, which was essentially providing the information and providing the direction, she interpreted to be pushiness and inflexibility, and not seeing her way. I tried several different tactics. One was to increase the face-to-face contact, which usually . . . at least in the past worked very well with me in my previous job, and in interviews at Fuqua for jobs, that was one of my strengths.
>
> What I found was that in increasing the face time, things were getting progressively worse, because the more I tried to apply myself and to build the relationship and to network and to communicate in the best way I knew how, the more she would withdraw and want to have as little to do with the project as possible. It was absolutely mystifying to me at the time. I would send a memo saying, "This is just to summarize what we talked about in the meeting last week," and I would get a memo back saying, "You're always pushing . . . you're pushing . . . you're pushing . . . you're pushing too hard."
>
> This was really disturbing to me. I just couldn't understand what it was I was doing. My manager was telling me that I was doing my job, that I was following up, and that I was providing direction and leadership for the project, but somehow, this leadership was not coming through in a positive way to my Italian marketing contact. Finally, the way we solved this, was that I found an intermediary, . . . an Italian manager. I communicated with him and he conveyed the information to my marketing contact, and vice versa.

For James, this experience and the sense that his repertoire of management tactics was insufficient—even counterproductive—were eye-opening. Building relationships had been an integral part of James's managerial style. Now, he found that his style could be so misunderstood that it impeded his success in managing others, particularly those outside the management group.

But, as James learned, that was only one cost. Previously, his relationships had served as an important conduit to information. As James described, even the physical environment in his German office seemed to create obstacles:

We work as assistants in Germany, in big rooms, a sort of bull-pen-type environment with the desks pushed together and everyone talking at once, which, for me, didn't create the most ideal of working conditions. We're more used to cubicles in the States, where you have contact with your colleagues on a daily basis, but you still have your own place where you can have some privacy and really concentrate on your work.

The Germans see [U.S. cubicle offices] as working in a prison cell. They would rather work in wide-open spaces. But the real purpose of this is to facilitate flow of information, particularly when you're new, in those first couple of years. This means you're sitting and working on your projects, but you're also keeping an ear open to what's going on with the next product.

Unfortunately, while I can conduct business in German, I would not consider myself completely fluent to the point where I can do two things at one time, . . . listen to people speak German . . . and also do my work.

James realized that he obtained significantly less information than his peers. Although he believes his difficulty picking up information in this "bull-pen" atmosphere has had an impact on his performance, the relationship between his access to information and his performance has been indirect. He explained:

It's a bit difficult to talk about this because it tends to sound as though I'm being discriminated against, and I'm not being afforded the same opportunities as the next person. On the surface, that's not true. But there are some subtleties that I've only noticed gradually as I've spent more and more time here. I can point to frequent examples where other departments are coming to a colleague on my product who has less experience than I do for information and advice. So they will first go to the German native before they go to me for information. . . . They're simply going to feel more comfortable going to somebody where they can just rattle off exactly what they want . . . and joke around . . . and make the whole circumstance a little bit fun. They feel more comfortable going to someone with whom they can communicate more confidently, where they can understand that person better. I may be more knowledgeable with information, but this person, my colleague, will be able to make himself better understood to the person asking the question than I could. It's a combination of language and familiarity.

For James, feeling like an outsider in the informal network has been a source of frustration. He sees relationships as a key way to make sense of formal communications, to get valuable translations of corporate decisions, but, in his case, relationships only go so far. As he described:

> From the German standpoint, just like you put on a suit every day
> and go to the office, you also put on your language. These are native
> German speakers and they have to go into this environment every
> day and they have to speak the official language of the company, so
> I think, psychologically, when I am speaking English with them,
> they feel that they are speaking it officially. This is the feeling I get
> sometimes.

Because Premium Products' formal performance evaluation process ensured that James's career advancement was affected by his progress relative to measurable goals, rather than his inclusion in informal networks, James did not feel that his career progress was directly impeded. Nevertheless, to the degree that his access to information affected managing his projects, his outsider status did increase the difficulty of meeting his performance objectives.

The solution to some of James's difficulties came in the form of a mentor. Because his experience with his first manager was not particularly positive, James needed help in finding his niche in the company. It took a full year for James to find a mentor, mainly because there were few of the most willing mentors—expatriate managers with longer tenure in the host country—in his division. Once he did hook up with a mentor, this more senior German manager was able to help James transition from one product area to another. His mentor took time to understand James's strengths, worked to identify how he could best be used in the organization, and helped him be more effective in his job. But most of all, James credited his mentor for:

> making me feel really part of the organization and not as much of an
> outsider as I felt with my manager. . . . It's this role of identification
> that was important in this mentor relationship. . . . This was some-
> one who was several levels higher than I was and he drew on a lot of

examples from his own career at Premium Products. . . . It was really the first time I could identify with someone in the organization.

Through his mentor, James began to recognize how he was viewed by others and how to better communicate. He also had access to someone who could help him make sense of his experience.

Reflecting on his two years in Germany, James feels strongly that being an expatriate manager has been valuable professionally and personally. As he explained:

> I think it has certainly made me more aware of myself in terms of how I come across to other people. It has made me much more thoughtful, . . . made me question my instincts more . . . [and] think more analytically and strategically daily about how to communicate and approach someone to achieve my objectives. It has made me question myself more about the way that I am acting or managing a situation. The second thing is that it has made me a better listener, a more active listener. I feel less anticipation on my part when I am listening to someone. I ask more questions. Sometimes I have to stop and say, "What you are telling me doesn't make sense to me; let's clarify."

James reported that personally he has become a more patient and tolerant person. In Germany, he has encountered differences in the way people think about social issues, work ethics, politics, and everyday life—a range of views that he rarely confronted in the United States. He has had to learn to accept these differences. James explained:

> It's very sobering to be in the minority rather than the majority when it comes to the way people are thinking. It makes you a more reflective person in general—more reflective of your own society, and more tolerant of other people's societies.

Since his arrival in Germany as a full-time marketing assistant, he has been promoted to assistant product manager and plans to continue working in Europe. He believes that having cross-border management experience early in his career and integrating it into the general management learning process builds "value added" for the future, whether in another expatriate assignment or working back in the United States.

Having weathered the difficulties of expatriate adjustment—without even being acknowledged as an expatriate—James finds himself instinctively helping new Americans who join his division. By mentoring them, he hopes to demonstrate some of the sensitivity he would have welcomed, and to share the lessons he has learned about successfully communicating across cultural barriers.

John Grabino

For John Grabino, taking an overseas assignment after graduating from Fuqua seemed natural. Lebanese by background, John had spent a semester studying in London during college and worked in Kuwait prior to attending Fuqua.

When the time came to begin his post-MBA career, John knew he wanted to work in investment banking and had a strong interest in taking a global assignment. Company culture and reputation were important to him. He paid close attention to how different investment banking firms recruited at Fuqua: the types of students the firms interviewed and selected, as well as the way top managers described the firm's culture and values.

John chose Trasella Bergen because, in his view, the firm selected people who were very well rounded, while other firms picked people who were more one-dimensional: at the top of the class academically, but with few outside interests. Trasella Bergen recruited John for a specific job: a position on the central bank and official institution's sales desk in the firm's London office. John recalled his feelings about the opportunity:

> They said they wanted me to come to London. And to cover the international franchise and so on. And that was the reason—I was very attracted to being in a foreign post doing these things. And in retrospect it turned out to be quite good, because the industry became more and more global, and if you looked at the revenue in the pie chart on how international compared to New York, it was very small and over the last ten years it continued to grow, so that now it's pretty much fifty-fifty. So that was where the growth was. And beyond that, it was, from my standpoint, a pretty interesting lifestyle— very cultural and so on.

John moved to London with his wife, Diane, also a Fuqua graduate. In his job, John immediately experienced life in a global industry and firm.

Working with predominantly British supervisors and a diverse group of peers, John noted that 28 nationalities were represented on a single floor of 100 people in his office. His customers also were extremely diverse: "all nationalities." The job itself presented exciting opportunities reflecting the global marketplace. As John described:

> It's become a twenty-four–hour market. In addition, a colleague of mine in New York would probably be specialized in a certain product. And selling to a specific client base. While here in London, you can sell any product that the firm can offer to a specific client base. So while in New York, you might be sitting there and you're trying to sell U.S. Treasury bonds, and the U.S. Treasury market is unattractive. Here, in London, you can say, "Well, the U.S. Treasury market is not attractive, maybe the French bond market is attractive." Or corporate market, or whatever it is. So the options are many and as a result . . . you do have a lot more choice here in London than you would in New York.

But these new opportunities were accompanied by new challenges. The first challenge was cultural. Despite all the diversity and novelty John faced in his new position, he received no training or preparation for his move. What training was available from the firm was aimed at acclimating spouses to what they would experience. This seemed reasonable to John. After all, Trasella Bergen is an American firm, and being in London, he would not have the difficulties associated with a language barrier. His orientation once he was in London consisted of a one-week rotation during which he spent approximately a half-hour shadowing each of the nearly eighty individuals he would work with in his new position.

Outside of work, John found that his social activities revolved around the community of other American expatriates. While there was mixing across groups, John found that groups formed around nationality and that other Americans became an important source of social support.

Like any new employee, John relied on his manager for help in settling into his new job and workplace. Here, his expectations were unmet. In investment banking—an industry focused on sales—managerial skills are typically not the basis for selection into managerial positions. Typically, managers in investment banking firms are people who formerly posted the highest sales numbers. To be a successful individual contributor is assumed to be sufficient preparation for a role as manager of other individual contributors.

Unfortunately for John, his manager's sales success did not translate into effectiveness in managing people. In recalling this manager, John said:

> I think his biases did sort of affect the way he went about doing things and I think I suffered because of that. And, really, for me, it was hard in the beginning to understand why. Now, I can see his shortcomings. He wasn't worldly enough. . . . I mean, it is one thing to have worked in Tokyo for two years, but it is a totally different thing to understand how different cultures work and so on, and to try to find the strengths and weaknesses [of one's employees] and sort of work with these attributes.

An ineffective manager is, of course, problematic for anyone, but when an office consists of the diversity represented in John's London workplace, making sense of poor management is more difficult and the effects are more dramatic. While trying to understand his manager, a Norwegian, and his style, John saw his career progress slow. Even in retrospect, John recounted:

> [My manager] was extremely xenophobic. . . . It's hard to explain, . . . very stubborn, and very inflexible. For me, that was very much of a nightmare. . . . I really had to solicit help and take a gamble, basically, a very big risk.

John was sufficiently concerned by his manager's performance that he approached the senior managers in the London office. For his first two years there, John felt that his potential was being wasted; he wasn't moving forward. In his third year, he felt the gamble was necessary and was willing to endure the potential costs: that senior management might not listen to him and, instead, maintain the status quo. The senior managers believed John and had observed enough other problems in the office so that, eventually, they fired his manager.

Up to this point, John had not been participating in the success of his division: "I was not really given an opportunity to do so." After the management change, people in his office took an interest in him and realized that there was an opportunity to include him—to tap his unrealized potential. Now, John had to deliver. His initial difficulties taught him a critical lesson.

A common denominator is that you've got to be good at what you do—very good. Typically, these firms have a very effective recruiting method, so that they do, in the end, find the people they think will succeed in this business. The one thing that 90 percent of the people do not realize when they get into this business, and I did not know, is that there are two parts to this job. The first part is that you sell Trasella Bergen—you sell the firm, to the client, to the world outside. And you try to do that better than anyone else. And you think that when you do that very well, then your manager is going to pay you, and is going to promote you, and is going to take care of you.

But your manager sometimes has a totally different agenda. Maybe he's busy, maybe he's got different priorities, or maybe you're an American and he's British. What you need to do is to sell yourself within the firm, inside the firm, on the trading floor, everywhere. You've got to network and sell yourself. For example, you do a great transaction where you sold a very difficult thing to a client, something that the firm has had a rough time selling for about six months. Finally, you sell it. And you think, "That's the end of it." That's what I used to think. Well, I've done something which is great. Somebody's bound to recognize what I've done. I will get compensated and I will get recognized for that. It's not really like that. . . . If you get four or five people to . . . go and alert the higher-ups to what you're doing, then I think you really can bridge these difficulties: that you sort of come across as an American and the other guy is French, you just can't relate to his sense of humor or whatever. In the end, you find that [selling yourself to others] is extremely effective in opening doors for you. People start to recognize what you're doing. They take an interest in you.

For John, who is still in London, things have turned around. His value has been recognized and he has been able to contribute to his division's bottom line. But for him, the transition from potential contributor to actual contributor was painful. While he recognized that he was initially consulted less because he was less experienced than some of his peers, he also realized that cultural familiarity affected consultation and information sharing. Had his manager been more proactive, John felt his impact would have been greater from the outset. Instead, the firm missed out on his contribution, and personally, he was "undercompensated and underpromoted."

In thinking about how he will manage others, John was enthusiastic:

I think I'll be a great manager!! I think, really and truly, . . . having gone through these problems, I'm now very aware of them. I think I'll make a lot of mistakes, because I think it's an art and not a science. . . . It's sort of a bit of both. . . . The most important thing is to be aware of that and try to solicit feedback from people who work for you.

In fact, John's firm now uses 360-degree feedback, which allows employees to comment on people they work with at the same, higher, and lower levels. The idea is to solicit feedback from the entire universe of people who may have constructive performance information.

John has ridden the waves of the investment banking industry and seen accompanying changes in the value placed on management, as well as the specific management practices (such as 360-degree feedback) used. With the enormous volatility in the investment banking industry, John has seen very good firms suffer. Firms have responded to the volatility through large-scale firing, downsizing, and cost cutting. Right now, his firm avoids using expatriates because of the enormous costs associated with sending Americans overseas (personal communication, Fuqua School of Business alumnus who previously worked overseas for the same firm).

During this downturn, the costs of poor management have become clear. As John described:

If you get things wrong, or if you do things wrong, you pay a very heavy price. So that is one reason why good managers are extremely important to us. . . . It's very hard for us, here in London, and I think in New York, to find the right people. It's extremely difficult to recruit the right kind of person. It's not easy. And once you get the right people, to hold on to them, and motivate them, is I think even more difficult.

Other industry changes also indicate that people-management practices will become more, not less, important. Mergers between commercial banks and securities firms, while sensible on paper, stimulate new management challenges. The cultures of commercial banks and investment firms are radically different, yet to obtain maximal benefits from a merger, some firm activities must be integrated and talent, ideally, should be shared. Managing the cultural differences between these two entities will require management talent that may be in scarce supply within the industry.

For John, the professional growth he has experienced since his early difficulties on the job, as well as the lifestyle that he and his wife have enjoyed in London, made his expatriate assignment worthwhile. In overcoming the initial challenges he faced on the job, John has recognized the importance of management practice in a way that is oftentimes more difficult when things go smoothly. And he is certain he will be a better manager as a result of his experience.

Chuck Wagner

Chuck Wagner, unlike John Grabino, started his post-Fuqua career as a corporate bond trader with Trasella Bergen in New York. After he had five years on the job, Chuck's boss, Dan Wright, a very successful trader, accepted a position in London and wanted Chuck to go with him.

The London operation was very small and needed talent and expertise from the New York office in order to grow quickly. Although using expatriate traders from New York in London cost twice as much as using local traders, the firm believed that the international business opportunities opening up in London justified the high cost of the imported employees. Trasella Bergen's strategy was to develop the London operation quickly, using some expatriates, and then staff it with local hires as appropriate talent became available and the business matured.

For Chuck, accepting such an assignment, while risky, provided an important opportunity to grow professionally. Although he had not previously planned or specifically envisioned going overseas, relocating to London enabled Chuck to trade nondollar government bonds, which he viewed as more intellectually challenging, requiring a more multidimensional approach to the markets. In addition, because the London office was being developed, Chuck saw this as an entrepreneurial opportunity unavailable in New York.

Nevertheless, Chuck knew that making the move to London would be a gamble. Taking the position involved severing his ties to the New York office: he would become an employee of Trasella Bergen in London. Furthermore, his London trading desk had no satellite in New York which could serve as a "home" for Chuck when he was ready to move back to the United

States. However, Chuck believed that, ultimately, the market would move toward twenty-four–hour, real-time, nondollar trading and this development would require the New York office to build a parallel trading desk. If that happened, the New York operation would need someone with the expertise that Chuck would gain in London. Under this scenario, Chuck's gamble would pay off handsomely. Under the alternative scenario—that 24–hour, real-time, nondollar trading did not develop—he had no obvious route back to New York that would provide him with the opportunity to use the expertise he would acquire in London.

After a site visit to meet his potential colleagues in London, he accepted the position. Chuck did not anticipate that a major adjustment would be required. To some degree, he thought that "London would be like the fifty-first state." After all, he spoke the same language and would be working in an operation which had connections to an American firm. In addition, Chuck had several close personal friends and professional colleagues who were based in London at the time and he was aware that there was a large American expatriate community. However, as he quickly learned, there were both industry and office-level differences. In London, the trading floor was less aggressive and Chuck found the business less relationship-oriented. European clients did not form allegiances to particular investment banks, opting instead to focus exclusively on price and execution. This made the competition within the dealer community "much more wide open." On the trading floor, Chuck found that his European colleagues construed American-style drive and leadership as "pushiness."

There were also differences inside Trasella Bergen's London office. Working with 60 to 65 percent non-Americans, Chuck found himself in the minority. He interacted with traders from many different countries: France, Spain, the Netherlands, China, Germany, and Italy. This diversity of native cultures and languages posed some adaptation challenges, but other dynamics in the office presented greater difficulty. Chuck arrived in London after there had been quite a bit of upheaval in the sales force. Many of the senior people had left and the people who remained were disgruntled. With the departure of so many senior people, the firm lost both valued expertise and key client relationships. Morale and the bottom line were adversely affected. Reflecting upon other conditions related to his introduction to the London operation, Chuck realized that the circumstances were less than ideal:

I think one of the problems was that I was the only one Dan brought over, and there was probably this perception that "he's bringing this guy in as his boy and we just don't particularly like that idea." It was a pretty close-knit group I was dropped into. And you know these guys, in hindsight, probably didn't really trust Dan, let alone trust me.

In fact, shortly after Chuck arrived, Dan, his one-time mentor, suggested that they not talk as much so that he could integrate himself into the office without any gossip that he was the boss's "spy."

The other traders were already suspicious of Chuck, or so it seemed to him. Chuck remembered that each morning for his first six months, the four German traders he worked most closely with would say "Hi" to him and then spend the rest of the day without uttering a word of English.

Although Chuck used his network of other expatriates as much as possible to get up to speed, he could learn the mechanics of the markets he was trading only from his German colleagues. He patiently worked and waited for his coworkers to help him. This was frustrating and painful for Chuck:

Looking back, it actually hurt my performance for the first year or two when I was over there. Now eventually things changed, people I worked with warmed up to me. . . . It took two years to work itself out and probably cost me a fair amount of money in terms of what I got paid at the end of the year as well as career advancement. I could have benefited greatly if they had been more helpful to me, getting me up to speed so I didn't have to learn so much on my own and learn from my mistakes as much as I did. I could have saved a lot of time and saved a lot of money if these guys had been a little more helpful. . . . [But] quite frankly, maybe they wouldn't have minded if I didn't succeed.

As difficult as this was for him, Chuck realized that he was not alone in being treated as an outsider. Often when Americans came to the London office, the European traders would essentially shut them out. Chuck observed how the Europeans in the office responded to the new Americans:

Sometimes you would see a new expat come in, and he's used to doing business in the style that's done on the New York trading floor.

And he would try and behave the same way in London, and the people would just freeze him out. [Imitating non-Americans in the office:] "Here comes another American, another person from the New York office who thinks that this is how business is going to get done." And it just didn't work. They would freeze him out. . . . They'd just ignore him . . . and not respond to any of his requests.

Chuck found that he had to "rewire" his brain in order to succeed. Ultimately, he did adapt and grew professionally as he had originally hoped. He learned to trade new products and be more entrepreneurial during the rapid growth of the London office. In London, he was able to wear not only "more hats" but also "bigger hats." Chuck knew his decision to go to London had been a gamble, but he felt the gamble had paid off.

After three years, Chuck expressed his interest in returning to the New York office. The London office had grown 300 percent since his arrival. Although Chuck had not visited the New York office during his tenure at Trasella Bergen in Great Britain, he was now flown back to talk about his planned return.

Unfortunately, several unexpected events delayed the repatriation planning process. His former sponsor, Dan, left the London office and took many people with him, causing enormous turmoil. As a result, Chuck opted to stay in London to shore up the business. It took six to seven months for things to normalize and management to again consider Chuck's request to return to New York.

Chuck was willing to wait for a good opportunity to open up, but with Dan's departure, he was left without a sponsor in London. As an employee of the London organization, Chuck had no formal ties to a manager in New York who would take responsibility for managing his transition back to the United States. As Chuck explained:

I think the biggest concern or the biggest impact that management and management practices have on an expat is when they come back to the United States. I think that's when you really care about management practices: "Now that it's time to go back, what can you do for me?" And I'll be quite honest, the repatriation process, for me, was difficult.

While Chuck had worked in London, 70 to 80 percent of his professional interactions had been with Europe-based traders and dealers. He had no regular contact with his former colleagues in New York during his expatriate assignment. However, one of his London colleagues, Marcelo Sorrelli, had previously transferred to New York. Fortunately for Chuck, Marcelo, who had been a managing director in London and had now assumed an administrative role in New York, took a personal interest in helping Chuck return.

It took a little more than a year to get Chuck back to New York. While the London office had grown exponentially, the New York office was on a different trajectory. Chuck recalled that, at the time:

> New York was stagnant and shrinking in terms of the number of professionals they had. The businesses were very mature. The people who stayed weren't going anywhere. So there were just not a lot of openings in New York. . . . It was very difficult for me to find a spot that leveraged my experience. It took a long time just to get two or three options to pursue.

Chuck returned to New York, working in his old trading job for one year. The job did not leverage Chuck's new expertise, but it did enable him to return to the firm and provided an opportunity for people to learn about his experience overseas. Although Chuck could have immediately exploited his knowledge by moving into sales, he wanted to stay in trading, and so he waited for an opportunity to move laterally within the New York operation. When two managers running the global high-yield department noted Chuck's experience, they asked him to work in emerging markets, a growing area of the firm. The job provided Chuck with an opportunity to use the expertise and professional network he had acquired in London, and to remain in trading. He accepted the offer.

Since joining the global high-yield department, Chuck has found that he interacts frequently with salespeople and traders in Europe. These professional relationships, as well as his insights into the characteristics of London accounts, have increased his effectiveness. Although he had to wait for this opportunity, Chuck feels that his expatriate experience has paid off:

> I acquired business skills and trading skills and knowledge that I don't think I would have acquired here in New York. That translates

into my being more productive, and in that sense, the firm is utilizing the knowledge I acquired over there.

Compared to many expatriates, Chuck has been fortunate. In Marcelo, he had an unofficial sponsor who was able to help him come back, and in his new position, he has leveraged some of the knowledge and expertise he gained in London. Looking back, Chuck explained:

> If I had it to do over again, I'd do it over again, even exactly the way it happened. . . . I had an opportunity to develop professional skills that I would not have developed in New York—without question. I'm a better trader for it. I'm a better businessman. I matured a lot more quickly professionally over there.

In using expatriate managers, Trasella Bergen was able to rapidly develop a foreign operation while the market and local talent matured. Today, approximately 50 percent of the firm's revenues come from nondomestic sources.

Local skill gaps are one of the most common reasons American multinational corporations send expatriates overseas. Other justifications for the use of expatriates include providing a firm-wide understanding and focus on goals and objectives, corporate control, and building knowledge of the global operation (Kobrin, 1988).

For Chuck, the reentry process was the most difficult part of his assignment. Since his return, Chuck has discovered that his repatriation experience was not atypical. A survey conducted by the firm showed that many expatriates had similar difficulties with the process.

Research on other companies shows that firms often do not prepare their expatriates for the difficulties involved with the repatriation process. Studies indicate that repatriation provides a number of specific challenges: cultural adaptation, career management, and leveraging newly gained expertise, to name a few. In fact, recent studies support Chuck's assessment that, for many managers, repatriation is often more difficult than expatriation.

All of these facts make it less surprising that 25 percent of repatriated employees leave their company within a year of returning (Black, Gregersen, & Mendenhall, 1992). The up-front expense of using expatriates, combined with the difficulty of retaining these employees, argues for a reconsideration of global assignments.

Or does it? Whatever concerns firms may have, the number of American executives going overseas increased 30 percent between 1993 and 1994 (*Fortune,* August 21, 1995, p. 129). And in 1995, it is estimated that 225,000 Americans will work overseas (*Wall Street Journal,* July 25, 1995, p. B1). For many firms, how they will manage global assignments and the repatriation of their employees so as to capitalize on these managers' knowledge, skills, and abilities is more than a matter of improved people management—it's a matter of competitive advantage.

Suggestions for the Use of Case 7.2

This case is a good example of some of the challenges that will need to be met while making the professional adjustment to a culture that is not one's own "native" culture. It addresses some of the critical issues facing the expatriation and repatriation process. While illustrating the dynamics of relationships between the expatriate and his or her coworkers and clients, it demonstrates problems that are inherent in cross-cultural interactions. It suggests that these problems are prevalent and can escalate without personal adjustment, management and organizational support, and appropriate mentorship.

Some of the issues for discussion and analysis in the case are listed below:

1. The case demonstrates the positive impact that a good mentor can bring to the expatriate's development and contribution to the organization.

2. The case shows the importance of language and of the distinction between language fluency and full proficiency of language.

3. The case illustrates subtle sources of disadvantage (for example, the effect of the "bull-pen" office style on James).

4. The case highlights the need to prepare managers to be effective in supervising expatriates (for example, the need for formal training even when the language is the same).

5. The case illustrates the need to pay attention to the repatriation process (which has at least two parts: assisting the expatriates with their personal career transitions and creating mechanisms for taking advantage of what they have learned to benefit others in the organization).

6. The case gives some examples of cultural differences. Can you identify them?

Cultural Differences: The Case of Work Specialization

Thus far in the chapter we have given attention to cultural differences as they relate to nationality, gender, and age cohort. In addition, cultural differences based on racioethnic groups will be addressed in Chapter Eight. Here, however, we want to conclude our study of the power of cultural differences by using an example based on a different, and rarely studied, basis of group identity: professional identity or work specialization.

● ● ●

Activity 7.3
WORK SPECIALIZATION AS A CULTURE GROUP

Objectives

1. To learn specific differences in culture (value structures and goal priorities) based on work specializations that are common in many organizations

2. To learn the implications of cultural differences based on work specialization for the effective performance of cross-functional teams

Procedure

Study the data shown in Tables 7.1 and 7.2, which were taken from the work of John Barnett. Using these data as a basis, either prepare written responses to the following questions or, if you are working in a facilitated group, discuss them in groups as directed by a facilitator. Group members may also want to prepare short written answers to each question to be shared with the full group.

1. Are these differences predictable? Why or why not?

2. What implications do these differences have for cooperation, consensus, and good interpersonal relationships in a product development team that contains both engineers and scientists?

TABLE 7.1. Cultural Differences Based on Work Function: Goal Priorities

Questionnaire Items	Engineer	Scientist
1. Contribute knowledge in my field	3.5	3.8
2. Participate in the business decisions of the company	3.9	3.5
3. Commercialize a product	4.2	3.6
4. Invent new products or processes	3.8	3.4
5. Be involved in money-making projects	4.1	3.8
6. Publish in technical journals	2.7	3.4
7. Take assignments that are stepping-stones	3.4	3.0
8. Reputation outside company is important	3.2	3.7

SOURCE: John Barnett, *Understanding Group Effects Within Organizations: A Study of Group Attitudes and Behaviors of Engineers and Scientists.* Santa Barbara, CA: The Fielding Institute, 1994.

NOTE: Scores are averages on a five-point scale, with higher numbers indicating higher importance. All differences were statistically significant.

Sample = 201 Ph.D. scientists and engineers in the same research and development firm.

TABLE 7.2. Cultural Differences Based on Work Function: Behavioral Styles

Self-Ranked Order of Attributes for Engineers	Top 10 for Engineers	Rank of Same Behavior by Scientists
Problem solver	1	9
Practical	2	23
Customer-focused	3	29
Guided by ethics	4	3
Analytical	5	5
Detailed	6	11
Cautious	7	24
Structured	8	26
Designer	9	28
Cooperative	10	15
	Average Difference in Ranks = 12.0	

SOURCE: John Barnett, *Understanding Group Effects Within Organizations: A Study of Group Attitudes and Behaviors of Engineers and Scientists.* Santa Barbara, CA: The Fielding Institute, 1994.

3. If the team is cross-disciplinary but dominated by one group or the other, what effects do you predict for group process and outcomes?

4. If these differences were known and made explicit in advance (which they normally would not be), how could this knowledge be used to build effectiveness on the team?

Suggestions for the Use of Activity 7.3

The data in the tables make it clear that there are real cultural differences between engineers and scientists. Indeed, the author of the research on which this activity is based has noted in his review of the data, "At worst, scientists are viewed as an out-group; at best, as a different culture from the company [culture]" (Barnett, 1994, p. 208).

The issue of dominance by a work-function-based identity group was a real one in the company from which these data were taken, which was engineering-dominated, and we have found that this same dynamic exists in other organizations, except that the function or work specialization of dominance may differ. When this occurs, some of the same outcomes (under-utilization, intergroup conflict, and so on) that have been observed for differences in gender and racioethnic identity can also apply to work specialization.

Ignorance of these culture-based differences leads to loss of effectiveness. If the differences are recognized, not only can the data be used to educate people on important characteristics of others in the team (essential for thorough team building), but also the differences can be better leveraged to improve work outcomes. For example, the tension between the engineers' push for immediate application and the scientists' quest to push the frontiers of knowledge can be useful to balance short-and long-term considerations in managing projects.

Summary Activity

As a summary to Chapter Seven, we again suggest an activity (Activity 7.4) that requires you to apply your learnings from the chapter to the full range of work tasks that were listed in the diversity competency model for individuals in Figure 1.2. The model specified seven task areas where diversity in work groups is known to have an impact. For your convenience, the model is reproduced here as Figure 7.3.

Figure 7.3. Diversity Competency Model for Individuals

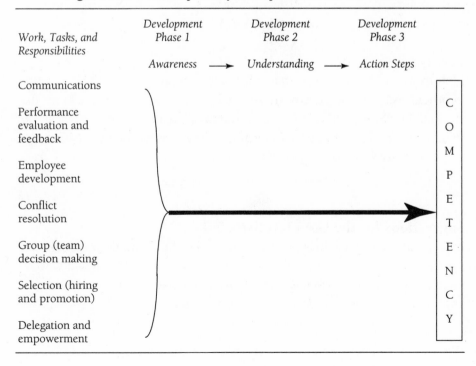

Activity 7.4
LINKING LEARNINGS ON CULTURAL DIFFERENCES TO THE DIVERSITY COMPETENCY MODEL FOR INDIVIDUALS

Objectives
1. To identify specific ways in which cultural differences can affect the performance of various work tasks and responsibilities
2. To identify steps that can be taken to minimize the potential for cultural differences to be a barrier to the effective performance of work tasks and responsibilities, and to leverage cultural differences to improve problem solving, creativity, and innovation in diverse teams

Procedure

Task 1
Working alone or in a group as directed by a learning facilitator, create a list of one to three ways in which cultural differences may have an effect on the performance of one or more (depending on how you wish to use the activity) of the task areas shown in Figure 7.3.

Task 2
Identify one to three actions that you could take, possibly with the support of others and your organization's leadership, to reduce the probability that cultural differences will be a barrier in the performance of these tasks, and/or to increase the probability that cultural differences can be better leveraged to enhance work-group outcomes.

Suggestions for the Use of Activity 7.4
Individuals can work through these two tasks alone and then request that they be reviewed with comments by colleagues whom they trust and who are more knowledgeable than they are on diversity issues. If you are facilitating a group, you may want to have each group work on a separate task area and

assign part or all of the seven task areas. You may also want to modify the task areas to fit the group you are working with better. For example, you may want to substitute coaching and counseling for delegation.

It will not be difficult to identify ways in which cultural differences could affect these tasks. For example, Reading 7.2, Activity 7.2, and Cases 7.1 and 7.2 provide some good insights on how culture can affect communications in diverse groups. Reading 7.1 has implications for task areas like delegation and empowerment. If it is available, we also strongly suggest that Chapter Seven of the theory book, *Cultural Diversity in Organizations* (Cox, 1993), be assigned in conjunction with this chapter to provide more information with which to do Activity 7.4.

SUGGESTED FILMS

Going International
Copeland-Griggs Productions
c/o Lewis Griggs
302 Twenty-Third Avenue
San Francisco, California 94121

This film presents vignettes illustrating how ignorance of cultural differences can become a major barrier to successfully conducting business outside one's home country. Insights into the national cultures of India, Mexico, Saudi Arabia, England, and Japan are highlighted. There is some humor in the film, but it also invariably leaves viewers with an appreciation of the link between being culture-savvy and achieving effective job performance in a global business context.

Discussion Questions
1. What specific cultural differences were illustrated?
2. How can the cultures of other nations be learned?
3. What should firms do to take advantage of the knowledge gained by professionals returning from overseas work assignments?
4. How can the presence of citizens born in other countries be leveraged to promote learning in this area?

The Colonel Comes to Japan
LCA Video/Films
Division of Learning Corporation of America
1350 Avenue of the Americas
New York, New York 10019

This video depicts the trials of an American company trying to break into the Japanese market. The introduction of Kentucky Fried Chicken restaurants into Tokyo was not a simple order. The video depicts how an American CEO had to adapt his way of thinking and doing business in order for his business to survive in the Japanese culture. Many adaptations of the American restaurant had to be made in areas such as marketing, advertising, and menu selections. In addition, the Japanese have various traditions that accompany the opening of a business, and these traditions must be carried out in order for a business to be respected and patronized. Overall, the video describes the expansion of thought and practice that must be addressed when attempting to be successful in global business ventures.

Discussion Questions

1. Identify some of the significant obstacles to the success of the American company in Japan.

2. What strategies were used by the American company to gain success in Japan?

3. Would some of the lessons learned in the Japanese venture be helpful and applicable to other global ventures? If so, what are they? If not, why not?

Developing Organizational Competency

In this part of the book we shift attention from the individual to the organizational level of analysis. A basic premise of the Interactional Model of Cultural Diversity (IMCD) theoretical framework from Chapter Three is that the effects of diversity, like those of other aspects of human behavior, occur as complex combinations (or interactions) of characteristics of individuals and characteristics of the environment. In this case, we are especially interested in the organizational environment.

As noted in Chapter One, we view organizational competency in managing diversity as having two components. First, a large percentage of members in the organization (especially managers) must have developed competency at the individual level, and second, the culture, policies, and structural characteristics of the organization must be aligned so as to support people in learning and displaying the behaviors that will create diversity competency. Organizations that achieve these two conditions will meet our definition of a multicultural organization.

We have dealt extensively with the first requirement in Part Two of the book; our focus here is on the second condition: supportive organizational culture, policies, and structure. We will address this requirement in two ways. First, in Chapters Eight and Nine, we will consider the specific aspects of the organizational environment that were mentioned in the IMCD framework. These include the organization's culture, its formal structure, and its informal structure (communications and social networks and processes). Of course, a full discussion of all aspects of culture, formal structure, and informal processes is beyond the scope of the book; therefore, we have selected for attention a sampling of relevant material.

Second, in Chapter Ten, we will provide a model for the design and implementation of an organizational change process to increase organizational diversity competency. As organizations begin to understand what it takes to foster a multicultural environment, many will identify a strategic gap between where they are at present and where they need to go. This chapter will offer a model and learning material to assist change leaders in closing the gap.

In the final chapter of the book, we provide some tools to assist people in continuing the learning process beyond this book, and we offer some brief comments on our view of the future of managing diversity as an area of practice and learning. After completion of this part of the book, you should feel more competent to:

1. Identify strategic gaps that require attention in order for your organization to achieve diversity competency

2. Personally support organizational change efforts for achieving diversity competency

3. Participate in designing and implementing organizational change strategies for achieving diversity competency

8

Organizational Culture

In Part Two, we addressed intercultural differences at the individual level of analysis, considering individuals as members of distinct identity groups. Here we revisit the central topic of culture, taking an organizational perspective. It is well established in both the academic and practitioner-oriented literatures that organizations develop distinct cultures and that organizational culture has profound effects on human behavior in the workplace (Trice & Beyer, 1993; Denison, 1984; Schein, 1990; Van Maanen & Barley, 1984).

The organizational culture defines preferred ways of thinking and behaving, and there is often enormous pressure to conform to these prescriptions, especially if one aspires to be upwardly mobile. Since both individuals and their employing organizations have cultures, the interface of these two cultures presents important dynamics for organizational behavior and effectiveness. When cultures overlap, the socialization of new entrants into an existing organizational culture is facilitated. On the other hand, cultural distance, the opposite of cultural overlap, sets the stage for culture-related conflict or culture clash. The resolution of cultural distance between cultural entities (in this case between individuals and their employing organization) is addressed by processes of acculturation.

Although there is clearly a potential for cultural distance between the norms and values of any individual and those of the organization, members who share the same primary social-cultural group-identity configuration (especially gender, racioethnicity, nationality, and work specialization) as the founders and historical leaders of the organization have a higher probability of achieving a "natural" cultural overlap than those from other cultural backgrounds. Thus the burden of acculturation is, in general, a much more serious problem for members of "minority" groups. These concepts and their implications for diversity competency are developed more extensively in the "Raising Awareness" and "Creating Understanding" sections of this chapter. We conclude the chapter with an activity and a case that ask you to apply the concepts to real organizations.

RAISING AWARENESS

Perhaps the most important aspect of organizational culture to understand in the context of managing diversity is that of acculturation. Reading 8.1 is intended to raise awareness about this important topic by providing, among other things, a typology of the different forms of acculturation.

Reading 8.1
THE PROCESS OF ACCULTURATION
IN DIVERSE ORGANIZATIONS

TAYLOR COX, JR., AND JOYCELYN FINLEY-NICKELSON

The globalization of business and the demographic trends of many nations of the world are creating markets and workforces that are increasingly culturally diverse. For example, it is estimated that in the next decade more than 40 percent of all net additions to the workforce in the United States will be ethnic minorities, including many immigrants from Asian and Latin American countries (Fullerton, 1987). Further, organizations based in many other countries of the world, including Canada (Frideres, 1989; Ramcharan, 1982), Italy (Olivares, 1987), the Pacific Islands (Renshaw, 1987), Germany (Antal & Kresbach-Gnath, 1987), and Japan (Steinhoff & Tanaka, 1987), are struggling with issues related to the increased presence of ethnic minorities or of women in management ranks. These trends highlight the need for understanding the impact of cultural diversity resulting from changing profiles of racioethnic, gender, and nationality identities on organizational behavior and effectiveness. While a significant number of articles have appeared in the management literature on gender issues, there has been far less attention given to racioethnicity and nationality identities of organization members. Moreover, the management literature on gender and racioethnicity has tended to focus on equal opportunity issues and has largely ignored the cultural aspects of workforce diversity. For example, a recent review of research published in twenty leading management journals indicates that of 201 articles dealing with racioethnicity, more than half dealt with the hiring and organizational policy aspects of equal employment opportunity (Cox & Nkomo, 1990).

Recently, a number of writers have called attention to the importance of the cultural dynamics of diversity (for example, Dunphy, 1987; Schneider,

Source: Adapted from Taylor Cox, Jr., and Joycelyn Finley-Nickelson, "Models of Acculturation for Intra-organizational Cultural Diversity," *Canadian Journal of Administrative Sciences, 8*(2), 1991, pp. 90–100. Used by permission.

1988; Cox, 1993; Fernandez, 1981; Ferdman, 1992; Triandis, 1995; Chen & DiTomaso, 1996).

A central theme in these writings is that different racioethnic, gender, and nationality groups represent distinct cultures within the broader culture of the society or organization in which they live and work. Persons with group identities in a minority culture can be expected to be influenced by norms of behavior and values that may be quite different from those of the dominant culture group. Therefore, a key to effectiveness for organizations with diverse workforces is to address the cultural differences between the various groups represented.

Acculturation

The term *acculturation* has been used to refer to the process of addressing cultural differences and to cultural change and adaptation between groups, especially where one or more minority groups (numerical minorities in a particular social context) are being merged with a majority group (Berry, 1980). Work in the fields of sociology and psychology highlight the importance of acculturation processes to understanding cross-group interactions in culturally heterogeneous societies. General or multiethnic-group discussions of acculturation processes include Berry (1983), Lambert and Taylor (1988), Padilla (1980), and Wong-Rieger and Quintana (1987). Writers have also addressed the importance of acculturation to understanding human behavior in diverse groups for specific racioethnic groups such as African Americans (Valentine, 1971), Mexican Americans (Hazuda, Stern, & Haffner, 1988), Japanese Americans (Kiefer, 1974), and French-Canadians (Breton, Burnet, Hartmann, Isajiw, & Lennards, 1975).

Although this previous research and theory has established the centrality of acculturation to understanding intercultural group dynamics, it has focused almost exclusively on societal diversity. The concept of acculturation has seldom been discussed in the context of organizational behavior. Recently, however, acculturation processes have been addressed in the literature on mergers and acquisitions (Malekzadeh & Nahavandi, 1990; Nahavandi & Malekzadeh, 1988; Siehl, Ledford, Silverman, & Fay, 1988). Nahavandi and Malekzadeh (1988) argue that the extent to which a merger will be successful is greatly influenced by the amount of congruence in preferred modes of acculturation between the acquired and the acquiring firm. Preferred modes of acculturation, in turn, are determined by such factors as the desire to preserve the culture of the premerger organizations, the extent to which the acquiring firm is tolerant of cultural diversity, and the degree of product-market relatedness among the firms. In a follow-up article, the same authors describe case examples of mergers which illustrate their theory (Malekzadeh & Nahavandi, 1990). Other writers who have addressed acculturation processes in the context of mergers and acquisitions include Buono and Bowditch (1989) and Sales and Mirvis (1984).

While the cited works on mergers and acquisitions focus on cultural differences between organizations, we believe they may be adapted to address intraorganizational cultural diversity. Accordingly, the remainder of this reading will address types of acculturation processes and factors that determine the type of acculturation process that is used.

Modes of Acculturation

Modes of acculturation are typically classified into four types as follows: (1) assimilation, (2) separation, (3) deculturation, and (4) integration (Berry, 1984).

Assimilation

Assimilation refers to a one-way adaptation process in which the culture of one group (the dominant culture) becomes the standard of behavior for all other cultures merging into the society. Everyone, regardless of cultural heritage, is expected to conform to the norms and values of the dominant group and little, if any, of the culture of minority groups is preserved. A number of writers have noted that this has been the predominant approach in Western organizations of the past (Domm & Stafford, 1972; Klein, 1980). Hampton, Summer, and Webber (1987, p. 93) have provided a good illustration of this approach in their advice to racioethnic minorities and women seeking careers in predominantly Anglo, male organizations:

> Conform to the culture style in appropriate ways such as language and dress. Learn to play golf or tennis and talk about stock prices or whatever is necessary to encourage the group to feel comfortable around you. Most [minorities] have made it by learning to behave like traditional white, Anglo-Saxon Protestant culture.

Separation

Separation refers to cultural merger situations in which the minority groups are unwilling or unable to adapt to the dominant culture and as a result seek cultural and often physical autonomy from the dominant culture (Berry,

1983). Under separation, cultural exchange between the two parties is minimal. At the societal level, this form of acculturation can be seen in the prevalence of residential segregation based on racioethnic group. It should be noted that separation is often reinforced by both the dominant and the minority group. For example, the residential segregation of African Americans and "Black" Hispanics in the United States is a function of both discrimination and prejudice against these groups by Anglos and the preferences of many members of the minority groups to live with others who share their cultural heritage (Massey & Denton, 1988; Massey & Mullan, 1984). A similar history applies to other groups such as Chinese Americans, as evidenced, for example, by the existence of "Chinatown" locations in San Francisco and New York.

At the interorganizational level of analysis, the merger of Shearson and American Express Company is an example of the separation mode of acculturation. Managerial and cultural exchanges between the parties were minimal and there was a mutual acceptance of partitioning (Malekzadeh & Nahavandi, 1990). A second example is the merger of the Urban and Suburban banks [pseudonyms] as discussed by Buono and Bowditch (1989). In that merger, members of the acquired Urban bank resisted assimilation into the culture of the Suburban bank, which they perceived as distinctly different from their own. The result was the development of a "counterculture" within the Urban bank that stood in opposition to the predominant culture of the postmerger organization.

Deculturation

The third mode of acculturation is deculturation, in which neither the minority nor the majority culture is highly valued by members or influential in framing the behavior of minority members of the society or organization (Berry, 1983). Thus there are members of society who experience a lot of confusion about cultural identity because they do not have strong ties to any cultural group.

Pluralism

Berry uses the term *integration* to refer to a two-way acculturation process in which both culture groups change to some degree to reflect the norms and values of the other. Although the term *integration,* as defined by Berry, may be an appropriate label, it has frequently been used with different connotations than the one intended here. Therefore, we prefer, in agreement with Triandis (1976), to employ the term *cultural pluralism*. The origin of the term *cultural pluralism* is found in the essays of the early 1900s by Horace Kallen (1924). In discussing the cultural landscape of America, Kallen emphasized both the interdependence among members of the merging groups and the importance of preservation of the minority cultures. The idea of a mutual appreciation for the contributions of each culture is also central to the meaning of pluralism.

In the organizational context, the term *pluralism* suggests an acculturation process in which minority-culture members assimilate on a limited number of behaviors while retaining substantial differences on other dimensions. A specific example of pluralism acculturation occurred in the acquisition of Rolm by IBM, in which IBM agreed to allow Rolm the independence that is needed to retain a culture which emphasized entrepreneurship (Malekzadeh & Nahavandi, 1990). A second example is the acquisition strategy of Dana Corporation. Instead of attempting a cultural "takeover," Dana attempts to honor the culture and heritage of an acquired firm and establish a dual identity in which "a new home is added to the Dana Family" (Buono & Bowditch, 1989, p. 172).

Organizational Factors Affecting Acculturation
Degree to Which Diversity Is Valued
One factor that is expected to influence modes of acculturation in organizations is the extent to which diversity itself is highly valued in the organizational culture. The importance of this factor has frequently been addressed in writings on pluralistic societies (Berry, 1984; Frideres, 1989; McLeod, 1979; Triandis, 1976) and has recently begun to appear in writings about multicultural organizations (Cox, 1991; Nahavandi & Malekzadeh, 1988; Sales & Mirvis, 1984). The literature on mergers and acquisitions also provides theory and some case examples indicating that modes of acculturation among merging parties will be partly determined by whether or not diversity is valued (Malekzadeh & Nahavandi, 1990; Nahavandi & Malekzadeh, 1988). If the acquiring firm does not value diversity (is unicultural), then the emerging acculturation mode will normally be deculturation or assimilation. Alternatively, if the acquiring firm does value diversity (multicultural organization), then either separation (individual-firm autonomy) or pluralism

will occur. The literature further shows that among multicultural acquiring firms, pluralism will be favored in mergers among firms with similar products, whereas separation will occur if products or markets are highly dissimilar. Similar rationales can be made for predicting likely acculturation patterns for intraorganizational cultural diversity. Organizations which do not place a high value on diversity will tend to impose pressure on all members to conform to a single system of existing organizational norms and values. In summary:

PROPOSITION 1: When the organizational culture does not place high value on cultural diversity, organizations will tend to display the assimilation mode of acculturation.

Alternatively, organizations which place high value on diversity will tend to favor either separation or pluralism in order to preserve the richness of the differences that members of different cultural backgrounds bring to the organization. In interorganizational acculturation (as with mergers and acquisitions), the separation mode is made feasible by the presence of two previously independent organizations, which, if desired, can remain relatively autonomous in the postmerger environment. However, in the context of intraorganizational cultural diversity, the opportunity for effective separation of cultural groups is severely diminished. Separation may be feasible to the extent that task interdependence among cultural groups is low. An example is the traditional structure of multinational organizations in which foreign affiliates are run by natives and managed largely as culturally autonomous units (Prahalad, 1990). However, to the extent that task interdependence is high, and/or organizations desire a high level of coordination among cultural units (as preferred by many multinationals in recent years), it is important that all members, regardless of cultural background, share a set of "core values" of the organizational culture (Ghosal & Bartlett, 1988). Under this latter scenario, the pluralism mode of acculturation is indicated because, in contrast to separation, the pluralism mode contemplates a balance of shared and divergent behavioral norms. By definition, pluralism provides for common norms in some behavioral arenas while tolerating substantial retention of minority-group norms and values in arenas where shared norms are not essential. In summary:

PROPOSITION 2: When the organizational culture places a high value on diversity and task interdependence and coordination requirements among cultural groups are low, organizations will tend to display the separation mode of acculturation.

PROPOSITION 3: When the organizational culture places a high value on diversity and task interdependence and coordination requirements among cultural groups are high, organizations will tend to display the pluralism mode of acculturation.

Organizational Culture-Identity Structures

Explanation of the Factor. Another organizational factor which is expected to influence organizational acculturation processes is the culture-identity structure of the organization. The literature on organizational culture implies that the concept of culture-identity structures, which is typically applied at the individual level of analysis, may also apply to organizations. For example, organizational cultures are sometimes characterized as "strong" and "weak," usually on the basis of the extent to which norms and values are clearly defined and rigorously enforced (Denison, 1989; Mitroff & Kilman, 1984; Pascale, 1985). An organization with a weak culture has ill-defined norms and values and/or low enforcement, so that pressure to conform to organizationally prescribed behaviors is relatively low. Alternatively, a strong culture is one in which organizational values and norms are clearly defined and much attention is given to member conformity, so that adherence is widespread (Weiner, 1988).

The matter of pressure to conform to organizational norms is also addressed by research on organizational socialization. For example, Schein (1984) reports that organizations place different levels of importance on different norms and values. Some are treated as norms to which members must conform in order to survive in the system, while for others compliance is strongly preferred but not mandatory for survival. Schein labeled the mandatory norms as "pivotal" and the nonmandatory norms as "relevant"; however, we will substitute the term *peripheral* to be more descriptive of the connotation intended by relevant norms (that is, nonessential). According to Schein, norms on such things as dress, decorum, and political party affiliation are normally treated as peripheral, but in some organizations even these areas of behavior have written expectations which are enforced by management.

Based on the foregoing discussion of previous research on organizational culture and socialization, it is suggested that organizational culture-identity structures be conceptualized as shown in Table 8.1.

It should be noted that both Types 3 and 4 satisfy the definition of "strong" culture in that both have a high influence on behavior in core norm areas (Weiner, 1988). However, the fact that organizations with Type-3 cultural identities do not impose conformity pressure in noncore behavioral domains may be a critical distinction in predicting acculturation processes. This will be explained further in the following section, where the relationship between organizational culture-identity structures and modes of acculturation is discussed.

Organizational Culture Identity and Modes of Acculturation. In organizations with weak cultures (Types 1 and 2 in Table 8.1), the pivotal norms and values of the organization are ill defined and poorly enforced, and the specific culture of the organization will therefore not be easily discernible. As a result, pressure for conformity on entering members will necessarily be minimized. Under these conditions, we would expect relatively little cultural change among minority-culture members entering the organization from backgrounds which are divergent from those of the majority group. By the same token, majority-group members would have little incentive to change to minority-group norms since the latter groups are less politically powerful and are often underrepresented in the power structure of the organization. In summary:

PROPOSITION 4: Organizations with weak organizational cultures will tend to display a deculturation mode of acculturation.

TABLE 8.1. Types of Organizational Culture-Identity Structures

	Conformity Required for Career Success	
	Pivotal Norms	*Peripheral Norms*
Type 1	No	No
Type 2	No	Yes
Type 3	Yes	No
Type 4	Yes	Yes

In contrast to Type-1 and Type-2 organizations, Type-3 and Type-4 organizations are characterized by a clearly defined system of norms and values which are rigorously enforced. Since minority-culture members are generally underrepresented in the power structure of the organization, pivotal norms are primarily established by majority-group members. Thus, to the extent that people enter these organizations from cultural backgrounds which diverge from the majority, a significant degree of conformity to the dominant culture may be required. However, the amount of adaptation required is less in the Type-3 organization because the conformity pressures are limited to pivotal norms. Therefore:

PROPOSITION 5: Organizations with Type-3 culture-identity structures will tend to display a pluralism mode of acculturation.

PROPOSITION 6: Organizations with Type-4 culture-identity structures will tend to display the assimilation mode of acculturation.

Propositions 1–6 specify types of acculturation that are predicted under different organizational environments. Exhibit 8.1 summarizes the previous discussions. Different approaches to acculturation are expected in mergers with cultural differences within organizations when those organizations feature an organizational culture and one or more subcultures.

Conclusion

This article has described a framework for predicting modes of acculturation for organizational cultural diversity. The discussion has two general implications for management practice. First, organizations are expected to be more effective in managing culturally different personnel if they adopt a mode of acculturation which fits their contextual conditions as specified in Exhibit 8.1.

A second implication is that as workforces become more culturally diverse in the United States and elsewhere, and as the incidence of mergers and joint ventures among parties with distinctly different cultures increases, organizations which have traditionally been monocultural will need to shift toward a multicultural environment. A pluralism form of acculturation has been identified as a primary characteristic of such an environment (Cox, 1991; Triandis, 1976). Pluralism has also been advocated as the appropriate

EXHIBIT 8.1. Summary of Propositions

Assimilation will be the predominant mode of acculturation when:

1. The degree to which the organization values diversity is low.
2. The organizational culture-identity structure is Type 4 (pressure for conformity is high for both pivotal and peripheral values and norms).

Separation will be the predominant mode of acculturation when:

1. The organization places a high value on diversity, and task inter-dependence and integration requirements between cultural groups is low.
2. Organizational cultures are weak (culture-identity structures Type 1 and Type 2).

Pluralism will be the predominant mode of acculturation when:

1. The organizational culture places a high value on diversity, and task interdependence and coordination requirements among cultural groups are high.
2. The organizational culture-identity structure is Type 3 (high pressure to conform to pivotal values and norms but low pressure for peripheral norms).

---

acculturation mode for modern multinational organizations which must build capability to respond to diverse national interests while simultaneously preserving the ability to coordinate and implement certain policies and activities worldwide (Bartlett & Ghosal, 1987).

The framework presented here suggests that pluralism will be facilitated by organizational culture and policies which reinforce the "value" in diversity, and by a strong organizational culture identity which strongly enforces pivotal values but permits high tolerance for differences on peripheral behaviors (Type 3). Organizations seeking to create multicultural environments must therefore take steps to foster these characteristics. For example, a valuing-diversity culture is fostered by rewarding managers for superior effort on managing diversity and by insisting on minority-group representation in key decision-making committees (Cox, 1991). Thus, to the extent that the ideas presented here can be empirically verified, they may assist organizations in identifying what they must do in order to establish pluralism and promote a multicultural organizational model.

Suggestions for the Use of Reading 8.1

This reading introduces the major forms of acculturation. Particular emphasis should be given to the contrast between assimilation and pluralism. It should be noted that in the longer article from which this reading was excerpted, additional (individual-level) factors that affect the mode of acculturation were discussed. Thus we do not mean to imply that the form of acculturation that will be effective is entirely determined by the few factors noted in the reading, but rather to focus attention on the most important organization-level factors.

The reading is intended to increase your understanding of the concept of acculturation and also to stimulate thinking about possible steps that organizations might take in order to more effectively address the implications of cultural distance for their members. Some suggested discussion questions follow:

1. What form of acculturation process is dominant in your organization? What are the pros and cons of the various modes of acculturation?

2. How do organizational norms and the pressure for conformity to them get communicated?

3. What outcomes would you predict to occur when the process of acculturation breaks down (that is, when cultural distance remains unresolved for a significant number of organization members)?

4. In the case of a merger between two organizations with very different cultures, what steps could be taken to reduce the potential for destructive culture clash?

CREATING UNDERSTANDING

Reading 8.1 gave an introduction to acculturation as a process for addressing cultural differences between organizations and their members. We will now build on the insights gained in Reading 8.1 by examining more closely the implications of acculturation for members of "minority" ethnic groups.

Reading 8.2
BICULTURAL SOCIALIZATION: FACTORS
AFFECTING THE MINORITY EXPERIENCE

DIANE DE ANDA

Over the past several decades, there has been a marked growth in both the proportion and diversity of ethnic minorities within the United States. With the nation becoming increasingly culturally pluralist, particularly in the larger urban centers, it is important to examine the complex factors affecting the interface between the white majority or mainstream culture and ethnic minority cultures.

The "discovery" during the 1960s of substantial populations of ethnic minorities that had remained differentiated from the mainstream culture, in many cases over a number of generations, signaled the death knell for the "melting pot" theory, the traditional American belief in the process of cultural homogenization. To fill the conceptual void, conflicting models were proposed to explain the continued existence of these diverse cultural groups despite the socialization forces exerted by the institutions of the mainstream culture.

Models of Cultural Socialization
The cultural deficit model had its heyday in the compensatory education programs that flowed from the War on Poverty in the mid-sixties. This conceptualization posited that norms and cultural patterns of minority groups that varied from those of the majority culture were for the most part deviant and destructive and led to a self-perpetuating "cycle of poverty and deprivation." However, a multipronged attack by social scientists from various fields criticized the data base from which the model was drawn, the use of mainstream cultural norms as evaluative criteria, and the underlying assumptions of the structural inferiority of minority cultures. This led to the

Source: Excerpted from Diane de Anda, "Bicultural Socialization: Factors Affecting the Minority Experience," *Social Work,* 39(1), 1984, pp. 101–107. Copyright 1984, National Association of Social Workers, Inc., *Social Work.* Used by permission.

discrediting of the cultural deficit model and the ascendance of the cultural difference model.

The cultural difference model focused instead on the uniqueness of each minority culture, viewed as an independent and internally consistent system, to be understood in its own context rather than judged according to its similarity to or difference from the majority culture. However, the cultural difference model drew criticism from commentators such as Valentine (1971) based on its inability to explain how minority-group members who were socialized within this totally distinct cultural context were able to function within the bounds of the majority society and its institutions.

To remedy this, Valentine formulated a bicultural model. He postulated a dual socialization process for members of minority groups, consisting primarily of enculturation experiences within their own cultural group, along with less comprehensive but significant exposure to socialization agents and forces within the majority culture—in other words, cross-cultural socialization. Thus, in addition to socialization into their own culture, Valentine (1971, p. 143) stated that

> members of all subgroups are thoroughly enculturated in dominant culture patterns by mainstream institutions, including most of the content of the mass media, most products and advertising for mass marketing, the entire experience of public schooling, constant exposure to national fashions, holidays, and heroes.

In this way, the individual from an ethnic minority group was instructed in the values, perceptions, and normative behaviors of two cultural systems.

In my opinion, the bicultural model holds the most promise for understanding the process by which an individual learns to function in varying degrees within two systems—the minority culture and the majority society. However, although this model provides an overall conceptual framework, it offers little information regarding the specific mechanisms through which dual socialization occurs. The objective of this article, therefore, is to explain the process of bicultural socialization and to trace the influence of significant variables that account for variations among and within different ethnic groups in their degree of biculturalism and successful interactions with mainstream society.

Six Factors

The bicultural model postulates that the minority individual learns two distinct behavioral repertoires for utilization in the minority and majority societies. This does not completely explain, however, the differential success of different ethnic minorities and of different individuals within these ethnic minorities, particularly when success in dealing with the majority society is not based on degree of assimilation. I posit that at least six factors affect the degree to which a member of an ethnic minority group can or is likely to become bicultural:

1. The degree of overlap or commonality between the two cultures with regard to norms, values, beliefs, perceptions, and the like
2. The availability of cultural translators, mediators, and models
3. The amount and type (positive or negative) of corrective feedback provided by each culture regarding attempts to produce normative behaviors
4. The conceptual style and problem-solving approach of the minority individual and her or his mesh with the prevalent or valued styles of the majority culture
5. The individual's degree of bilingualism
6. The degree of the individual's dissimilarity in physical appearance from the majority culture in such things as skin color and facial features

As will be described in the following sections, the variation in these six factors and their interaction accounts for different levels of biculturation. These variables can serve to facilitate or impede dual socialization.

Cultural Overlap

Valentine's concept of biculturalism focused on the ability of the minority individual to step in and out of the repertoires of two cultures that were seen as totally distinct and separate.

On the contrary, the bicultural experience is possible only because the two cultures are not totally disparate. Dual socialization is made possible and facilitated by the amount of overlap between two cultures (see Figure 8.1). That is, the extent to which an individual finds it possible to understand and predict successfully two cultural environments and adjust his or her behavior according to the norms of each culture depends on the extent to which these two cultures share common values, beliefs, perceptions, and

Figure 8.1. Biculturalism

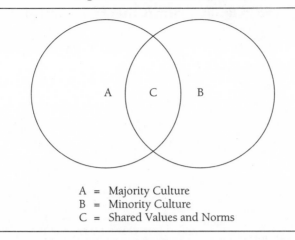

A = Majority Culture
B = Minority Culture
C = Shared Values and Norms

SOURCE: Diane de Anda, "Bicultural Socialization: Factors Affecting the Minority Experience," *Social Work, 39*(1), 1984, pp. 101–107.

norms for prescribed behaviors. This explains to some extent why the melting pot theory was applicable for many of the European immigrants but not for other minority groups such as African Americans, Hispanics and Asians. (See Figure 8.2.) The European immigrants, in contrast to the other minorities, had a much larger area of shared values and norms and thus were able to identify or had familiarity with a far greater number of the cultural expectations of the mainstream society.

Cultural Translators, Mediators, and Models

The availability of certain types of socializing agents is another factor that can determine the extent of the individual's biculturation. Three main types of agents are posited who serve to facilitate the socialization of the minority individual to the norms of the majority culture: translators, mediators, and models.

Translators are probably the most effective agents in promoting dual socialization. A translator is an individual from a minority individual's own ethnic or cultural group who has undergone the dual socialization experience with considerable success. The translator is able to share his or her own experiences, provide information that facilitates understanding of the values and perceptions of the majority culture, and convey ways to meet the

Figure 8.2. "Melting Pot" Theory (European Immigration) Versus Biculturalism (Other Immigration)

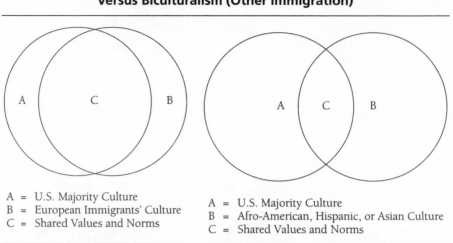

A = U.S. Majority Culture
B = European Immigrants' Culture
C = Shared Values and Norms

A = U.S. Majority Culture
B = Afro-American, Hispanic, or Asian Culture
C = Shared Values and Norms

SOURCE: Diane de Anda, "Bicultural Socialization: Factors Affecting the Minority Experience," *Social Work, 39*(1), 1984, pp. 101–107.

behavioral demands made on minority members of the society without compromising ethnic values and norms.

Mediators are individuals in the mainstream culture who serve as providers of information and guides for ethnic minority persons. They may be persons who serve formal socializing functions, such as teachers, counselors, and [job orientation trainers], or may be informal agents of socialization, such as peers and mentors. Mediators, unlike translators, cannot offer extensive information about the points of convergence and divergence between the two cultures or methods for dealing with the resulting value conflicts. However, mediators offer valuable instructive information about areas that the minority individual might not have ready access to on her or his own, might misinterpret, or might have to learn about by painful trial and error.

Models are individuals in the minority person's environment whose behavior serves as a pattern to emulate in order to develop a behavioral repertoire consistent with the norms of the majority or minority culture. For the individual to learn the ways of the minority culture, obviously, the models must be of the same ethnic group. For learning the normative behavior of the mainstream culture, however, the models can be of either group. Research indicates that the modeling process can be enhanced by perceived similarities between the model and the observer or by recognition of the model as a controller of resources (Bandura, 1969; Bandura, Ross, & Ross, 1963).

Learning through modeling, however, is not devoid of potential cultural conflict. Problems can occur when there is conflict between the behavioral norms presented by different models, particularly models from two different cultural groups. The behavior of the mainstream model may clearly offer more tangible rewards within the mainstream culture, whereas the minority model may evoke affective responses associated with the person's primary socialization experiences. For example, the Japanese American adolescent may note that the assertiveness of the mainstream model is instrumental in obtaining a desired object. However, the Japanese American model's expression of *enryo* (hesitancy and reserve) evokes a positive emotional response based on the positive experiences with this type of interaction in the Japanese community. If this response is seen as less instrumental and devalued by the mainstream culture at the same time that it is emotionally appealing, the bicultural process can be disrupted as the individual struggles to find a means of resolving the conflict.

Corrective Feedback

Although an individual may become acquainted with the norms of a particular culture by observing the behavior of cultural models, the shaping of his or her behavioral repertoire requires corrective feedback as to the accuracy of the modeled response. The greater the availability of corrective feedback, the better the chance that the individual's behavior will more accurately conform to cultural norms. Without corrective feedback, the individual might engage in behavior which he or she feels is appropriate, but which in actuality is viewed as unacceptable or incongruous by members of the cultural group with which he or she is attempting to interact. Corrective feedback is particularly important to clarify which behaviors are appropriate in particular contexts. For example, corrective feedback may be necessary to indicate to the minority individual that a formal type of communication is expected with coworkers while on the job, whereas a very different form of communication is appropriate outside of the job situation.

Biculturation of the minority individual will be facilitated by interaction with socializing agents who (1) provide corrective feedback that is specific, (2) offer corrective feedback regarding both errors the individual has committed and more appropriate behavior, (3) tie the specific information to a general rule for use in future situations, and (4) indicate positive aspects of the individual's performance and use this as a source of motivation for future performance.

For example, over the past few years a notable percentage of the Hispanics I have taught at the master's level have indicated that they felt that part of their success in the mainstream culture (as measured by their educational level) was due to their parochial school education. For these students, parochial education offered a clear-cut socialization experience with specific rules and significant amounts of corrective feedback regarding both normative and non-normative behavior. In fact, the principal aim of their primary-level parochial education was the shaping of values, beliefs, and behavior. Thus, consistent and clearly specified criteria for judging appropriate and inappropriate behavior and beliefs were repeatedly presented.

Problem-Solving Skills

The mesh between the dominant cognitive style fostered within each culture and that of the mainstream culture may also affect the degree of bicultural socialization possible for the minority person. Within the mainstream culture, an analytical cognitive style appears to be the most valued approach to understanding one's environment. Consequently, individuals from minority cultures that foster this style are most likely to be successful in engagements with the majority culture. In addition, there is a considerable divergence *within* cultures regarding cognitive styles. Thus, many minority individuals may also exhibit a cognitive style that is predominantly analytical, regardless of the dominant cognitive style for their particular culture, due to idiosyncratic elements of their socializing environment.

In any case, individuals whose analytical skills are well practiced have the best chance of successfully interpreting the demands of the majority culture, of discriminating between the most and least acceptable behaviors in a variety of contexts, and, ultimately, of predicting the requirements of and appropriate responses to the mainstream cultural environment. Moreover, this style of organizing experience may also help to alleviate some of the problems engendered by conflict between the two cultures because it permits the individual to compartmentalize behavior and affect, allowing him or her to selectively focus, interpret, and respond to the demands of the specific situation.

Facility with the analytical mode may also enhance the process of dual socialization because the concepts and rules about the environment are less bound to culturally specific contexts. An approach that is highly bound to a specific context probably offers the most useful preparation for successfully interacting with the object environment and particularly the interpersonal environment of one's own culture, and the least useful preparation for dealing with cross-cultural situations. In other words, the degree to which concepts and rules are contextually embedded may affect the facility of the minority individual in understanding and successfully responding to the socialization demands of the majority culture.

Degree of Bilingualism

The extent of an individual's proficiency in the language of a particular culture can either enhance or impede the socialization process. That is, an individual conversant in the language is more likely to be exposed to a greater number of models and mediators and to a wider range of learning situations. She or he will be better able to understand and even to request corrective feedback.

Obviously, the bilingual person has the greatest opportunity to become a bicultural individual. However, the greatest percentage of ethnic minority persons are probably not coordinate bilinguals—that is, they do not display equal facility in both languages. Instead, most minority individuals can be placed along a continuum from monolingual through various degrees of subordinate bilingualism. The language of the subordinate bilingual is characterized by interference and dominance. *Interference* refers to the entrance of elements from one language into the other, such as phonetic elements that result in a "foreign accent," and to grammatical mistakes that result from an interchange of grammatical structures, such as use of the double negative from Spanish when speaking English.

The term *dominance* indicates a differential degree of competence in the two languages. Competence in the language determines to some extent the socialization experiences available to the individual, limiting, for example, access to institutions such as those of higher education. Limitations in vocabulary reduce the chances of understanding information imparted by models and mediators, particularly regarding problem-solving processes within the culture. Obviously, monolingual minority individuals have the least opportunity to learn the norms of the majority culture, because the lack of any working knowledge of the language of the mainstream culture automatically shuts off important sources of socialization. Moreover, intrusions of incorrect grammatical structures and of accents (such as those of Spanish or Black English) serve to further accentuate and continually re-inforce the dissimilarities between the two cultures and the belief that minority individuals cannot display the competence necessary to meet mainstream norms.

Appearance

The dissimilarity of physical appearance between individuals in the minority and majority cultures is a self-evident obstacle to the process of bicultural socialization. It appears obvious that pronounced differences, such as those of skin color and distinguishing facial features, are not likely to be easily "melted" into the mainstream. However, it is important to note possible ways in which similarities or dissimilarities in physical appearance affect the socialization experiences of the minority person.

Similarities in physical appearance made it easier for the European immigrant to blend into the American populace and, thereby, be privy to an "insider's" socialization experiences. By contrast, ethnic minorities whose physical appearance is dissimilar are more likely to experience socialization as *pressure* exerted upon "outsiders." Messages offered to outsiders ("them") in contrast to insiders ("us") are likely to be less complete and initiated less frequently, thereby limiting socialization opportunities. If this is the case, the service of translators becomes particularly salient.

Because there is generally substantial variation in physical appearance within ethnic groups, a portion of each minority population will be closer in appearance to individuals of the majority culture. These individuals have more mobility within the mainstream culture, particularly in situations where people are essentially anonymous participants, for example, as customers in a large department store. Not only are these individuals treated similarly to members of the majority culture, but they also can be exposed to disparaging remarks about members of their own ethnic group. Although such an experience produces conflicting emotions for the individual, it also offers information that is not usually available to minority-group members, particularly regarding specific behaviors or beliefs that conflict with mainstream cultural norms.

Implications

Individuals and families from minority cultures make up a significant portion of the clientele served by those in the field of social welfare [and many other fields]. Many of the functions workers perform for their clients, therefore, relate to problems of conflict between majority and minority cultural demands or mutual lack of understanding between people regarding cultural differences. Therefore, one of the social worker's primary functions is to facilitate a process of dual socialization that, ideally, provides the minority client with information and skills needed for interacting within mainstream culture and institutions, along with affirmation of the basic values of the minority culture. To accomplish this task, the worker must first recognize and accept her or his role as an agent of socialization and the responsibilities attendant on this role.

To foster the development of behavioral repertoires for dealing with the demands of both the majority and minority cultures, the worker needs to examine the impact of the six factors previously discussed to determine whether they are serving to facilitate or impede the process of bicultural socialization for the client. The components of this complex task include:

1. Determining areas of interface between the two cultures that can serve as "doorways" between them

2. Noting the major points of conflict between the two cultures and the negative consequences for the client

3. Searching out and providing translators, mediators, and models who can offer guidelines for dealing with such conflicts and offer critical experiential information

4. Arranging, when possible, for increased corrective feedback for the client in the environment

5. Working to expand the client's repertoire of problem- solving skills, particularly those that are the least context-bound, and helping to develop a larger repertoire of context- specific problem-solving skills

6. Educating people of the majority culture about the significant characteristics, values, and needs of minority cultures, as well as serving as an advocate of greater flexibility and adjustment in the mainstream culture's institution

In the complex process of socialization, there are obviously numerous possible points of intervention. The points of intervention that are appropriate for each client are determined by the specific factors that interfere with the bicultural process for that individual. Ideally, the social worker [or manager] will help a bicultural client [employee] to maintain his or her cultural identity and values while functioning successfully within the basic institutions of mainstream society.

Suggestions for the Use of Reading 8.2

We suggest that this reading be used as preparation for doing Activity 8.1. Perhaps the most important point of the article is that it illustrates differences in degrees of cultural overlap and the implications of these differences (for example, assimilation is more difficult for people with less overlap). The discussion on similarity of appearance is also quite insightful and raises sensitive issues that deserve attention. The following discussion questions are suggested:

1. If we take the arguments of de Anda at face value, what implications do they hold for understanding the experience of people from different cultural backgrounds who are being socialized into the same organization?

2. Should we take the arguments at face value? Do you agree or disagree with the main conclusions of the reading? Defend points of disagreement with an argument of your own.

3. What problems does biculturalism pose (especially if it is not coordinate biculturalism, in which people have equal knowledge of and identification with both cultures) for the members of minority groups?

4. We find significant numbers of minority-culture members who are bicultural but relatively few majority-culture members (see research on this subject in Cox, 1993, pp. 53–56). Why is this? Would it help organizations to have more bicultural majority-culture people? If so, what can be done to increase biculturalism among majority-culture members?

Exploring Cultural Overlap and Distance

Readings 8.1 and 8.2 have explained more fully the concepts of culture, cultural overlap, and acculturation that were given in the introduction to the chapter. We have found Activity 8.1 to be fun and also effective as a tool to get an even deeper understanding of these concepts. The activity explores cultural differences in your own work group.

Activity 8.1
EXPLORING CULTURAL OVERLAP AND DISTANCE

Note to participants: This activity is intended to be done in a facilitated group. For purposes of the activity, you will be asked to work in an identity-based group (for example, Anglo-American men, African Americans, East Indian women, or Jewish Caucasians). These assignments are not intended to reinforce stereotypes but rather to provide identity groupings that have been found to produce strong examples of cultural differences within work groups. If you are not comfortable with the exercise, you may request to be assigned as an observer.

Objectives
1. To learn about cultural differences and similarities between individuals and the organizational culture and among different culture-identity groups
2. To learn about the implications of cultural distance in assimilation-based acculturation systems (this objective may or may not apply to any specific organization, but assimilation has been the typical acculturation mode in Western organizations for centuries)

Procedure
Using group identities that are salient in your group (if possible, based on the results of Activity 4.1), organize the full group into four to eight small groups that share some culture-relevant identity as described above. When one person represents a distinct cultural group, such as Korean or Cuban, and prefers to work alone rather than in a more broadly defined group (such as Asian or Latino), this should be done. People who prefer not to be assigned to a group may be assigned as observers, although we have used the exercise many times and have rarely seen this happen.

Each group will be asked to complete the Cultural Profile Form shown in Exhibit 8.2. An "X" (company culture) and "Y" (group culture) should be placed on each line of the profile form based on the company culture profile. An "X" on each scale signifies what the group views as the typical norm or value in the organization (that is, the organizational culture where they work), and the identity group profile ("Y" on each scale) signifies their view of the norms of the group (not their individual norms but their view of what is typical for the group represented). This is sometimes difficult, especially for people who rarely think of themselves in terms of group memberships. When this occurs, the process can be facilitated by having members fill out the sheet individually and then (after some discussion) average their answers. Before beginning the work on the profiles, each person should be provided with a copy of the definitions of the behavioral areas shown in the Cultural Profile Form (see Exhibit 8.3).

On the profile form, the organizational norms ("X") should be indicated in one color and the group norms ("Y") written in a different, "high-contrast" color. If possible, the completed profile forms should be enlarged (or done originally on large sheets of poster board) and, when completed, posted

EXHIBIT 8.2. Cultural Profile Form

Individualism		Collectivism
Emotion should be expressed		Emotion should be repressed
Competitive nature		Cooperative nature
Task orientation		Relationship orientation
Written communication		Oral communication
Aggressive behavior		Nonaggressive behavior
Conflict resolved by confrontation		Conflict resolved by diplomacy
Talking loudly and with much animation		Talking softly and with limited animation
Words and true feelings go together		Words and true feelings are often different

EXHIBIT 8.3. Definitions of Terms for Cultural Profile Form

Individualism versus collectivism. Individualism places emphasis on standing out from the group, personal achievement, and personal consequences in motives for behavior. Collectivism places emphasis on group outcomes and responsibility to a group, with individuals sacrificing for the good of the group.

Emotion. Here we are speaking of the desirability of showing one's feelings in communicating about issues and events as opposed to a more dispassionate expression of one's position. The expression of love as well as anger or negative emotion in the workplace is also included.

Competitive versus cooperative nature. Here we are referring to a competitive nature within one's own company or work group. Competition against other organizations is not included. People with a cooperative orientation tend to think in terms of working with others for mutual benefit. Competitive people tend to define situations as win-lose propositions, while the cooperative orientation is to go out of one's way to find a win-win solution.

Task versus relationship orientation. In seeking to get work done, the task-oriented person focuses initially on the task at hand; relationship building is pursued to the extent that it seems necessary or when natural friendships develop. To the relationship-oriented person, it is necessary to work on building relationships first in order to lay the groundwork for approaching the task. Further, relationships themselves (in their own right and independent of their use in performing the task) are more important to some people than to others. Both task- and relationship-oriented people can be equally concerned about job performance.

Written versus oral communication. Some people prefer to give and receive communication orally rather than in writing. In addition, some are more effective with one method than with the other. Which form of communication comes more naturally or receives greater emphasis? At the organizational level, some companies make greater use of written communication. For example, organizational change efforts may be communicated by memos instead of staff meetings. Similarly, written reports may be more utilized than oral presentations.

Aggressive versus nonaggressive behavior. This refers to work style. Some people are more forceful, active, and driven to have their say than others. One manifestation of this is that aggressive people are usually more comfortable engaging in self-promotional behaviors, whereas nonaggressive personalities are reluctant to call attention to their own achievements and abilities. At the organizational level, there are differences in the extent to which self-promotional behaviors and forceful communication styles are rewarded and expected.

EXHIBIT 8.3. Definitions of Terms for Cultural Profile Form, cont'd.

Conflict resolution. Direct confrontation does not necessarily mean fighting, but it does suggest a blunt exchange of views between the conflicting parties. Some people prefer to get the point across by more indirect communication or even by talking to someone else who may relay the word. At the organizational level, there may be norms about how conflict is best resolved. Acceptable levels of confrontation vary among organizations.

Congruity of words and feelings. This is not simply a matter of truth versus lying. The issue is more one of taking communication at face value compared to having to "read between the lines." Perhaps it is fair to say that some people (and organizations) put a greater value on the thoroughness of truth and openness in communication than others.

---

around the room. Then a representative of each identity group should talk the members of the larger group through their sheet, highlighting insights from their group discussion as they go.

When all of the groups or individuals representing a specific culture have reported, the facilitator will lead the full group in a discussion of what was learned and the implications of the learnings.

Suggestions for the Use of Activity 8.1

In addition to the cultural content that will be revealed by these reports, differences between profiles and differences between the group-level profiles and the profile of the organization will usually be evident. All of these patterns should be discussed. Usually there will be a fair amount of consensus about the organizational culture but wide differences in the norms for the identity groups. This happens because the behaviors chosen for the profile have been shown in theory and research to differ based on racioethnic, nationality, and gender background.

The differences between the group norms and the organizational norms and the differences among the groups represent cultural distance. Discuss the implications of large differences in norms between the organization and, for example, members of a Latino culture group in the organization. Discuss the fact that, although assimilation places a burden of conformity on all members, the burden may be greater for people from cultural traditions that are different from those of the founders and historical leaders of the organization.

The activity will also reveal the fact that there are significant differences within groups. This is also a learning and should be discussed as such. Ultimately, we should see that when we talk about intercultural differences, we are acknowledging differences in the distribution of characteristics and not differences between individual data points within those distributions.

Ignorance of cultural differences can lead to miscommunication, conflict, reduced cooperation, and other dysfunctional outcomes in groups. By contrast, awareness of cultural differences is the first step toward improving our capacity to function as a diverse team. What additional steps should be taken? The following additional discussion questions may be helpful:

1. Between which groups do the largest cultural gaps occur?
2. Which culture seems to come closest to the organizational culture?
3. Was this a difficult activity to do? Why or why not?
4. What implications do the differences have for work behavior and relationships?
5. To what extent were participants aware of these cultural differences? Why isn't there more knowledge in this area?

TAKING ACTION

Because organizational culture is the sociological background against which all work behavior is enacted, many organizations find that their cultures must change in order to better support the strategic goal of leveraging workforce diversity. Although changing culture is a long and difficult process, a useful starting point is to create a descriptive profile of the current organizational culture. Then, if we can create a vision of the desired culture, the difference between the two will form a basis for planning.

Like other core competencies of organizations (such as Total Quality Management and effective teamwork), managing diversity requires specific ingredients in the organizational culture in order to succeed. A question that requires attention, therefore, is: Does our organizational culture support the goal of leveraging workforce diversity? We have found Activity 8.2 to be useful in beginning to answering this question.

Activity 8.2
ASSESSING THE ALIGNMENT OF
ORGANIZATIONAL CULTURE

Objective
1. To assess the extent to which the culture of the organization is aligned with the goal of diversity competency

Procedure
This activity can be done in as little as forty-five minutes, or it can (with embellishments) provide the foundation for several days of in-depth work. The following instructions are for use with facilitated groups.

Short Form
Ask participants to create a list of the words or phrases that first come to mind if they are asked to describe the culture of the organization as they experience it. If you have concerns about your ability to get candid responses, the activity can be done through an anonymous written process and the results posted on a board. If the activity is done with students or others who are currently unemployed, they can be asked to think of the last place they worked on a full-time basis.

When new items for the list begin to dry up, focus the attention of the group on the extent of their agreement about the various descriptions. The process can be stopped once a list of twelve to twenty-five descriptive words or phrases has been created about which there is some degree of consensus. (*Note:* If the participants do not work for the same organization, the consensus process should be omitted.)

Next, ask participants to examine each item and give an opinion as to whether it would tend to hinder (–), help (+), or be neutral ("0") in terms of developing competency to manage diversity for competitive advantage. If the group is divided on an item, get a show of hands as a voting mechanism. When this process is completed, add up the number of pluses, minuses, and zeros to get a quick idea of where the present culture stands. Our experience is that very few organizations will have more pluses than minuses.

Long Form

In order to further develop thinking around the output of the first part of the activity, small groups may be assigned to develop a plan of action that will change the culture by addressing the minuses that were identified. Each team can then report to the full group. The facilitator may also want to lead the group in a discussion of barriers to the proposed changes and ways they might be overcome. In addition, teams can work on ways to further leverage the pluses for greater impact. If you are working alone, it is still possible to follow the instructions above, deleting those items that require a group (for example, the reference to forming consensus).

Regardless of which form of the activity is used, it should conclude with a summary of major drivers of cultural change. We believe the three most important drivers are the following:

1. *People.* Cultural change happens when people with core values, goal priorities, and preferred styles of behavior that are different from those of the past come into positions of leadership. The CEO and other high-level managers are most important here, but all members of organizations contribute to the formation and preservation of culture to some degree. Thus one way to promote cultural change is by managing entry and exit processes for organization members.

2. *Education.* Education (if it is properly designed and implemented) has the potential to change the beliefs, values, and behaviors of people. We purposely use the word *education* and not *training* in order to communicate that education can be implemented in an organization in many ways.

3. *Reward systems.* Reward systems, especially compensation and the opportunity to do progressively more challenging work, influence what people set as work priorities and the kinds of behaviors they display. Also included here is the idea of established accountability for participation in making the change happen. Because rewards typically change behaviors but not necessarily attitudes and beliefs, this lever for change should never be used without the previous two.

Suggestions for the Use of Activity 8.2

This activity serves a number of purposes. First, it starts people thinking about the relevance of culture to the change process and makes more specific the content of culture that is relevant to managing diversity. Second, it creates the beginnings of an "as is" (the analysis of the present culture of a specific firm). Third, it usually makes the point that significant change in the present culture is needed in order to properly support the goal of leveraging diversity.

Action Planning: Diversity of Religion

Case 8.1 is an example of how diversity of religion in the workplace can create challenges for managers. The issues in this case pertain to the conflict resulting from an apparent incompatibility between the religious practices of an employee and the policies of the organization. It is included in Part Three of the book because of the interplay between the individual and the organizational context.

Case 8.1 was written as a class assignment by a student in an MBA class taught by one of the authors. The case is based on the actual experiences of this student; however, names have been changed to protect the identity of the student and the organization involved. The case is used here with the permission of the student author.

Case 8.1
DIVERSITY OF RELIGION IN THE WORKPLACE

I am a manufacturing engineering supervisor at an automotive parts plant. "Gary" works for me as a process engineer and is responsible for the engineering of the manufacturing processes for a new product. This new product will replace an existing product in the plant. The processes and machinery required to manufacture these products are similar and in some cases are the same. Process trials for the new product cannot be performed while the existing product is being manufactured because the machinery is shared. As a result, the trials for the new product are often performed on weekends. Gary's role during these trials is to perform ongoing analysis of the trial results and determine adjustments that should be made to process variables such as time and temperature and to provide direction for alteration of the tools and machinery used during the trials.

Planning for the new processes was performed over a period of months prior to the commencement of the process trials. Gary performed the necessary planning; however, because he is a trainee, he is inexperienced and required more than the usual amount of time for planning. His inexperience, combined with a proclivity for details and an engineering education that is outside of the mainstream, caused him to work many hours of overtime during the week and on weekends in order to complete the planning on time.

Knowing that Gary is Jewish (as he stated during casual conversation), I offered him the option of doing the work whenever he wanted to on the weekends; apparently in response to my flexibility, he said that he preferred to do the work on Sunday so that he could observe *shabbat* but would charge the time to Saturday because, in his words, "My Sundays are everyone else's Saturdays, and my Saturdays are everyone else's Sundays." By charging this Sunday overtime as "Saturday time," he would be paid 1.5 times his normal pay rather than twice his normal pay for Sunday overtime. I told him that, as long as he didn't mind, that seemed like a fair arrangement. Gary worked Saturdays as he saw it to be necessary when working only on Sunday meant that his assignments would not be completed on time. On those occasions he charged his time as it was worked without complaint.

This arrangement continued for several months until three events occurred nearly simultaneously.

The first event was the arrival of "Phil," our new department manager. Phil had a well-deserved reputation for getting into details normally reserved for the supervisor or engineer. The second event was Gary's attendance at a Jewish wedding, where one of his family members related a story about a high-ranking executive in his family whose desire not to work Saturdays, even though his job would occasionally require it, was facilitated by his employer (the company where Gary, Phil, and I work). These events happened within days of the beginning of the process trials, the last of the three events.

During this period I was out of the plant at supervisor training, and while I was in class I was paged by Phil. I left class and called him and was told that Gary had told Phil that he would not work the upcoming Saturday because of his religious convictions. Phil said that he had never heard of such a thing and asked what I had done in the past. I told him about the arrangement between Gary and me, and he stated that apparently something had changed because Gary was adamant about not working on the upcoming Saturday. He asked me to meet with him on the following day, after my training ended, so that we could develop a plan for managing the situation "in the long run" and staffing for the upcoming weekend. I suggested that he invite a manager from employee relations, because I had been told repeatedly during supervisor training that, if a situation arose that I did not know how to handle, I should ask for assistance from employee relations.

We met the next day as planned. At the meeting, Phil reiterated that he had never been in this situation before and asked "Suzy," the employee relations supervisor, to tell us the official company policy. Suzy stated that she was not aware of an official policy and that she would have to contact headquarters and ask if one existed. She also said that Gary had stated on his application that he was available to work any shift on any day and, if he refused to work, we could "fire him if we wanted to for lying on the application." Phil and I said that this wasn't the goal; we just wanted to know the company's policy regarding these situations so that we could manage them appropriately. When I told Suzy about the previous arrangement between Gary and me, she stated that we were wrong to do this and should pay for the day and time when hours were worked. When Phil asked me how I wanted to support the upcoming weekend trial, I told him that I would work on

Saturday to avoid a conflict with Gary. Phil then asked Suzy again to get the official company policy.

The following day, Suzy, Phil, and I met again. Suzy stated that she had found that the company did not have an official policy. I mentioned the story about the Jewish executive that Gary had mentioned, and Suzy stated that the company did not have to accommodate Gary just because a special accommodation had been made for someone else.

To this day, we have not developed a plan for handling Gary's request not to work on Saturdays and have been fortunate that we have not had a situation where Saturday work was required. Gary has worked on Sundays and has been paid the Sunday overtime rate.

Suggestions for the Use of Case 8.1

This can be done by individuals working alone or in groups with a learning facilitator. Address the following three tasks and questions:

1. Develop a plan to present to this manager for handling Gary's request to avoid Saturday work.

2. Should there be a company policy on this? If so, prepare a draft of what the policy should say.

3. Did the manager handle the immediate problem (the current weekend) correctly? If not, what should she or he have done?

9

Formal and Informal Structure of Organizations

You will recall that the interactional model of cultural diversity (IMCD) given in Chapter Three depicted the impact of diversity on organizational outcomes as a result of the joint effects (interaction) of individual characteristics and factors in the organizational environment. The model identified culture and acculturation, structural "integration," informal "integration," and human resource systems as key organizational factors. Culture and acculturation were the points of focus in Chapter Eight. We now turn our attention to structural and informal integration (the remaining factor, human resource systems, will be addressed in Chapter Ten).

The formal structure of organizations is a defining characteristic of diversity competency in several ways. First, the profile of members along dimensions of diversity (gender, physiological ability or disability, work specialization, racioethnicity, age, and so on) is, in itself, an important aspect of the formal structure of organizations. This dimension of structure is often referred to in the management literature as organizational demography. A second, related, aspect is the distribution of these various identities among the positions of significant power in the organization. We will address these issues of organizational demography and power distribution by means of a reading and a case on affirmative action and an activity on differences of organization levels.

Organizations also have an informal structure, and the activity that takes place in these informal networks has important consequences for organizational behavior and outcomes. One such activity is mentoring. This subject has been chosen for attention in this chapter because there is extensive evidence that it is influenced by the dynamics of diversity and has powerful effects on worker career outcomes (for a review of some of the relevant literature supporting these points, see Kram & Hall, 1996).

RAISING AWARENESS

In this chapter we will deal extensively with affirmative action as a common tool for changing the structure of organizations. We have chosen this point of focus not only because of the central place that affirmative action has historically occupied in organizational planning and decision making related to diversity, but also because its continued use is probably the single most contentious issue with relevance to managing diversity today. The goals and operationalization of affirmative action also deal very directly with both organizational demography and power distribution, the two points of focus named earlier.

In this section, Reading 9.1 is given to clarify the definition of affirmative action. Later in the chapter, Case 9.1 will provide a vehicle for practice in decision making in this difficult area of management.

● ● ●

Reading 9.1
WHAT IS AFFIRMATIVE ACTION?
FRANCES A. HOLLOWAY

The term *affirmative action* carries many meanings in today's society. Often the term elicits strong feelings, both positive and negative. Frequently these feelings derive from a misunderstanding of what affirmative action is all about.

Executive Order 11246

Most older people became acquainted with the term *affirmative action* in the late 1960s and early 1970s when federal contractors were first required to devise and carry out affirmative action programs. Executive Order 11246, signed by President Lyndon Johnson on September 24, 1965, required that federal contractors "take affirmative action to ensure that applicants are employed, and that employees are treated during employment, without regard to their race, color, religion, sex, or national origin." The order goes on to say:

> Such action shall include, but not be limited to, the following: employment, upgrading, demotion, or transfer; recruitment or recruitment advertising; layoff or termination; rates of pay or other forms of compensation; and selection for training, including apprenticeship.

Enforcement of Executive Order 11246 and of the subsequent executive orders and federal laws pertaining to affirmative action is the responsibility of the U.S. Department of Labor's Office of Federal Contract Compliance Programs (OFCCP). Equal opportunity specialists in the OFCCP and affirmative action officers in organizations that have contracts with the federal government rely on a thick manual (U.S. Department of Labor, 1979) as well as on the Code of Federal Regulations (Title 41 CFR Chapter 60) to determine whether or not a federal contractor is in compliance with the law.

Source: Excerpted from Frances A. Holloway, "What Is Affirmative Action?" in F. Blanchard and F. J. Crosby (Eds.), *Affirmative Action in Perspective* (New York: Springer-Verlag, 1989), pp. 9–19. Used by permission.

Executive Order 11246 specifies that affirmative action is one of the conditions of agreeing to do work for the government, but it does not define affirmative action. The OFCCP's manual does. According to the manual, affirmative action consists of:

> those results oriented actions which a contractor by virtue of its contracts must take to ensure equal employment opportunity. Where appropriate, it includes goals to correct underutilization, correction of problem areas, etc. It may also include relief such as back pay, retroactive seniority, make-up goals and timetables, etc.

Essentially the same definition occurs in Title 41 of Chapter 60 of the Federal Regulations, where the regulations outline what constitutes an affirmative action *program*. The language that appears in the regulation states that:

> An affirmative action program is a set of specific and results-oriented procedures to which a contractor commits itself to apply every good faith effort. The objective of those procedures plus such efforts is equal employment opportunity.

Since the onset of affirmative action programs, two groups have been identified as "target groups"—women and members of minority groups. The definitions of targeted minority groups used by the federal government are:

American Indian or Alaskan Native—Persons having origins in any of the original people of North America, and who maintain cultural identification through tribal affiliation or community recognition.

Asian or Pacific Islander—Persons having origins in any of the original peoples of the Far East, Southeast Asia, the Indian Subcontinent, or the Pacific Islands. This area includes, for example, China, Japan, Korea, the Philippine Islands, and Samoa.

Black, not of Hispanic Origin—Persons having origins in any of the Black racial groups of Africa.

Hispanic—Persons of Mexican, Puerto Rican, Cuban, Central or South American, or other Spanish culture or origin, regardless of race.

What exactly are the requirements of affirmative action? First, the contractor is subject to certain broad ground rules. A contractor must maintain a workplace that is not segregated by race or sex. Subcontractors and vendors with whom the contractor does business must also comply with the nondiscrimination and affirmative action requirements to which the contractor is obligated. The contractor's collective bargaining agreements may not discriminate on the basis of race or sex. Employment selection criteria may not discriminate on the basis of race or sex.

By accepting a federal contract the employer also agrees to permit the federal government to conduct periodic compliance reviews of its employment policies, practices, and affirmative action program.

The OFCCP requires contractors to develop, maintain, and update annually a written affirmative action plan (AAP) targeting the employment of women and members of minority groups. The AAP must contain certain data and data analyses. These data include a workforce analysis, a listing by job title (ranked from lowest-paid to highest-paid) and by department, showing the number of men, women, Blacks, Asians, Hispanics, and Native Americans for each job title.

Finally, the contractor must monitor employment activity—for example, referrals, placements, transfers, promotions, and terminations—for each job group. The contractor must report and analyze these data in its annual affirmative action program report. During a compliance review OFCCP also will analyze the data.

Along with data requirements, the AAP must contain specific policy and procedural commitments. The contractor must formulate a written policy on nondiscrimination and affirmative action and disseminate it widely within the company and the neighboring community. An executive in the organization must be identified as the EEO Coordinator and his or her role made known to employees and potential applicants. The contractor must develop monitoring and reporting systems to measure the progress or lack of progress of its affirmative action program in meeting its goals and timetables.

Other required components of an affirmative action program include the identification of problem areas, the development of action-oriented programs, and the active support of local and national groups which focus on aiding the employment of women or minority-group members.

Handicapped and Veterans
Legislation enacted in the 1970s broadened the scope of affirmative action originally established by President Johnson's executive order. The Rehabili-

tation Act of 1973 and the Vietnam Era Veterans Readjustment Assistance Act of 1974 require federal contractors to develop, maintain, and update written AAPs for the employment of handicapped persons and for disabled veterans and veterans of the Vietnam era. The regulations pertaining to Section 503 of the Rehabilitation Act of 1973 define a handicapped individual as:

> any person who (1) has a physical or mental impairment which sub-
> stantially limits one or more of such person's major life activities, (2)
> has a record of such impairment, or (3) is regarded as having such
> an impairment. A handicapped individual is "substantially limited" if
> he or she is likely to experience difficulty in securing, retaining, or
> advancing in employment because of a handicap.

Although some of the affirmative action requirements of the Rehabilitation Act and the Veterans Readjustment Act diverge from the requirements of the executive order, some are similar. A major difference is that the contractor need not provide a workforce analysis, estimate the availability of persons with disabilities and Vietnam-era veterans, determine if it under-utilizes them in its workforce, or set goals and timetables for hiring handicapped persons and veterans. Similarities exist, for example, in that the contractor must work only with vendors and subcontractors who do not discriminate on the basis of these factors.

Affirmative Action and True Equality

Given the lack of definition in the original Executive Order 11246, it may not be surprising that many people have distorted and misinterpreted the meaning of affirmative action. Some people equate the terms *affirmative action* and *equal opportunity.* Others think that an employer cannot simultaneously practice affirmative action and equal opportunity because affirmative action means discriminating against or not providing equal opportunity to White males.

It is true that equal opportunity means not discriminating against a particular group because of that group's race, sex, religion, ethnicity, disability, or Vietnam-era veteran status. Employers must evaluate applicants solely by those performance criteria which directly describe the requirements of a particular position of employment or academic program for which they are applying. This sounds easy. The problem arises when persons responsible for hiring or admissions decisions carry with them their own experiences and prejudices. Criteria are often subjective, and people's presumptions affect their judgments. A supervisor may, for example, believe that any blind person is unable to perform secretarial tasks such as typing and filing. A college admissions director may review the high school grades of a dyslexic student in the same way he or she reviews those of a student who is not dyslexic. A supervisor may review the résumé of a woman who is returning to the workforce after ten years of staying at home with her young children in the same way he or she reviews that of a man who has had continuous employment. A college admissions officer may review the application of a disadvantaged Black student who has taken care of younger siblings and worked part-time to contribute to the family's income in the same way he or she reviews the application of a more affluent applicant.

A common misunderstanding about the meaning of affirmative action is that a person selected as a result of affirmative action is an inferior employee [or student]. People with this view operate on the assumption that minority-group members in their company are less qualified than Whites, or that minority students are less qualified than White students. It is not only White men who have this misconception about affirmative action; many women and members of minority groups want it known that they were selected for their conventional qualifications rather than through affirmative action procedures. The presumption that women are continuously inferior to men is also revealed when the rejected male applicant tells his friends that he was not selected for a position because "they had to hire a woman."

Conclusion

Most companies now view affirmative action as one of many tools for effective management. In academe the rejection of the "old-boy network" for filling faculty positions and the use of broader advertising networks have probably increased the total quality of the pool of candidates in most disciplines. Also, the statistical requirements of the federal regulations have produced improved personnel data for faculty and staff positions, a key element in the planning function of a college or university. Affirmative action requirements have also forced employers to attend more carefully to the validity of performance criteria in job descriptions and in job interviews.

Affirmative action is just that: action; it is an employer doing something to remedy the effects of past discrimination against women, minority-group members, persons with disabilities, the veteran. This action is more than hiring a few more Blacks or women to meet a goal. Affirmative action is a mandate to employers to first discover the barriers to the employment of those underrepresented in the workforce and then to remove these barriers. It is a tool for employers to use in evaluating all their programs and policies and to ensure that their impact on targeted groups is known and understood. Finally, it is a temporary program to guide employment practices and policies only so long as targeted groups are underrepresented in the workforce.

Suggestions for the Use of Reading 9.1

The following are recommended as points of focus for discussion of the reading. First, the main purpose of this reading is to provide a factual statement of the original definition and intent of affirmative action. We find that contemporary discussions of affirmative action do not reflect a good understanding of the legal definition of the term. A knowledge of the original executive order and subsequent legislation is necessary for informed dialogue about the use of affirmative action.

The reading also raises several of the strongest objections to affirmative action, namely, that it actually encourages the behavior (discrimination) that it is designed to prevent and that it creates a stigma for members of the underutilized groups, who must wonder about the true reasons for their selection.

We believe that the apparent contradiction between the language of the executive order and the behavior of priority treatment (based on a group-identity factor) should be discussed and debated. We also believe that it is important to focus attention on the distinctions between affirmative action and quotas, between affirmative action and hiring of unqualified applicants, and between affirmative action (a tool to achieve equality) and equal opportunity (the goal itself). Differences in the use of affirmative action at different stages of the selection process should also be discussed. For example, there is a marked difference between action to ensure that a candidate pool is demographically diverse and action to select an individual over another person based on membership in a demographic group. This reading and the discussion of it should be referred to again when working on Case 9.1.

CREATING UNDERSTANDING

This section will present two vehicles toward achieving a deeper understanding of the structural aspects of organizations that affect diversity competency. First, in Activity 9.1, the issue of power distribution is examined from a somewhat different perspective than that of the affirmative action debate. The fact that organizations are authority hierarchies creates "we-they" dynamics around identity groups based on organizational level.

Next, we shift to the informal organization with Reading 9.2 on mentoring. The reading provides information about how cultural groups may be relevant to the effective design of organizationally supported mentoring programs. This information will better position you to proceed to the material in the "Taking Action" section of the chapter.

● ● ●

Activity 9.1
ORGANIZATIONAL LEVEL AS A DIMENSION
OF WORKFORCE DIVERSITY

Objectives
1. To identify barriers to cross-level teamwork
2. To identify the sources or underlying causes of barriers to cross-level cooperation and teamwork

Procedure
Working alone, in small groups or in the full group:

1. Make a list of at least six, and no more than a dozen or so, individual behaviors, individual attitudes, or organizational policies and practices that tend to create barriers between people of different organizational levels.
2. Using the list generated in step 1, determine the three most serious barriers to cross-level teamwork in *your* organization or work unit.
3. Answer the following questions:
    a. What is the origin of these behaviors, attitudes, policies, or practices?
    b. Why and how have they been sustained over time?

Suggestions for the Use of Activity 9.1
The more work on diversity we do in companies, the more convinced we are that improving work relationships among people of different levels in organizations is one of the most pressing challenges in managing diversity that we face. The reason that this work relates to managing diversity and not simply to managing subordinates or to interpersonal relations is that significant elements of the problem are based on group identity rather than taking place at the individual level. For example, a common problem in research laboratories is conflict between research technicians and the professionals to whom they report on projects. Technicians often complain that the scientists treat them like "second-class citizens" and that their ability and

contributions are undervalued and underutilized because technicians are viewed as "a pair of hands." The scientists who supervise them often express concern that technicians are not as productive as they could be and that they don't have an accurate understanding of their assigned role in performing research.

As a second example, when we interview secretarial and clerical staff in organizations, we frequently hear that managers do not treat them with respect. In one organization, where one of us was recently conducting a focus group of such workers, they summed up their comments about the work climate by saying, "We don't respect management and they don't respect us." To these examples we can add the well-known acrimony between management and the unionized blue-collar labor force in many countries of the world, and the list goes on. Despite the poor quality of interlevel relationships in many companies, they are now doing more and more work in teams composed of three or more levels in the chain of command. In light of these circumstances, it is imperative that organizations develop a climate that fosters better cross-level relationships.

We note with interest that managers at or near the top of organizations are often reluctant to engage in introspection on the problems in cross-level relationships, expressing surprise that people below them apparently treat subordinates in a condescending manner and "wondering aloud" where this style of supervision came from. Activity 9.1 is designed to force this kind of reflection. It can be done with groups from different organizations, because most people are familiar with this problem on some level. It will work best in mixed-level groups within the same organization if there is enough candor for the lower-level people to challenge statements of denial by higher-level participants. There is a risk in very status-conscious organizations that lower-level members of the organization will go into extreme withdrawal behavior during this activity, but in most organizations the support of four or five other people at their level will be enough to bring out a balance of perspectives.

An obvious next step to this activity is to brainstorm action steps to overcome the barriers, but the main focus here is to really *understand* the problem. In facilitated groups, the facilitator may, after the group has worked with the activity for a while, want to use the following topics for a debriefing. They consist of behaviors, attitudes, policies, and practices that tend to create or reinforce barriers to cross-level relations.

1. Lack of social or informal contact between people at different organizational levels

2. Differential benefits or incentive compensation plans for which level is an eligibility criterion

3. Assigned parking spaces

4. Access to different dining facilities based on level

5. Failure by higher-level people to greet or verbally acknowledge people at lower levels

6. Shouting at or using profane language in addressing people at lower levels of authority

7. Using intimidating messages such as "If you can't get the job done, we'll find someone who will"

8. A tendency to give more response to comments or ideas offered by higher-ranking people in mixed-level meetings

9. A tendency among lower-level people to blame higher-level managers for work problems, regardless of the actual reason for them.

● ● ●

Reading 9.2
MENTORING FOR THE HISPANIC
Mapping Emotional Support
JACK DAVIS AND EDUARDO S. RODELA

A remarkable transition is occurring in the U.S. workplace in the 1990s. America's workforce is becoming much more "culturally diverse," which means that by the end of the decade a much higher percentage of minorities will be making up the nation's labor picture (Johnston & Packer, 1987). Playing a leading role in this dramatic shift is the Hispanic. Hispanics represented 6.2 percent of those employed in the United States in 1982 and 7.6 percent in 1990 (Haugen & Meisenheimer, 1991). By the year 2000 they are forecast to comprise 10 percent of the country's employees (Fullerton, 1989). This 10 percent figure equates to 14.3 million Hispanics working in the United States in 2000, an increase of more than 5 million from the end of the 1980s (Fullerton, 1989).

Even though these data offer the Hispanic population hope for employment in the future, some current issues may prevent Hispanics from fully enjoying this expanding job market. These intermingled issues include the Hispanics' (1) high rate of unemployment, (2) lack of job training, and (3) limited job advancement in organizations. The latest Bureau of Labor Statistics information clearly shows for the 1980 decade a much higher Hispanic unemployment rate, compared with that of the Anglo male group (Haugen & Meisenheimer, 1991). The American Society for Training and Development has reported that for every $100 spent on training by U.S. organizations, $90 goes to the Anglo male and less than $3 goes to the Hispanic (Carnevale & Gainer, 1989). Labor statistician P. Cattan, in describing "occupational upgrading" during the 1980s for Hispanics, states Hispanics "are still somewhat more likely than the overall workforce to be employed in lower skilled, lower paid occupations" (Cattan, 1988, p. 13).

It is with this third issue of Hispanics' not moving up within U.S. organizations that this reading is broadly concerned. More specifically, the reading looks at the role that mentoring may play in aiding the advancement opportunities of Hispanics. By way of a definition, a mentor is "someone in a position of power who looks out for you, or gives you advice, or brings your accomplishments to the attention of other people who have power in the company" (Fagenson, 1988, p. 186); "a mentor supports, guides, and counsels" (Kram, 1985a, p. 2); and a mentor is "a higher ranking, influential, senior person providing upward mobility and support to a protégé" (Ragins, 1989, p. 2). Given the underlying or implicit reference to support in the definition of mentoring, the reading closely examines one significant aspect of the mentoring process: providing emotional support, as mentoring is applied to Hispanics.

In the chapter, we raise and then begin to answer a critical mentoring question for the Hispanic: Is the emotional or motivational makeup of the Hispanic such that distinctive attention needs to be given to the emotional support aspect of mentoring for the Hispanic?

One Organization's Planned Use of Mentoring

Cultural diversity is requiring U.S. organizations to pay greater attention to the establishment of programs that truly assist minority employees in their jobs. This major employment trend is causing organizations to look beyond the scope of past EEO and affirmative action requirements (Thomas, 1990). Legal arguments are being transcended because the survival of organizations and the maintenance of our nation's standard of living are at stake. Writers are indicating that it will be quite difficult for an organization to survive in a fiercely competitive world when its culturally diverse workforce is not integrated and not developed to its fullest potential (Loden & Rosener, 1991; Thomas, 1990).

A prominent Western bank corporation is an example of an organization that has recognized the implications of America's coming extensive cultural diversity and has set about taking serious steps to deal with it. (The name of the bank was changed to ensure confidentiality.) In 1988 the bank appointed a large, high-level task force to take a hard look at its past and present philosophies, values, behaviors, and actions as they pertained to the employment and utilization of minorities. After a rigorous self-examination over the cultural diversity issue, the task force issued a report in 1989. Many of its conclusions are eye-opening. According to the report, the organization:

1. "does not accommodate minorities and women at all levels of the organization, especially in line and leadership roles"
2. "[has] achieved compliance with the law, but a multicultural environment does not exist"
3. "[has] little, if any, overt discrimination, but there is a true lack of understanding of the problems, cultures and needs of minorities and women"

The task force's overall recommendations include establishing a broad cultural diversification plan with (1) a communications program that states clearly the organization's diversity mission and goal, (2) a career development system to train women and minorities, and (3) a program that identifies high-potential employees, including women and minorities, and mentors them into senior positions. The bank recognizes in the task-force report several difficulties associated with undertaking a serious career development and mentoring endeavor that is driven by the cultural diversity issue: senior management values must change, managers at all levels must be evaluated and held accountable for the advancement of minorities, and "a clear reward system" is needed to "spur innovative efforts in the management of the minority-female-white interaction." The task force's ending statement addresses the question, How will we know when we're there? The part of the task force's answer striking at the mentoring process was: The organization will know it is there when it "assures appropriate role models, indicates opportunity for upward mobility and eliminates misunderstandings caused by exclusively white-white, male-male, minority-minority vertical communications."

Mentoring, Emotional Support, and Hispanics
After reviewing the [relevant] information, it is not unreasonable to conclude that mentoring is an appropriate method for organizations to use to uplift Hispanics and other minorities in their organizational job hierarchies. Anglo males have had positive experiences with the mentoring process (Clawson & Kram, 1984). Some organizations may, because of the rising pressure of cultural diversity and because of the favorable recommendations of such companies as the bank just mentioned, rush into the institution of mentoring programs. We believe it is important to be aware that questions do exist concerning the mentoring process. These questions range from, what are the key parts to the process [of mentoring] (Kram, 1983; Kram 1985b; Kram & Isabella, 1985; Noe, 1988; Olian, Carroll, Giannantonio, & Feren, 1988;

Shapiro & Farrow, 1988)? to, what distinctive treatment, if any, needs to be given to a minority group such as the Hispanic in mentoring (Domino & Acosta, 1987; Rodela, 1990; Vernon & Roberts, 1985)? Also, it is important for the sake of objective research to bring out that some have published criticisms concerning mentoring. These criticisms center around (1) many organizational cultures' not valuing personal development and these cultures being too difficult to change; (2) forced coupling between a mentor and a protégé that leads to harmful resentment, discontent, and suspicion; and (3) many managers' being psychologically unprepared or unable to be a mentor (Kizilos, 1990; Kram, 1985b).

Bringing forward these questions and criticisms is not meant to downgrade the overall value or worth of mentoring. Good evidence indicates that mentor assistance programs provide these very positive results:

1. Higher productivity and performance ratings for both mentor and protégé
2. More accurate selection and training of new personnel
3. Greater retention of highly qualified people
4. A greater probability of a person's being promoted to a senior rank
5. Higher earnings and job satisfaction for the mentored individual (American Society for Training and Development, 1986)

[Research has shown the value of social support for career outcomes, including mentoring (American Society for Training and Development, 1986; House, 1983; Collins, 1983), and the particular relevance of social and emotional support for advisory activity with Hispanics (Rodela, 1990; Barrera & Ainlay, 1983).] As a consequence, I believe that whether counseling or mentoring is involved, emotional support plays a crucial role in understanding and helping the Hispanic.

The underlying argument established with this line of thinking sets up very probably a long-term research requirement to support the significance of emotional support in mentoring, not only for Hispanics but for all other groups as well. A crux of this research is how to identify and measure emotional support.

Likert and others at the University of Michigan's Institute for Social Research have developed, through an organizational survey, one general form of identifying and measuring support in the work setting (Likert, 1967).

Gottlieb's research offers guidance in pinpointing with more exactness what a person does in being more supportive in a counseling situation (House, 1983). But as House has pointed out, the question of precisely what it is, either in the work or the counseling effort, that the supportive person does and what causes the person to behave in this way still remains unanswered. House views the answer as having the highest importance:

> If we could validly assess the traits giving rise to a supportive personal orientation, we could select supervisors and therapists at least in part on the basis of these traits. We could also try to provide more training and experience in giving and receiving social support, as well as other interpersonal skills, in the socialization and education of children in our society. (House, 1983, p. 96)

Identifying and Measuring Emotional Support in a Corporate Setting—A Start
Procedure
At this stage we would like to introduce a way to conceptualize and measure two critical intrapersonal and interpersonal characteristics that are thought to affect greatly the processes of emotional support in mentoring. The innovative method used to assess these characteristics is the Birkman Method, and the two human personality characteristics that are viewed as highly essential for the effective execution of emotional support in mentoring are (in Birkman terminology) esteem and empathy (Birkman & Associates, 1991).

Since 1951 the Birkman Group, a management consulting firm, has been evolving a comprehensive system of perceptually based instruments. This battery establishes a basis to bring your perceptions of values, motives, and interests into a framework of how you adapt and cope with life with "normal" active and outwardly directed behavior and also reactive behavior or behavior that you desire from the person you are interacting with, which occurs when your needs are not met or while you are experiencing stress. Validation of the method has been extensive although not widely published (Mefferd, 1975).

The Birkman battery results permit the measurement of your needs in eleven behavior areas, including esteem and empathy. The Birkman Method provides you with two ways of viewing your behavior with regard to these eleven areas. The first way, as noted above, refers to how you actively behave toward another individual on the basis of the social and self-perceptions in question. In this case you provide or emit certain behavior to another person while performing your work. The second way of viewing your behavior is concerned with how you behave or act in a reactive manner when your needs are not met or while experiencing stress. In this case you need the other person with whom you are engaged to behave toward you with the particular behavior described by the same behavior dimension. In the case of esteem, you may desire respect and sensitivity or frank, open, and direct behavior. In other words, the Birkman system reveals how you see your needs, drives, or motives while actively behaving toward another person in work situations and also how you desire or expect the other person to behave toward you within this dimension of possible behaviors. This perceptual two-way street is most revealing as emotional support and mentoring are more closely examined in the practical setting. As esteem and empathy are defined or described operationally, this dual-direction characteristic becomes clearer and more meaningful (Birkman & Associates, 1991).

Esteem. Esteem from the Birkman point of view is the amount of sensitivity, respect, and appreciation you (1) provide (active behavior outwardly directed) to another person in a one-to-one relationship, and (2) expect (need or inwardly desired behavior) from that same person or from any other individual when dealing with the person singularly, as opposed to dealing with a group.

Outward Direction (Actively Emitted Behavior). The Birkman scoring uses a percentile range of 1 to 99. Considering the "outward direction" (active behavior provided to others) of the behavioral characteristics associated with esteem (you demonstrate sensitivity, respect, and appreciation to another within an individual relationship), a low score of 1 to 35 would mean that you see yourself actively behaving in a very frank, open, direct, and matter-of-fact way when dealing with another person. Conversely, a high score on esteem would mean your being sensitive to another's feelings and showing respect and appreciation.

Inward Direction (Need or Stress Reactive Behavior). When looking at the "inward direction" (behavior expected or needed from others) of the esteem characteristic (expecting the other person to be sensitive, respectful, and appreciative toward you), a low score means you expect and/or want another person to be open and frank with you; you particularly do not care for "yes-people" who tell you what they think you want to hear or who beat around the bush and are not up-front. Conversely a high score on esteem in the "inward direction" (desired or needed behavior) means you expect or desire sincere respect and appreciation. Criticism needs to be well considered and infrequent. You do not need back-talk but rather would like to have communication that takes your personal worth into full consideration.

Empathy. Empathy, according to Birkman, is the amount of objectivity and/or emotional support you (1) provide someone else and (2) expect from that person.

Outward Direction (Actively Emitted Behavior). Looking at the characteristic of empathy and its outward direction (emitted or provided to another), a low score means you see yourself as detached, competitive, objective, and logical with another person in a one-to-one relationship. Your insight into the feelings of others is filtered by a strong belief in others' practicing self-help. A high score on empathy in the outward-direction aspect of the Birkman (active provider behavior toward another) means you see your behavior as sympathetic, warm, and filled with genuine feelings toward others. You come across as definitely caring for and involved with others.

Inward Direction (Need or Stress Reactive Behavior). The inward direction (behavior needed or desired from another) low score on empathy indicates you need to be treated in a matter-of-fact way. You do not care for excessive emotional reactions or attention. On the other hand, a high empathy inward score (behavior expected or desired from another) indicates you need people to be aware of your personal feelings. You want to express your ideas and feelings and know others are really listening and responding to you in this regard.

Sample

We are currently conducting preliminary research into the area of emotional support, and we offer the following to illustrate these concepts. Table 9.1 presents the actual esteem and empathy scores for thirty-three Hispanic and forty Anglo males from a major Southwestern corporation. The total population of the corporation numbered approximately 10,000. These men came from management and nonmanagement ranks and were selected randomly from a group of 1,000 in the 35–50 age range for a study initially having to do with job stress, in which the Birkman Method was a primary research instrument. (This stress study has not been concluded, and as a result no data have yet been published.)

Results and Discussion

The outward scores of the two characteristics [esteem and empathy] for both groups are all low (23.8–34.4 range), indicating a possible difficulty for both Hispanic and Anglo males (in this age bracket and within this Southwestern corporate environment) to actively provide sensitivity, appreciation, and recognition to someone else.

In a corporate setting like the one just discussed, it would appear that a thorough education and training effort regarding this esteem and empathy phenomenon would be helpful for a Hispanic or Anglo male about to be involved in a mentor-protégé relationship (either as mentor or protégé) (Birkman & Associates, 1988; House, 1983). If an organization is able to determine ahead of time that a potential mentor would likely demonstrate a low level of emotion, sensitivity, or recognition and be matter-of-fact and objective in communicating and dealing with the protégé, tailored training could be developed and provided in order to create a good deal of awareness. In this way training and assignment issues could be better managed. For example, an Anglo mentor with scores as just described would need to be made aware of these qualities and given special training, especially if a Hispanic protégé has high inward (expectation or desired) esteem and empathy scores. Case studies from the counseling literature would suggest that individuals can alter the way they relate to others in interpersonal situations. The male Anglo mentor (low active provider) working with a male Hispanic protégé (high expectation and low provider in both esteem and empathy) certainly would need to be cognizant of the likelihood that the Hispanic male may be plainspoken and not respond to sensitive, caring, and warm words or actions by the mentor. The mentor needs to understand that the Hispanic would not have a hidden motive for this behavior (such as "I do not like this Anglo") but is merely being himself or herself or motivationally treating everyone in the same manner. As the reader can conclude readily, a mentor and protégé having the knowledge of specific esteem and empathy outward (active provider behavior) and inward (need or desired) scores and being thoroughly educated and trained to the meaning and significance of these scores [may] have the potential to create a more productive and effective mentoring relationship. Before looking at some of the actual and definite scores of individuals found in Table 9.1, a few observations must be made concerning the data that are striking. In Table 9.1 are six Hispanic males (out of thirty-three), as opposed to two Anglo males (out of forty), who have all four of their scores under thirty. In addition, ten individuals in both groups may be considered as low in the outward (active provider) scores for esteem and empathy and moderate to high for the inward (expected or desired) scores on these two characteristics. As a consequence, one out of two Hispanic males and one out of four Anglos will have potential mentoring difficulties. These data suggest a need for special consideration regarding emotional support in mentoring.

As an example that illustrates the Birkman application to the emotional support aspect of mentoring, we examined Table 9.1 to begin to "map" realistically the problems and opportunities for mentoring Hispanics in the workplace. Assume your organization has five up-and-coming technically competent Hispanics whom senior managers want mentored. Their esteem and empathy scores are represented by Hispanic individuals 1 through 5 of Table 9.1. Also assume you are to select their mentors from the forty Anglos in Table 9.1. Assume that all forty Anglos are technically competent in their respective fields. Do you really want to set up mentoring relationships for Hispanics 1 and 3? If so, how will you make sure both of them (mentor and protégé) understand fully the contrasting perceptual patterns or forces within them that may possibly prevent the process from working well? For Hispanic 2, a mentor may be needed who sees the individual as being candid, private, and unemotional (low provider) but possibly with a strong need for the mentor to show personal warmth and concern (given the 70 score on empathy, need, or inward direction). Certainly Hispanics 4 and 5 will welcome having a mentor, given their esteem and empathy scores. Whom do you select, however, for these two or the other three? As you go down the list, several good candidates appear who can supply a natural emotional supportive environment: Anglos 3, 12, 18, 20, and 35. Anglo 35's protégé would be well served by being informed that the mentor's normal communication is terse and candid but otherwise will convey the needed emotional support.

What do the Birkman data from these midlife Hispanic and Anglo males mean in terms of the challenge of providing adequate social-emotional support to Hispanics and in terms of future research? In a sense these data were the result of an initial journey to discover the importance of patterns of perceptions corresponding to emotional support in the mentoring process for Hispanics and others. Because of this early sojourn, some rough routes may have been drawn for a map of the steps that need to be taken next. Since the data of Table 9.1 suggest that Anglos and Hispanics may have somewhat different relational needs, especially on esteem, it appears that Hispanics should be more thoroughly studied to see whether support is sufficient given their different emotional and motivational makeup, thus increasing the chance of their being mentored effectively (Griffith & Villavicencio, 1985). Researchers interested in the mentoring process need to be gaining more familiarity with the Birkman Method, testing its value in both training and research contexts. With these kinds of efforts taking place, it would then seem possible for a complete and strong theory of mentoring Hispanics, fully considering the role of emotional support, to be developed. Over time such a theoretical map could guide others to greater success in traveling the mentoring road.

Conclusions

Cultural diversity, of which the Hispanic is a large part, is gaining attention as an American organizational issue. Mentoring is possibly one way to deal effectively with the issue of developing the Hispanic in the organizational setting. Mentoring, however, is not a fully understood and researched process. Emotional support, indicated by social and self-perceptions, is apparently a significant part of mentoring that must be identified more fully and measured in a viable way. The Birkman Method as discussed here is one viable means of aiding in the study of mentoring, especially as it relates to Hispanic employees. The information and data from the Birkman Method presented in this reading, involving a sample of Hispanic and Anglo males from a major corporation, possibly serve as a relevant example of how mentoring Hispanics is a complex but manageable matter. The Birkman esteem and empathy scores provide a path for understanding and researching emotional support. We are encouraged strongly by the possibility of preparing a map with these data for mentoring Hispanics in order to ensure that these valuable human resources are developed and utilized to the fullest in organizations. In order to develop a better map to guide organizations in the use of emotional support in mentoring, more research is definitely needed.

TABLE 9.1. Birkman Esteem and Empathy Scores for a Group of Hispanic and Anglo Males (Aged 35–50) from a Major Southwestern Corporation

	Hispanic					Anglo			
	Esteem		Empathy			Esteem		Empathy	
	Outward	Inward	Outward	Inward		Outward	Inward	Outward	Inward
1.	8	19	3	12	1.	5	95	20	45
2.	8	28	36	70	2.	3	57	12	45
3.	5	5	1	3	3.	76	40	70	45
4.	40	76	85	70	4.	19	28	70	7
5.	40	57	85	85	5.	40	19	3	7
6.	40	28	36	45	6.	57	76	20	85
7.	28	57	7	45	7.	28	57	12	12
8.	19	76	36	92	8.	95	95	7	36
9.	40	3	12	3	9.	57	95	70	12
10.	28	76	85	60	10.	28	57	7	36
11.	95	95	92	92	11.	57	19	70	12
12.	19	76	36	97	12.	76	95	97	99
13.	5	95	1	45	13.	40	57	60	60
14.	3	40	1	12	14.	40	40	1	20
15.	57	28	7	12	15.	19	95	12	45
16.	8	28	1	1	16.	19	95	3	85
17.	13	19	45	45	17.	13	76	60	85
18.	5	57	1	36	18.	76	95	60	60
19.	3	13	7	7	19.	28	13	36	12

	C1	C2	C3	C4	C5	C6	C7	C8
20.	5	13	7	7	76	95	85	45
21.	28	95	20	45	19	76	20	97
22.	5	13	45	20	40	76	12	85
23.	28	40	7	12	1	57	1	20
24.	28	76	70	97	19	19	3	7
25.	76	95	92	99	3	19	36	45
26.	57	76	60	70	28	57	1	20
27.	3	28	1	1	57	95	3	7
28.	28	28	45	20	5	19	1	7
29.	8	95	12	92	19	57	36	45
30.	1	5	36	70	76	95	12	45
31.	40	40	70	45	28	95	45	60
32.	8	76	7	60	8	76	92	45
33.	8	19	12	45	57	40	45	45
34.					8	95	36	20
35.					28	76	70	70
36.					40	76	3	7
37.					57	95	20	45
38.					13	40	1	20
39.					5	95	7	36
40.					13	57	3	7
Av	23.8	47.7	32.2	45.9	34.4	65.4	31.2	41.6

SOURCE: Jack Davis and Eduardo S. Rodela, "Mentoring for the Hispanic: Mapping Emotional Support," in Stephen Knouse, Paul Rosenfeld, and Amy Culbertson (Eds.), *Hispanics in the Workplace* (Newbury Park, CA: Sage, 1992), pp. 137–150.

Suggestions for the Use of Reading 9.2

This reading is intended to provide you with some information about cultural differences that are potentially relevant for the effective design of a mentoring program in organizations with significant Hispanic populations. Do not feel limited by the authors' interpretations of the data. Use the data and definitions to draw your own conclusions. The reading is preparation for Activity 9.2.

Some suggested questions for discussion of the reading follow:

1. Do you agree with the conclusions of the authors based on the data presented? Why or why not?

2. The data in Table 9.1 do show some differences between Hispanics and Anglos. Given the definitions of the terms offered, do you see these differences as relevant to mentoring? If so, how?

3. Aside from the interethnic differences, the reading suggests that many people are simply not suitable to be mentors. Do you agree that some kind of self-assessment should be used to screen mentors? What are the pros and cons of this?

TAKING ACTION

Structural Integration: "Glass Ceiling" Issues

As indicated earlier in the chapter, an important aspect of the formal structure of organizations with implications for diversity competency is the distribution of power among gender, race, and nationality groups across different levels of organizations. In this regard, a frequently observed structural dynamic of organizations is the so-called "glass ceiling" effect, whereby women, racial-minority men, and foreign nationals continue to be underrepresented at the top levels of organizations compared to their representation at lower levels and in the qualified available labor pools in various countries. The notion is that members of social-cultural minority groups encounter an invisible boundary to upward progress that keeps them, with very few exceptions, from advancing beyond middle management.

Affirmative action is the best-known, and many would argue the most effective, tool for breaking the glass ceiling that has been developed to date. Yet, after more than twenty-five years of use in the United States, affirmative action has yet to achieve worldwide application, and it is presently under a severe legal challenge in the United States. California has already made it illegal in state government employment and state-supported college admissions and has a proposal on the ballot to bar its use among all employers in the state.

Case 9.1 provides data on a real organization that we think illustrates both sides of the debate as well as many of the nuances of effective versus ineffective implementation of affirmative action plans.

Case 9.1
AFFIRMATIVE ACTION IN BIRMINGHAM, ALABAMA
LaRue Hosmer

Birmingham, Alabama, was founded in 1872 during the Reconstruction of the South following the Civil War. Northern investors were attracted to the area by the abundant deposits of iron, limestone, and coal that were found in the region. Iron, limestone, and coal are the raw materials for steel, and the city was formed around the first steel mill in the southern states. It was named for Birmingham, England, the largest steel center in Europe.

The city grew rapidly. Jobs were plentiful, in the mills and on the railroads and at the mines that served the mills, though most of the jobs were hard and dangerous, and they tended to attract a workforce that could also be described as hard and dangerous. The jobs were segregated from the start. Skilled positions were reserved for whites; only the menial tasks were open to blacks. There were, however, many menial tasks in the steel industry before it was mechanized: shoveling ore and coal, lifting ingots, riveting girders, loading rails, laying tracks, and cleaning cars. Many black laborers migrated to the city from the rural sections of the South, and Birmingham became one of the first metropolitan areas in the United States to have a substantial black population. Members of that population, however, were strictly segregated in housing, education, employment, and government. Until 1958, for example, all job applications for governmental positions in the city of Birmingham were marked "whites only."

> With a population of 350,000, Birmingham was in 1960 Alabama's largest city. A steel town, it was one of the region's major business centers. Blacks accounted for 40 percent of the city's population, but were three times less likely than white residents to hold a high-

Source: LaRue Hosmer, "Affirmative Action in Birmingham, Alabama, Case," in LaRue Hosmer, *Moral Leadership in Business* (Burr Ridge, IL: Richard D. Irwin Publishers, 1995), pp. 178–189. Used by permission.

school diploma. Only one of every six black employees was a skilled or trained worker, as opposed to three quarters of the whites. The median income for blacks was $3,000, less than half that for white people. (Williams, 1987, p. 185)

Continued income and educational inequality and a growing resistance to change marked the early days of the civil rights movement in Birmingham. In 1962, for example, the city closed sixty-eight parks, thirty-eight playgrounds, six swimming pools, and four golf courses rather than comply with a federal court order desegregating all public facilities. In 1963, after a handful of downtown merchants had removed the "whites" and "colored" signs on separate restrooms and drinking fountains, the head of the Public Safety Commission—a person soon to become known nationwide as "Bull" Connor—sent city inspectors to fine those stores for building-code violations. Eighteen bombings occurred in black neighborhoods during the same year; these were not investigated by the public safety commissioner due to an alleged lack of staff.

Black civil rights leaders in Birmingham were frustrated and angry in the spring of 1963. They had received no assistance from the city officials, and they expected no help from the state governor, George Wallace, who had ended his inauguration speech in January of that year with the words "Segregation now! Segregation tomorrow! Segregation forever!" The local leaders turned to the Southern Christian Leadership Conference, whose director, Dr. Martin Luther King, another person soon to become known nationwide, offered to organize civil disobedience demonstrations aimed at getting blacks hired as clerks in the downtown stores and at desegregating public facilities in the downtown area.

The black community started a boycott of the downtown stores on April 2, 1962, and conducted marches through the downtown area, but the public safety director acted with restraint and avoided violence, and little public sympathy was generated for the cause of greater equality. Reverend King was arrested as he led one demonstration, but instead of offering support, members of the white clergy within the city took out a full-page ad in the *Birmingham News* the following day to criticize him as an "outside agitator" and to denounce his ideas as "unwise and untimely." Dr. King responded with his famous "Letter from the Birmingham Jail":

My dear fellow clergymen:

While confined here in the Birmingham city jail, I came across your recent statement calling my present activities "unwise and untimely." Seldom do I pause to answer criticism of my work and ideas. If I sought to answer all the criticisms that cross my desk, my secretaries would have little time for anything other than such correspondence in the course of the day, and I would have no time for constructive work. But since I feel that you are men of genuine goodwill and that your criticisms are sincerely set forth, I want to try to answer your statement in what I hope will be patient and reasonable terms.

I think I should indicate why I am here in Birmingham, since you have been influenced by the view which argues against "outsiders coming in." I have the honor of serving as president of the Southern Christian Leadership Conference, an organization operating in every southern state, with headquarters in Atlanta, Georgia. . . . Several months ago the affiliate here in Birmingham asked us to be on call to engage in a nonviolent direct-action program if such were deemed necessary. We readily consented, and when the hour came we lived up to our promise. So I, along with several members of my staff, am here because I was invited here. I am here because I have organizational ties here.

But, more basically, I am in Birmingham because injustice is here. Just as the prophets of the eighth century B.C. left their villages and carried their "thus saith the Lord" message far beyond the boundaries of their towns, and just as the Apostle Paul left his village of Tarsus and carried the gospel of Jesus Christ to the far corners of the Greco-Roman world, so am I compelled to carry the gospel of freedom beyond my own home city.

Moreover, I am cognizant of the interrelatedness of all communities and states. I cannot sit idly by in Atlanta and not be concerned about what happens in Birmingham. Injustice anywhere is a threat to justice everywhere. Whatever affects one person directly, affects all persons indirectly. Never again can we afford to live with the narrow, provincial "outside agitator" idea. Anyone who lives inside the United States can never be considered an outsider anywhere within its bounds.

You deplore the demonstrations taking place in Birmingham. But your statement, I am sorry to say, fails to express a similar concern for the conditions that brought about those demonstrations. I am sure that none of you would want to rest content with the superficial kind of social analysis that deals merely with effects and does not grapple with underlying causes. It is unfortunate that demonstrations are taking place in Birmingham, but it is even more unfortunate that the city's white power structure left the Negro community with no alternative. . . .

If I have said anything in this letter that overstates the truth and indicates an unreasonable impatience, I beg you to forgive me. If I have said anything that understates the truth and indicates my having a patience that allows me to settle for anything less than brotherhood, I beg God to forgive me.

I hope this letter finds you strong in the faith. I also hope that circumstances will soon make it possible for me to meet each of you, not as an integrationist or a civil rights leader but as a fellow clergyman and a Christian brother. Let us all hope that the dark clouds of racial prejudice will soon pass away and the deep fog of misunderstanding will be lifted from our fear-drenched communities, and in some not too distant tomorrow the radiant stars of love and brotherhood will shine over our great nation with all their scintillating beauty.

> Yours for the cause of Peace and Brotherhood,
> Martin Luther King, Jr.

The "Letter from the Birmingham Jail" provoked an immediate response. Volunteers, black and white, came to demonstrate in front of the Birmingham City Hall. Black high school students from the surrounding counties joined the demonstrations en masse. Bull Connor reacted. The students were arrested and forced into police cars and then school buses, and finally National Guard trucks. The city and county jails were filled, and then a stockade was erected to hold the overflow at the state fairgrounds.

Students and volunteers kept coming, television cameras kept recording, and Bull Connor kept reacting. He ordered the Birmingham Fire Department to turn their hoses on the demonstrators. These hoses had 100 pounds of pressure per square inch; they were powerful enough to knock demonstrators off their feet and wash them down the street. He ordered the Birmingham Police Department to use their dogs on the demonstrators. These were large German Shepherd animals; they were also strong enough to knock demonstrators off their feet. The hoses and dogs turned back the demonstrators, but only so far.

> In 1963, I remember being washed down Fourth Avenue by Bull Connor's fire hoses. They [Dr. King and his organizers] told us to just fall down and protect ourselves, but my parents were scared that if you got caught they'd bomb your house, so I'd run. You couldn't fight the hose, but it could wash you down the street just so far. I was fortunate I never got bitten by the dogs. I was fast then. I got up and flew. (Statement of a black fire fighter, quoted in the *Los Angeles Times*, February 7, 1990, p. A-1)

President Kennedy dispatched the assistant attorney general for civil rights, Burke Marshall, to Birmingham. With Burke Marshall watching and the television cameras recording; with the downtown merchants fearing major riots, looting, and damage; with the members of the Birmingham Police and Fire Departments growing increasingly exhausted by the long hours and constant turmoil; and with the ranks of the demonstrators undiminished by the continual arrests, the city agreed on May 10 to desegregate the department stores, lunch counters, drinking fountains, and public washrooms in the downtown area.

The next night the Ku Klux Klan rallied in anger just outside Birmingham. Bombs exploded in homes and churches within the black community and at the hotel where Dr. King was staying. Riots broke out, seven stores were burned and looted, and forty were injured. President Kennedy sent troops from the U.S. Army to restore order. Demonstrators were released from jail. Bull Connor was removed from office. Robert Kennedy, the brother of the president and the attorney general of the United States, drafted the Civil Rights Act of 1964.

The Civil Rights Act of 1964 was a landmark in equal rights legislation. With numerous parts—called "titles"—the document was over 100 pages long and dealt with everything from discrimination in voting to segregation in housing. Title VII focused on discrimination in employment, and in Section 703a it stated:

It shall be an unlawful employment practice for an employer:

1. to fail or refuse to hire or to discharge or attempt to discharge any individual, or otherwise to discriminate against any individual with respect to his compensation, terms, conditions, or privileges of employment, because of such individual's race, color, religion, sex or national origin; or
2. to limit, segregate, or classify an employee in any way which would deprive or tend to deprive any individual of employment opportunities or otherwise adversely affect his status as an employee, because of such individual's race, color, religion, sex, or national origin. (Civil Rights Act of 1964, p. 255)

Just ten paragraphs later, Section 703j specifically rejected an intent to create preferential treatment based upon race, color, or previous denial of opportunity:

Nothing contained in this title shall be interpreted to require any employer to grant preferential treatment to any individual or to any group because of the race, color, religion, sex, or national origin of such individual or group, or on the account of an imbalance which may exist with respect to the total number or percentage of people of any race, color, religion, sex, or national origin employed by any employer in comparison with the total number or percentage of persons of such race, color, religion, sex, or national origin in any community, state, section, or other area. (Civil Rights Act of 1964, p. 257)

It was not until 1968, four years after the passage of the Civil Rights Act of 1964, that the first black was hired by the Birmingham Fire Department. He joined four hundred white firemen within that department. No further blacks were hired until 1974, when the local chapter of the National Association for the Advancement of Colored People (NAACP) filed suit in federal court against the City of Birmingham, the Birmingham Fire Department, Jefferson County (the county surrounding the city of Birmingham), and the Personnel Board of Jefferson County. Three days later a second class-action suit was filed against the same defendants on behalf of three black individuals who had been denied jobs at the Birmingham Fire Department.

Jefferson County and the Personnel Board of Jefferson County were included in the suits because of the hiring and promotion procedures followed by the City of Birmingham. All applicants interested in working for the city went to the Personnel Board and filled out an application that listed the specific departments where they wished to work. Then, periodically throughout the year, the Personnel Board administered certification tests for the different positions within each of the departments to screen out unlikely candidates. The Personnel Board would then draw up a certification list of the passing applicants, ranked by the test scores from top to bottom, and would pass along the names of the first three people on the list for hiring interviews by the City.

The Board and the City followed a similar process for promotions. Those interested in moving up would take a promotional exam offered by the Board once each year. The score on the exam, plus a point added for each year a person had served within a particular department, would determine the three people who would be recommended to the City for promotional interviews.

Everyone, then, seeking employment or promotion within any of the City's departments had to take and pass the appropriate test. The Board argued that the tests were very objective, and that they were the best way to determine who should or should not be employed or promoted by the City.

Pressured by the lawsuits, the Board and the City began to certify and employ more black workers. Eight more blacks were hired by the Birmingham Fire Department between 1974 and 1976, bringing the total number to 9 out of a total staff of more than 400. The NAACP, however, continued to argue that the tests and the interviews were biased, and that the percentage of applicants of each race who passed both the tests and the interviews supported their view:

	Black	White
Total taking test	285	1,530
Total passing test	69 (25 percent)	1,263 (82 percent)
Total offered employment	9 (3 percent)	215 (14 percent)

In January 1977, the suits of the NAACP and the three black individuals who had been denied employment at the Birmingham Fire Department came to trial. The judge, Samuel Pointer of the U.S. Northern District Court of Alabama, ruled that the tests were not job-related, had a "severe adverse impact on black applicants," and were therefore in violation of Title VII of the Civil Rights Act of 1964. He commented that while there seemed to be no design or intent on the part of the Board to discriminate, the effect had been to discriminate.

Judge Pointer ordered the Board to take whatever steps were necessary to make certain that in the future the tests did not have an adverse impact upon black applicants. He stated that the tests should certify a percentage of blacks equivalent to the percentage of blacks taking the exam. Since 18.6 percent (285/1,530) of the recent examinees were black, 18.6 percent of the examinees certified for hiring by the City needed to be black or there would be de facto evidence of racial discrimination. The City and the Board quickly appealed Judge Pointer's ruling to the Fifth Circuit Court of Appeals in New Orleans.

Three and one-half years later, in May 1980, the Fifth Circuit Court of Appeals upheld Judge Pointer's original ruling. The City and the County began negotiations with the NAACP and the black litigants to reach an out-of-court settlement that would resolve future problems but not cause either the City or the County to be liable financially for past actions. This out-of-court settlement eventually took the form of two consent decrees that were accepted by all parties in the spring of 1981.

The text of both consent decrees was over 100 pages long, but the five key points affecting the hiring and promoting of black fire fighters at the Birmingham Fire Department could be summarized briefly as follows:

Long-term goal. The City would hire and promote fire fighters in percentages which would approximate their respective racial divisions in the civilian labor force of Jefferson County. Since the civilian labor force of Jefferson County was 28 percent black in 1980, this became the long-term target for the Birmingham Fire Department.

Short-term goal. In order to reach the long-term goal in a reasonable amount of time, it was agreed that over half the fire fighters hired by the City or promoted to lieutenant in any given year would be black.

Certification goal. The Board would certify enough blacks in any one year to meet the City's hiring needs.

Expiration date. The consent decrees would be dissolved after six years, when, it was felt, the long-term goal would have been met.

Qualifying clause. The consent decrees would not require the Board to certify or the City to promote a less qualified person in preference to a person who was "demonstrably better qualified."

Judge Pointer, whose court had to either arrange for a consent decree or enforce his earlier order that the Board should certify and the City should hire a percentage of blacks equivalent to the percentage taking the exam (18.6 percent in the period 1974–1976, but much higher at this time), approved of the terms:

> The settlement represents a fair, adequate, and reasonable compromise of the issues between the parties to which it is addressed and is not inequitable, unconstitutional, or otherwise against public policy. (Judge Pointer, quoted in *Federal Reporter, United States Court of Appeals,* 1984, p. 1492)

The decrees were signed by the contending parties in June 1981, and a community fairness hearing was held in August of that year. Some white fire fighters objected to the provisions on promotion, but Judge Pointer again emphasized that the settlement was not "inequitable, unconstitutional, or otherwise against public policy" and the two decrees became binding on August 18, 1981.

The Board and the City stated that they intended to observe both the letter and the spirit of the two consent decrees, and by March 1988 the Birmingham Fire Department had come close to meeting the 28 percent long-term goal in total employees; by February 1989 it did meet that goal in officer positions:

Fire Department	Total Employees	Number Black	Black (Percent)	Goal (Percent)
August 1981	453	42	10.2	28.0
March 1988	492	124	25.2	28.0

Fire Department	Officer Positions	Number Black	Black (Percent)	Goal (Percent)
August 1981	140	0	0.0	28.0
March 1988	136	38	27.9	28.0

Some of the white fire fighters, however, objected strongly to being passed over for promotion. They claimed that they had scored well on the tests but then had not been promoted because of the short-term goal of ensuring that at least 50 percent of all fire fighters promoted each year were black. Fourteen white members of the Birmingham Fire Department sued, claiming that this reverse discrimination was detrimental to their careers and that it was clearly illegal under Title VII of the Civil Rights Act of 1964. The attorneys for these men made four major points:

1. The white fire fighters were being denied promotion on the basis of their race, not on the basis of their competence or performance. The Fire Department admitted that it was promoting equal numbers of the highest-ranking whites and the highest-ranking blacks, regardless of where the whites and blacks fell on the list relative to each other. The City did not release the actual scores or the relative rankings of the people taking the tests; it did, however, notify each individual where he or she stood on the list, and the relative rankings could then be reconstructed by the individuals' "comparing notes." The fourteen white fire fighters involved in the legal action had all either determined or been told that they were high enough on the list in a given year to have been promoted were it not for the short-term 50 percent goal of the consent agreement.

> Chief Gallant told me I was number three on the list, but due to the fact that he had to promote more blacks, I was to be number six. Five men were promoted. (Statement of white fire fighter, quoted in the *Birmingham News,* December 17, 1985, p. A-4)

> Chief Gallant told me he didn't have anything against promoting me, but that I probably wouldn't be promoted because of the consent decree. He said my position would probably change from seventh to about sixteenth. (Statement of white fire fighter, quoted in *Birmingham Post-Herald,* December 18, 1985, p. C-1)

> Chief Gallant congratulated me but said he wasn't going to promote me because of the consent decree. I was very discouraged. (Statement of white fire fighter, quoted in the *Birmingham News,* December 19, 1985, p. A-4)

One of the white fire fighters reported that he had been eighth on the promotion list in 1982, when twelve men were promoted, but he was not one of them. He was third on the list in 1983, when five were promoted, but was again passed over. He was ninth on the list in 1984 when eleven were promoted, but was not among them that year either. He did not bother to take the test a fourth time.

2. The white fire fighters had no control over the format or content of the test and had to assume that it was not biased in their favor. They admitted that adding one point to the test score for each year of service did give them an advantage because they had been employed longer than the blacks, but they argued, first, that seniority was not a hollow issue—a fire lieutenant needed years of experience to safely lead other fire fighters into a dangerous situation—and, second, that they were willing to give up those points because they did not greatly affect the relative rankings.

> We are not wedded to the current paper test. It's up to the City to choose (and redesign the test if necessary). But then apply the results evenly. (Statement of white fire fighter, quoted in the *Los Angeles Times,* February 7, 1990, p. A-14)

3. The white fire fighters were being punished for a situation that they did not create. The fourteen whites involved in the lawsuit were all too young to have actively participated in the overt discrimination that existed against blacks in the City of Birmingham up until 1965, or to have been responsible for the covert discrimination that existed against blacks in the Birmingham Fire Department up until 1981. They claimed that consequently it was not "fair" to deny them the promotions they deserved on the basis of the test scores:

> Hell, it's not fair, it's not right to give jobs or promotions on the basis of skin color. We didn't discriminate against anyone. Don't hang it on us. We weren't the ones who put up those "no blacks need apply" signs. I want to shake those people now and say to them, "So you're going to do it to me now, discriminate against me on the basis of race, but now it's all right?" It wasn't all right then, and it isn't all right now. (Statement of white fire fighter, quoted in the *Los Angeles Times,* February 7, 1990, p. A-14)

> Your Honor, there is a human factor here. There are people behind these goals and quotas. The plaintiffs are human beings who have

been pushed aside. We feel that the City has been far too aggressive in pushing aside some employees in favor of others. (Statement of an attorney representing the white fire fighters, quoted in the *Birmingham Post-Herald,* December 29, 1985, p. A-2)

4. The white fire fighters did not participate in the discussions that led to the consent decrees. The officers of the white union, the Birmingham Fire-fighters Association, were never invited to attend any of the meetings, and none of their members were permitted to be present. Officers from the black union, the Black Firefighters Association, were invited to attend, and many times they took members of their union with them.

Legally, this was an important issue because it seemed to indicate that the white fire fighters had not been a party to the decrees, and consequently that they had a right to now legally challenge those decrees in court. This issue was also important from the standpoint of democratic processes; the white fire fighters felt that the terms of the decrees had been dictated to them without their participation and were resentful of that method of reaching a decision. They claimed that they were being asked to make sacrifices they weren't prepared to make, and had never agreed to make.

Attorneys for the black fire fighters, along with representatives of the City of Birmingham and the Personnel Board of Jefferson County, defended the existing consent decrees. They made three major points:

1. The black fire fighters should not be forced to wait for normal changes in age patterns to create promotion opportunities, nor for gradual improvements in the regional school system to raise test scores. The last was a critical point. Lower test scores were not, it was claimed, an indication of lower competence; they were just a proof of poorer education. Schools in the predominantly black sections of the South, it was said, even forty years after the end of formally segregated education in that region, tended to place less emphasis upon the basic skills of reading and writing than did schools in the predominantly white areas. Consequently, the black fire fighters read and responded to the questions on the tests somewhat more slowly than did the whites and had much less experience in the psychological pressures of doing well on written exams.

Are we qualified for promotion to fire lieutenant? All I can tell you is that there has been no increase in the loss of property or the loss of life caused by fires within the City of Birmingham since the consent decrees went into effect and black firemen were promoted to command positions. (Statement of black fire lieutenant, quoted in *New York Times,* June 14, 1989, p. A-10)

2. The black fire fighters needed active antidiscrimination steps to redress past wrongs. No black officers existed prior to the consent decrees, even though there had been a few black fire fighters since the early 1970s. It had to be expected that the future pace of promotions for black fire fighters would have continued to be slow without the short-term goals of the consent decrees.

> They're not totally fair, but was it fair that I couldn't be a fireman back in the '60s. If there had been black firemen in the 1960s, there wouldn't have been consent decrees in the 1980s. (Statement of black fire fighter, quoted in the *Los Angeles Times,* February 7, 1990, p. A-15)

> Could we have been less intrusive? What you're really asking is, could we have done it over thirty years instead of six? Well, sure, yes we could have. But then we wouldn't have dealt with the problem for two whole generations. (Statement of attorney for the black fire fighters, quoted in the *Los Angeles Times,* February 7, 1990, p. A-14)

> For years now I have heard the word "Wait!" It rings in the ear of every Negro with piercing familiarity. This "Wait!" has almost always meant "Never!" We must come to see, with one of our distinguished jurists, that "justice too long delayed is justice denied." We have waited for more than 340 years for our constitutional and God-given rights. (Martin Luther King, "Letter from the Birmingham Jail," p. 8)

The fourteen white firemen filed the suit charging racial discrimination in both the hiring and promotion policies of the City and the Board. Judge Pointer ruled in December 1985 once again that the consent decrees were not "inequitable, unconstitutional, or otherwise against public policy" and he noted that the decrees were limited in duration and consequently in effect, and could not be that damaging to anyone's career for very long, if at all.

Judge Pointer's decision was appealed to the U.S. Circuit Court of Appeals. That court ruled in December 1987 that the relief intended by the consent decrees was expected to come from the City and the County, and not from the individual fire fighters. It ruled that Birmingham might actively recruit black people to apply for positions and might offer classes or tutorials to ensure that black candidates would be able to qualify for open positions, but that the City could not, as part of an affirmative action program, ignore higher test results from equally qualified white candidates.

The City and Board appealed the circuit court's decision to the U.S. Supreme Court. In June 1989 the Supreme Court upheld the decision of the circuit court and found against the City, the Board, and the black fire fighters. The white fire fighters were now able to file suit against the City and the County for monetary damages. They did so in 1990.

At the same time, the racial composition of both the City of Birmingham and Jefferson County had changed since the 28 percent black hiring and promotion goal had been set in 1980. Birmingham was now over 50 percent black, and Jefferson County over 40 percent. Black civil rights groups, consequently, sued to continue the consent decrees beyond the six-year limit and to raise the hiring and promotion goals to 42 percent. It was expected that both lawsuits would continue for at least five years, eventually reaching the Supreme Court once again:

> The city has been put into a situation where they'll be defending their position no matter what they do. I anticipate seeing both reverse discrimination and traditional discrimination suits tried at the same time, maybe in the same court. We are on the horns of a dilemma. All we know is that whatever we do, the losing side is going to sue us. This might never end. (Statement of attorney for the City of Birmingham, quoted in the *Los Angeles Times*, February 7, 1990. p. A-15)

> As I sat in the Supreme Court today, I wondered how long would this type of thing go on, and how many different stumbling blocks will be put in our path before they correct the wrongdoings. Back in 1963 when I was demonstrating, I had hopes that within some short term—two or three years—some of these things would be resolved. But here we are in 1989, and we're still talking about some of the things I was demonstrating against back in 1963. When does it stop? (Statement of black fire fighter, quoted in the *Birmingham News*, January 19, 1989, p. B-1)

Where's affirmative action going to end? I say end it now. My kids shouldn't have to pay for the past. There's got to be an end. Sooner or later you pay off the car. (Statement of white fire fighter, quoted in the *Los Angeles Times*, February 1990, p. A-15)

Suggestions for the Use of Case 9.1

We recommend that the case be analyzed in gender-and race-diverse teams of no more than five people and with no less than thirty minutes of discussion before recommendations are presented. Give the groups the following instructions:

> You have recently been appointed the chief of the Birmingham Fire Department. The effectiveness of the department has declined markedly over the past four years as a result of the constant turmoil and legal squabbling. What do you do to end the turmoil and increase the effectiveness of the department?

The synopsis and time line of events shown in Table 9.2 may be helpful in preparing for a discussion of the case. It outlines the sequence of events that led to the current hiring practices as well as those that contributed to the prevailing turmoil and ineffectiveness of the Fire Department.

It is important that the group not limit itself to just the options of keeping the program as is or discarding it. A question that warrants attention is: What could the department do to promote the objective of increasing employment opportunities for minorities and women if the affirmative action program outlined in the case is scrapped? This is an especially important question because in the summer of 1996, the Supreme Court ruled that the original affirmative action plan of the department was illegal and must therefore be discontinued.

TABLE 9.2. Affirmative Action in Birmingham, Alabama: Time Line of Events

April 2, 1962	The black community started a boycott of the downtown stores and conducted marches throughout the downtown area. Dr. Martin Luther King, Jr., was jailed and criticized as an agitator.
May 10, 1963	The City agreed to desegregate stores, lunch counters, drinking fountains, and public washrooms.
May 11, 1963	The Ku Klux Klan rallied outside of Birmingham.
1964	The Civil Rights Act of 1964 was drafted. Title VII focused on discrimination in employment. Specifically, it became unlawful to: 1. Refuse employment, discharge, or discriminate against an individual with respect to compensation, terms, conditions, or privileges of employment because of such individual's race, color, religion, sex, or national origin. 2. Limit, segregate, or classify an employee in any way which would deprive an individual of employment opportunities or otherwise adversely affect his status as an employee (Civil Rights Acts of 1964, p. 255). In addition, it specifically rejected any intent to create preferential treatment based on race, color, religion, sex, or national origin.
1968	The first black fire fighter was hired by the Birmingham Fire Department (1 out of 400).
1974	The NAACP filed suit in federal court against the City of Birmingham, the Birmingham Fire Department, Jefferson County, and the Personnel Board of Jefferson County, arguing that the entrance tests and interviews were biased. Three days later a second suit was filed against the same defendants on behalf of three black individuals who had been denied jobs at the Birmingham Fire Department.
1974–1976	Eight more black fire fighters were hired by the Birmingham Fire Department, bringing the number to 9 out of 400.

**TABLE 9.2. Affirmative Action in Birmingham, Alabama:
Time Line of Events, cont'd.**

January 1977	The suits of the NAACP and the three black individuals came to trial. The judge ruled that the tests were not job-related, had a severe adverse impact on black applicants, and were therefore in violation of Title VII of the Civil Rights Act of 1964.
	The judge ordered the Board to make certain that the tests did not have an adverse impact upon black applicants and that they certified a percentage of blacks equivalent to those taking the exam. The City and Board appealed this ruling.
May 1980	The Fifth Circuit Court of Appeals upheld the original ruling of January 1977.
August 18, 1981	An out-of-court settlement was reached that took the form of two consent decrees that were accepted by all parties. Five key points affecting the hiring of black fire fighters at the Birmingham Fire Department were as follows:
	1. *Long-term goal.* The City would hire and promote fire fighters in percentages that would approximate their respective racial divisions in the civilian labor force. (This was 28 percent black in 1980 and became a long-term goal.)
	2. *Short-term goal.* To reach the long-term goal in a reasonable time, it was agreed that over half of the fire fighters hired or promoted in any given year would be black.
	3. *Certification goal.* The Board would certify enough blacks to meet the City's hiring needs.
	4. *Expiration date.* The consent decrees would be dissolved after six years when the long-term goal would have been met.
	5. *Qualifying clause.* The consent decrees would not require the certification or promotion of a less qualified person in preference to a person who was "demonstrably better qualified."
	Some of the white fire fighters objected strongly to being passed over for promotion because of the short-term goal. Fourteen white members of the

**TABLE 9.2. Affirmative Action in Birmingham, Alabama:
Time Line of Events, cont'd.**

	Birmingham Fire Department sued, claiming that this reverse discrimination was detrimental to their careers and that it was illegal under Title VII of the Civil Rights Act of 1964. They charged racial discrimination in both the hiring and promotion policies of the City and the Board. They made the following four points: 1. They were being denied promotions on the basis of their race, not on competence or performance. The Fire Department admitted that they were promoting equal numbers regardless of where they fell on the list relative to one another. 2. They had no control over the format or content of the test and had to assume that it was not biased in their favor. 3. They were being punished for a situation that they did not create. They were too young to have participated in the overt discrimination. 4. They did not participate in the discussions that led to the consent decrees. The officers of the white union were never invited to attend any of the meetings; however, officers of the black union were invited to attend.
December 1985	The judge ruled that the consent decrees were not inequitable, unconstitutional, or otherwise against public policy. The decrees were limited in duration and consequently in effect. The verdict was appealed.
December 1987	The U.S. Circuit Court of Appeals ruled that the relief intended by the consent decrees was expected to come from the City and the County, and not from the individual fire fighters. The City could actively recruit black applicants or offer classes to candidates, but it could not ignore the higher test results from equally qualified white candidates. The City and Board appealed the court's decision to the Supreme Court.
February 1989	The Birmingham Fire Department met its 28 percent long-term goal in officer positions.
June 1989	The Supreme Court upheld the circuit court's earlier decision.

TABLE 9.2. Affirmative Action in Birmingham, Alabama:
Time Line of Events, cont'd.

1990	The white fire fighters were now able to file suit against the City and County for monetary damages.
	The racial composition of both Birmingham and Jefferson County has changed since 1980, when the original hiring and promotion goal had been set to 28 percent. Birmingham was now over 50 percent black, and Jefferson County was over 40 percent black.
	Black civil rights groups sued to continue the consent decrees beyond the six-year limit and to raise the hiring and promotion goals from 28 percent to 42 percent.
	It was expected that both lawsuits would continue for at least five years.
August 27, 1995	Rick Bragg of the *Dallas Morning News* reported that "fire fighters can show how affirmative action can foster resentment, prejudices that Alabama program was meant to end still divide group."

Source: LaRue Hosmer, "Affirmative Action in Birmingham, Alabama, Case," in LaRue Hosmer, *Moral Leadership in Business* (Burr Ridge, IL: Richard D. Irwin Publishers, 1995), pp. 178–189.

Activity 9.2
DEVELOPING A MENTORING PROGRAM

Objectives
1. To apply knowledge of cultural differences to a specific organizational task
2. To gain experience with organizational actions that affect the informal structure of organizations

Procedure
After studying Reading 9.2 and other material in the book, such as Chapter Seven, as well as any other resources on cultural differences between Anglos and Mexican Americans that is available to you, complete the following assignment:

1. Imagine that you are a member of a task force composed of representatives from various line units in your company and you have been assigned to design a mentoring plan to be used in a group of technical and semiprofessional employees that is 90 percent male, 55 percent Mexican American, and 45 percent Anglo American. Because of the demographics of the work unit, the vast majority of protégés who are matched with mentors at higher organizational levels will end up paired with Anglos.

2. Create the basic outline of a mentoring program. Then prepare a written answer to the following question: How, if at all, would the makeup of the work group affect your planning? Be as specific as you can. For example, instead of simply saying "provide training to mentors and protégés," indicate what information needs to be conveyed in this training.

Suggestions for the Use of Activity 9.2
The intent of this activity is to apply data on cultural differences to the design of the mentoring program. The response should be based on the data presented in Reading 9.2 and other relevant information. For example, the Hispanic scores on esteem are much lower, in general, than those of Anglos.

What implications, if any, does this have for preparing people to mentor Hispanics as opposed to Anglos? How could Anglos mishandle the types of interactions that typically occur in a mentoring relationship, given their typically higher scores on esteem and their ignorance of the probable cultural differences between them and their Latino protégés.

Another example of how the data from the article can be used is in addressing the question of whether the scores on this (and similar assessments) should be used, as suggested in Reading 9.2, for creating mentoring matches. Ask for feedback of opinion on this question.

10

A Process for Organizational Change

Our model of the effects of diversity on organizational performance, as explained in Reading 3.1, indicates that these effects occur as a function of the interaction of the characteristics of people and the characteristics of the organization (environment) in which they work. In Chapters Eight and Nine we addressed specific features of the organizational environment that require attention if diversity is to be a positive factor in organizational performance. As leaders become more knowledgeable about the conditions necessary in order for the culture, formal structure, and informal structure of organizations to support diversity competency, they often become aware of the need for significant organizational transformation if these conditions are to be created and sustained. Changing organizations to enhance diversity competency is therefore the subject of this chapter. In the chapter, we specify a process for organizational change and a set of related learning tools designed to help you to apply the process.

RAISING AWARENESS

Figure 10.1 summarizes the change model that we have found useful in our consulting work in transforming organizations toward diversity competency. The specific components of the model will be explained in the following sections; here, however, we would like to highlight several features of the

283

model. First, the model illustrates that managing diversity has many similarities with other forms of transformational organizational change. The model shown here (or something similar to it) could be, and is, used for all types of transformational change involving the human resources of organizations.

Second, the model has five primary components and twenty-four secondary components, highlighting the need for a comprehensive approach to change. In our experience, organizations too often approach organizational change with a one-dimensional strategy focusing on doing training or changing compensation systems. Real and lasting change, however, requires sustained effort on all five components of the model.

Finally, it is very important to acknowledge that the components of the model are interrelated. For example, measurement is needed to determine the success of education efforts; the follow-up evaluation process involves application of the results of the measurement phase; the educational work and measurement plan must be consistent with the vision for diversity established by the leadership of the organization; and so on.

In order to make it easier for you to use the material in the remainder of the chapter to learn and apply the model, the "Creating Understanding" and "Taking Action" sections are organized around the five components of the change model.

CREATING UNDERSTANDING
Leadership

In the best-case scenario, every organization member takes personal responsibility for the process of change in his or her organization. Nevertheless, often the best case is not possible; in addition, leaders have special responsibilities. By *leaders,* we mean the CEO and his or her direct reports, heads of departments or other definable organizational units, project leaders, and members of diversity change teams, steering committees, or task forces. These people must take the initiative for change and take responsibility for the six items listed under the leadership component of Figure 10.1.

By *management philosophy,* we mean the core beliefs set forth about managing diversity, such as how it should be defined and why it is a priority for the business. Recall from Chapter Two that we defined *valuing diversity* as viewing diversity as an organizational resource that can bring a competitive advantage if it is properly leveraged. As a management philosophy, valuing

Figure 10.1. Model for Guiding Organizational Change for Managing Cultural Diversity

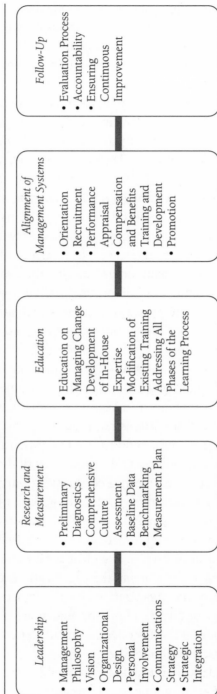

Leadership
- Management Philosophy
- Vision
- Organizational Design
- Personal Involvement
- Communications Strategy
- Strategic Integration

Research and Measurement
- Preliminary Diagnostics
- Comprehensive Culture Assessment
- Baseline Data
- Benchmarking
- Measurement Plan

Education
- Education on Managing Change
- Development of In-House Expertise
- Modification of Existing Training
- Addressing All Phases of the Learning Process

Alignment of Management Systems
- Orientation
- Recruitment
- Performance Appraisal
- Compensation and Benefits
- Training and Development
- Promotion

Follow-Up
- Evaluation Process
- Accountability
- Ensuring Continuous Improvement

Source: Adapted from Taylor Cox, Jr., and Stacy Blake, "Managing Cultural Diversity: Implications for Organizational Competitiveness," *The Executive,* 5(3), 1991, 52–54.

diversity has very different implications for the practice of management than a philosophy of tolerance or acceptance. For example, valuing diversity implies that we should be proactive in creating and sustaining cultural diversity in work groups, whereas a philosophy of tolerance does not.

A *vision* is a statement of what success looks like. It answers the question, What kind of organization are we trying to create in order to support diversity competency? Among other things, a vision for managing diversity gives guidance to the measurement process that will tell us the extent to which the change process is effective. The vision should be explicit, but brief and easy to understand. One of the authors recently heard a client say that if a vision statement cannot be explained with clarity to an entry-level employee in five minutes or less, it should be scrapped. This is good advice.

Leaders are also charged with assigning responsibility and providing the resources (staffing, training budget, and so forth) to allow the work of change to move forward. In many organizations, the design includes creation of a position for a limited period of time, such as director or manager of diversity, and establishment of planning groups such as diversity steering committees or action teams. This set of issues is referred to in Figure 10.1 as *organizational design*.

The *personal involvement* dimension of the leadership component refers to the fact that leaders must make a personal commitment to lead by example. This means that they must invest in personal development for diversity competency. When training is required, they should be the first to sign up. Speaking engagements should be used as opportunities to reinforce the importance of managing diversity to the success of the business. When leaders are asked to serve on steering committees, large blocks of time should be devoted so that the work gets off to a good start.

Although the technical work may be delegated, leaders have responsibility for the creation of an ongoing, organization-wide *communications strategy*. Effective communications will make clear what managing diversity is, how and why it is being approached in the organization, and what it means for individual workers. Some organizations have assigned task forces to develop communications for change efforts on managing diversity. Common tools for implementation of these strategies include letters and videos from CEOs, newsletter articles, and brochures.

Finally, because leaders are ultimately responsible for the operational results of the business, they must take responsibility for seeing that the change effort for diversity is linked to both the business strategy and other aspects of the strategic plan. In addition, in order to avoid investing resources for little or no return, they must ensure that the other components of the change plan (education, measurement, systems alignment, and follow-up) all take place. This set of responsibilities is what we have labeled *strategic integration* in Figure 10.1.

In order to extend your learning about the leadership component of the change model, we propose that you work through an activity for one of the subcomponents of leadership. Since detailed attention to all six components is beyond the scope of this book, we have selected the first dimension, management philosophy for diversity, as the point of focus in the activities on leadership, Activities 10.1 and 10.4.

● ● ●

Activity 10.1
MENTAL MODELS FOR DIVERSITY

Note: If you are facilitating a group, it is very important that participants do not read the Suggestions for the Use of Activity 10.1 before doing the exercise.

Objectives

1. To examine assumptions and patterns in the way you think about diversity

2. To illustrate some common problems in patterns of thinking about diversity that can be barriers to developing diversity competency

Procedure

Read the following list of twenty statements about diversity. Circle or list the numbers of statements that you have thought or said in the recent past (that is, statements that you more or less agree with). This is an individual assignment, and there should be no discussion about the statements with any other person. Go through the items quickly, without giving them much thought, and indicate those you tend to agree with by circling the number on the left.

When you have finished this task, the facilitator will lead your group in an assessment of your answers (or, if you are working alone, use the "Suggestions for the Use of Activity 10.1" to help you to interpret your answers).

1. I treat people as individuals, not as members of a group.
2. Women have equal job opportunities with men here.
3. Qualified members of racial minority groups have job opportunities equal to or better than those of Whites here.
4. The issue of "cultural" differences has little relevance in our predominantly U.S. workforce.
5. Our employment practices are color-blind.
6. Good managers have always been sensitive to differences when interacting with others.
7. When it comes to career opportunities, we tend to focus strictly on merit here.
8. Job status is not given a lot of emphasis here.

9. Age does not affect one's ability to have an impact here.

10. Diversity is not really an issue of much importance here.

11. Everyone tends to engage in stereotyping to some extent.

12. I'm sure that gender discrimination and sexual harassment do sometimes occur here.

13. All other things being equal, all people tend to favor others they see as like themselves in making selection decisions.

14. In many cases, racial differences do have an effect on human interactions.

15. Even some of our highest-rated managers would not necessarily know how to handle a discussion with an employee about how being a member of a minority group affects her or his work experiences.

16. Being well liked by the right people is an important factor in promotions here.

17. In cross-level meetings, people at lower job levels are often reluctant to speak up.

18. People who are younger than their peers often have to work harder to be heard and to have an influence in group meetings.

19. Different work departments sometimes represent different cultures and this contributes to misunderstandings and conflict in the workplace.

20. There tends to be a "glass ceiling" here, that is, a level beyond which very few women and non-White men advance.

Suggestions for the Use of Activity 10.1

In the well-regarded work on mental models done in the organizational learning literature by Peter Senge and colleagues (Senge & others, 1994), they point out that one way to help people learn is to help them become more aware of their own assumptions and ways of thinking about a particular management idea or approach. Senge and others tell us that people often hold contradictory thoughts and beliefs about phenomena without knowing it because they seldom examine the combination of thoughts and beliefs that they hold as a set. We believe that this is nowhere more true than in the area of managing diversity. Activity 10.1 is designed to help us build on this idea by surfacing apparent contradictions in how we think about the topic of diversity. We have noticed in our work on diversity that certain contradictions in thinking are especially prevalent. Our collection of these contradictions, obtained by listening to employees and managers, led to the creation of the list of statements in this activity. Although you may get some argument about whether or not certain combinations are really contradictions, we have found that most people who have a genuine openness to learn get some important insights from this activity.

The activity should be scored by use of the matrix shown in Table 10.1. An "X" in the matrix indicates statements that are contradictory. For example, statement 1 ("I treat people as individuals, not as members of a group") and statement 11 ("Everyone tends to engage in stereotyping to some extent") cannot both be true. People tend not to recognize this contradiction because they think of themselves as able to avoid the mistakes made by others (even when "others" means nearly everyone else) and because people tend to think that a "little" stereotyping somehow is okay. This contradiction also occurs because many people don't really understand what stereotyping is (for example, they think that it is the same thing as being prejudiced). An individual's score is simply the sum of the contradictions shown by analyzing the set of statements that he or she agreed with.

TABLE 10.1. Scoring Matrix for the Mental Models Activity

	11	12	13	14	15	16	17	18	19	20
Item										
1	X									
2		X	X							X
3			X							X
4										X
5			X							
6					X					
7						X				
8							X			
9								X		
10		X	X	X	X		X	X	X	X

If you are working with a group, the facilitator should take a reading of the distribution of scores (for example, by asking how many had scores of 0, less than 3, and so on). Our experience is that most people will have more than one contradiction and a significant number will have as many as eight or ten.

Of course the "scoring" is not the critical thing here, but rather the discussions that can be generated about the ease of simultaneously holding contradictory beliefs or assumptions and about some of the specific statements.

Research and Measurement

Measurement plans are a powerful tool for managers, and nowhere is this more relevant than with managing diversity. Too often managers we talk with have a hard time thinking beyond traditional equal opportunity numbers when the subject of measurement is addressed. What we have in mind is much more comprehensive. Measures of things such as organizational culture profiles, employee turnover, and employee survey data on diversity-relevant factors are equally important. In addition, too many organizations are limiting measurement to initial diagnostics, setting baselines, or benchmarking with companies that are ahead of them in the process of change. Although these measurements are all necessary and important, the missing link in most organizations is the existence of a formal plan for ongoing measurement that is implemented and given priority attention at the top of the organization. Reading 10.1 is suggested to increase understanding of this approach to measurement.

Reading 10.1
A COMMENT ON MEASUREMENT IN CHANGE PROCESSES ON DIVERSITY

TAYLOR COX, JR.

My advice to organizations is to develop measurement plans for diversity in stages, as shown in Figure 10.2. "Work climate" refers to the overall work environment in terms of its effects on employees and is largely measured by perceptual data taken from a cross-section of people who work in it. Of particular interest here are measures that are most directly connected to the effects of diversity in work groups, such as perceived fairness, perceived multiculturalism, stereotyping, intergroup conflict, and intergroup differences in employment satisfaction.

Although the importance of this type of data is sometimes questioned by managers, it must be remembered that perceptions determine behavior, and therefore creating the right perceptions among members of the organization (as long as they are true impressions and not deceptions) is a vitally important task for leaders. Research has shown that employees' perceptions of their work environment have a significant effect on performance measures such as innovation (Eisenberger, Fasolo, & Davis-LaMastro, 1990), customer satisfaction (Schneider & Bowen, 1985), and employee productivity (Russell, Terborg, & Powers, 1985). Other aspects of the work climate include measures of the diversity itself, such as traditional equal opportunity profiles or profiles of national origin or age distributions, and action steps taken to implement strategic plans for diversity (for example, the percentage of the work

Figure 10.2. Managing Diversity: Stages of Measurement

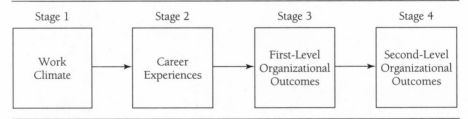

Stage 1	Stage 2	Stage 3	Stage 4
Work Climate	Career Experiences	First-Level Organizational Outcomes	Second-Level Organizational Outcomes

population that has participated in diversity awareness training). If the change effort is effective, the first area in which measurable results should occur is in the work climate.

"Career experience" measures are tangible indicators that group identity is affecting the contribution levels of employees toward achieving organizational goals as well as toward achievement of their own career goals. This includes such metrics as job performance ratings, job mobility and promotion measures, and gender gaps in compensation. These measures are not based on perceptions but should be taken from personnel records. These stage-two measures will not respond as quickly as the perceptual measures of stage one, but as the change process proceeds, measures in this area should improve.

"First-level organizational outcomes" has the same meaning here as in the Interactional Model of Cultural Diversity given in Figure 3.1 and includes such things as employee absenteeism and turnover and measures of creativity, innovation, productivity, and customer satisfaction. Once progress has been made on perceived work climate and on removing the effects of group identity on employees' career experiences and outcomes, these measures should begin to improve.

Finally, "second-level organizational outcomes" addresses the bottom-line results of market share, profits, and accomplishment of the organizational mission. These outcomes are clearly the most long-term in the expected timing of occurrence given success at managing diversity. Moreover, cause and effect are much less tightly coupled here than with any of the other stages of measurement. Although improvements in these organization-level financial measures should be expected and measured accordingly, attributing either increases or decreases in them to any single organizational change effort is risky business. Indeed, the cause-and-effect assumption between improvements in managing diversity and increases in the metrics proposed here gets successively weaker as one moves from left to right in Figure 10.2. We therefore recommend that managers focus their greatest attention, at least in the short term, on the first two stages of measurement.

The framework shown in Figure 10.2 should help you to construct a conceptual foundation for measurement in your organization. Later, in "Taking Action," you will want to refer back to this reading as a basis for actually working on a measurement plan to fit your situation.

EDUCATION

We view education as one of the three most important drivers of change. To realize this potential, however, the education must (1) be ongoing and (2) be well designed and implemented. Moreover, in planning education related to diversity competency, organizations should pay attention to:

1. Learning and development on managing change in addition to content on diversity
2. Developing internal expertise to teach about managing diversity
3. Revising existing training courses to reflect a knowledge of diversity dynamics
4. Moving beyond awareness training to address the understanding and action dimensions of the learning process

Based on our experiences to date, we believe that the most important requirement is that education should be ongoing. A one-or two-day workshop, however powerful, simply does not provide sufficient exposure on complex topics such as this one. Additional advice on developing educational plans for diversity is given in Reading 10.2.

● ● ●

Reading 10.2
TEACHING ABOUT DIVERSITY

RUBY L. BEALE AND TAYLOR COX, JR.

Diversity continues to be a reality and an important factor in contemporary society. With changing demographics, changes in the political climate world-wide, and technological advancements that facilitate communication and access between cultures and nations, the topics, issues, and outcomes that diversity and multiculturalism affect seem to grow exponentially almost daily. The topic of diversity and multiculturalism has engendered much talk and discussion. Though discussion is an important first step, much more needs to be done to effectuate development and change in order to facilitate positive and effective outcomes for organizational and group effectiveness as well as individual well-being.

Diversity and multiculturalism make up an area of study that is worthy of examination, discussion, and development as a stand-alone topic; it also needs to be integrated within the content of other subjects. Education in matters of diversity is an imperative for the knowledge base and skill set of today's professionals and citizens. In some organizations and schools, diversity teaching and training have become popular. An increasing number of trainers, educators, and consultants (some very qualified and prepared and others whose qualification is less apparent) profess to have expertise on the topic. Conversely, many individuals within the teaching and training professions state that they know virtually nothing about diversity and therefore cannot cover it or address it within the context of their classes, workshops, or work units. Indeed, teaching about any subject requires some knowledge of the topic and some focus on key learning points. In addition to subject and content knowledge, other important skills need to be developed by organizations, teachers, trainers, and managers to effectively teach about and manage diversity.

In order to better link this reading to other material in Part Three of the book, we will use the organizational change framework shown in Figure 10.1 and will address the four points listed under the education component and process. The four points are (1) the change process, (2) development of in-house expertise, (3) modification of existing training, and (4) addressing all phases of the learning process.

The Change Process

Education can facilitate the change process. New information or knowledge about different ways of observing and interpreting old information is critical for continuous learning and quality improvement that will affect the bottom-line objectives of the organization. In addition to the cognitive or knowledge content of diversity, there are also affective and behavioral dimensions. Not only does a teacher, trainer, or manager need to have an understanding of what diversity is; he or she also must understand, and to some extent be able to deal with, what discussing the topic of diversity can evoke affectively and behaviorally in people. Some people come to the classes or sessions thinking that they know a lot about the subject but are not necessarily willing to acknowledge, or perhaps are not even consciously aware of, the affective or emotional dimensions that influence their thoughts and actions about the topic.

It is important to note that some people will need not only to learn but also to unlearn things they may have been taught by their families and friends or other elements of society. They may have been taught incorrect information (which sometimes is manifested in stereotypes as well as biases or prejudices) through a variety of sources and mechanisms. Although they can readily identify some of their thoughts and feelings, others may make them so uncomfortable that they cannot readily acknowledge them. Their conscious knowledge may lead them to intellectually understand that they need to engage in the change process, but they may be ultimately unwilling to engage in behavioral change. Resistance to almost any change process is a common phenomenon in people and in organizations; it is manifested in many avoidance or sabotage techniques. While an individual is trying to avoid personal discomfort, other conflictual or withdrawal behavior may surface in or during discussions. Teachers and managers should anticipate and plan how to manage such behavior.

Development of In-House Expertise

Development of in-house expertise is a concrete indicator that the organization not only has an interest in but is willing to invest in a more effective diversity change process. It is critical for highly skilled people within the organization to be committed to the organization *and* the diversity process, and to be in place to carry out the initiatives in the day-to-day operations of the organization. Securing external expertise often leads to obtaining the most current knowledge, strategies, and processes, which can be transferred to internal employees or consultants to assist in further developing and institutionalizing that expertise. The development of in-house expertise in diversity can be leveraged to promote skill development throughout the organization.

Modification of Existing Training

Modification of existing training is made easier by utilizing in-house expertise in diversity. Human resource units or people within human resource or training units will generally have knowledge of the content and process of existing trainings. Training courses on teamwork, communications, the people aspects of total quality, performance management, and recruiting are among the most easily adapted to include content on diversity. As training courses are modified, the following tips should be taken into account.

1. Plan an activity or method to get people to agree, at the beginning of a session or class, to establish an environment in which people feel safe enough to discuss controversial matters and in which conflict can be handled in a balanced and responsible manner. The teacher or trainer should invoke ethics (personal and/or professional) and have the class members agree not to identify people by repeating elsewhere remarks that are made in the session.

2. Include material that acknowledges differences in interests, values, skills, and professional orientations based on differences of experiences in the group.

3. When planning about teaching diversity issues, it is important to be aware that it may touch "hot buttons," thoughts heavily laden with emotions and feelings. This is due partly to a history of elitism over race, sex, age, physical ability, and class, among other categories, in many countries of the world.

4. In designing and using training material, take care to acknowledge that victims of oppression should not be blamed for their oppression, and people should not be demeaned, devalued, or put down for their experiences. Human resource or training sessions should focus on responsibility rather than blame. That is, people should not be blamed for the misinformation that they have heard, but should be held responsible for repeating the misinformation after they have learned otherwise. There should be a basic tenet

in the training session or class that people try to do the best they can, both to learn the material and to behave in multiculturally productive ways. Teachers/trainers/facilitators have an obligation to actively combat myths and stereotypes about different groups that would prohibit skill development and cooperation.

While external consultants can be very helpful in the modification of existing training courses to reflect knowledge of diversity dynamics, certain aspects of the process of changing course designs would be most efficiently addressed by internal experts. They would more readily understand the politics and issues of their organization and also be better able to anticipate issues and concerns that might arise in the implementation process.

Addressing All Phases of the Learning Process

A common error in teaching about diversity is terminating the learning plan prematurely at the awareness stage of the learning process. Therefore, it is important to develop an educational plan that goes beyond awareness to build understanding and to provide help on action steps to change behavior. As you develop material and training and teaching techniques to extend learning toward building true competency, the following suggestions should be helpful:

- Focus each session on a small number of key learning points.
- Have a plan to deal with emotions that may arise.
- Give attention to what needs to be unlearned as well as what needs to be learned.
- When possible, use an exercise that puts people in touch with their own values or predispositions as a teaching "kickoff."
- Use a universal responsibility-for-change approach rather than a "blaming" approach.
- Model the behaviors that you are trying to teach.
- Do an inventory of your own feelings, knowledge, and beliefs about the topics and think about how they should be managed (that is, revealed, balanced, and so on) in the teaching sessions.
- Establish ground rules governing the session that all participants should commit to abide by.
- Encourage participation without applying undue pressure on silent participants.

- Intervene if the level of conflict appears to be getting out of hand, and protect individuals from personal attack and undue censorship.
- Develop negotiation and conflict resolution skills in order to more effectively handle conflict arising in educational sessions in a manner that is sensitive and equitable to all people.

Teaching about diversity can present some challenges for the teacher or trainer as well as the manager. However, when one is flexible, understands that cultural differences do exist, encourages constructive communication about differences, and commits to treating people equitably but not uniformly, she or he can provide an exciting, effective, and productive experience for the participants that can have a positive ripple effect in their professional, personal, and social environments.

Suggestions for the Use of Reading 10.2

This reading is intended to serve as background material for thinking and discussion about teaching diversity. It gives some further depth on subdimensions of the education component of the change model. Among the questions you may want to discuss are the following:

1. Why is this kind of teaching so difficult? What are the differences and similarities between teaching about diversity and teaching any other work-related topic?

2. How does the "identity" of the trainer or instructor affect the teaching of diversity-related topics, and what can be done to "manage" this?

3. In addition to those mentioned in the reading, what other ground rules could or should be established for teaching sessions on diversity?

4. What are the qualifications needed to teach about diversity? How does one acquire these qualifications?

Systems Alignment

The idea behind *systems alignment* is that once a strategic plan is set for the firm, all management practices and policies must reinforce that plan. This can be facilitated by a careful assessment of all major people management systems such as recruiting, employee development, and compensation.

Often, such assessments reveal that current management practices and policies are not well aligned with the future strategic priorities of the business. Bringing them into alignment therefore becomes the focus of action plans in the change process. We can illustrate these points by an example from a recent consulting project one of us conducted.

Company X has recently determined a set of strategic priorities that includes excellence in employee development as one of its critical competencies for the future. However, development, especially the development of *other* people, was not a priority in the company in the past. As a result, many of the management practices and policies did not emphasize development. For instance, managers were not held accountable for developing their direct reports, there was no organizational support for mentoring, developing others was seldom represented in the performance appraisal forms of managers, and there was very little mandatory training that focused on ways to develop others. Our consulting team therefore made recommendations for changes in some of these areas that would allow the management systems to better reinforce the new strategic priority of excellence in developing people.

This scenario is not unusual. In our work with organizations on culture change, we find that poorly aligned management systems are a major barrier to change. If the initial assessment work for systems alignment is done well, it is a major project, especially for decentralized, diversified firms, but it is absolutely critical to do this if we are to expect long-term change.

Activity 10.2 is suggested to help you prepare to do systems alignment work.

Activity 10.2
STAFFING AND REWARDS AS DRIVERS OF CHANGE

Objectives
1. To develop a better understanding of the use of staffing and rewards to drive organizational change
2. To gain practice with doing systems alignment work for diversity change processes

Procedure
Task 1

Carefully read the following short briefing about drivers of organizational change:

Earlier in this chapter, we stated that we viewed education as one of the three primary drivers of organizational change. Here we want to focus our attention on the other two, staffing and rewards. *Staffing* refers to the actual personnel who staff the system. Whereas education focuses on changing the mindset or knowledge of people who currently work in the organization, staffing focuses on changing the organization by managing carefully who gets hired, who gets fired, and who gets promoted into positions of high influence. The selection of people for movement into and out of the organization is a major factor in organizational change.

Rewards is defined broadly to include any positive recognition given for work performed. Primarily this includes performance feedback and compensation, but it can also mean nonfinancial awards, the opportunity to be promoted, and the opportunity to receive certain highly valued, but scarce, job assignments or development opportunities.

Task 2

Working alone or in small groups:

1. Identify the pros and cons of changing organizations through staffing policies rather than by manipulating rewards.

2. Identify and discuss (if working in a group) the barriers that hinder the use of the drivers of change in organizations.

3. Answer the following question: Of the three primary drivers of change (education, staffing, and rewards), which do you view as the most powerful? Why?

Suggestions for the Use of Activity 10.2

Note: If you are facilitating with a group, use the material shown in Task 1 of the activity to present a brief introductory lecture on drivers of organizational change. If you are working alone, you may simply read this material.

Depending on the time available, you may either have a general discussion about the items identified by the discussion groups or call for formal reports from each group. You may also want to ask each of three groups to focus on a different question (1 through 3 in Task 2). If you have more than three groups, you may add questions of your own or have two groups work on each of the questions.

The outcome of the activity should be a clearer understanding of the implications and strengths and weaknesses of these drivers of change. The intent here is to discuss change in organizations in general. When we move to action planning (Activity 10.7), you will be asked to become more focused on your specific organization.

Follow-Up

Earlier in this chapter we addressed the importance of measurement plans for diversity. However, as many change agents have learned, having a measurement plan is one thing; using it is another. An evaluation process requires not only that data be generated but that they be used to assess levels of success. Follow-up on measurement seems axiomatic, but we have found just the opposite. For example, one of us recently designed a measurement plan for diversity training for a client. The plan was based on assessing shifts in ways of thinking about diversity that hopefully would occur as a result of the training. Although the data were collected more than six months ago, the client still has not analyzed the information and is unable to say whether the training created movement or not. Nevertheless, that module of education has now been used in the rest of the organization, and thus one of the most critical objectives of the measurement plan, namely, to determine whether or not the training was effective enough to warrant rolling it out to the total organization, has already been lost.

In another case, a comprehensive measurement plan was developed for a client and presented in a written report. Despite warnings of the dangers of baseline contamination (when too much intervention takes place before the first comprehensive measurement, providing no way to know where the organization was at "ground zero"), this client did nothing with the report for six months. Some organizations have begun to take the issue of measurement more seriously and have done some interesting work in recent years. Pillsbury, General Electric Company, U S West Communications, and Avon Products come to mind in this regard.

Another issue of importance in this area is how much progress on a given measure is enough. For example, survey data often reveal order-of-magnitude discrepancies in percentages of favorable responses between lower-level workers and managers. Should we be satisfied to narrow these margins to, say, ten points, or should we be striving for zero difference (the equivalent of zero defect in Total Quality Management). We acknowledge as debatable the question of whether the marginal benefit of top-end improvements in these measures justifies the cost of obtaining them. At the same time, we argue that where the principle of continuous improvement has become policy, as it has in many organizations in the last ten years, it should apply to managing diversity just as it does to other major strategic issues.

The core issue in the previous discussion is the need for *accountability*. Accountability essentially means that members, and especially managers, take personal responsibility for seeing that progress is made on managing diversity. This is often mentioned in our conversations with managers about the requirements of effective change processes. They all agree that without it change efforts will fail, but how do we know whether or not accountability exists and, if it doesn't, how do we create it? Unless we can answer these questions, we run the risk of having accountability take on a mystical quality, something that everyone agrees is important but that somehow never seems to happen. Activity 10.3 is designed to address these important questions.

● ● ●

Activity 10.3
MAKING ACCOUNTABILITY CONCRETE

Objectives
1. To identify the specific conditions that define accountability for managing diversity
2. To identify why achieving genuine accountability seems so elusive in organizational change efforts for diversity competency

Procedure
Complete the following two tasks.

Task 1
Working alone, complete the following sentence with at least two or three different phrases:

I will know that real accountability for managing diversity has been established in my company when . . .

1. _____.

2. _____.

3. _____.

Task 2
Working alone or in teams as indicated by the facilitator, address the question of what gets in the way of the requirements of accountability as you have defined them. You might begin this with the following sentence-completion task:

The reason or reasons that we don't have _____
(one of the items listed in Task 1) is/are _____
_____.

Another approach to this activity is to use the outcomes of Task 1 as the main-line problems or goals of a fishbone chart analysis (see Figure 10.3) and then to complete the chart with the second-and third-level causes and reasons. Once everyone is satisfied that the root causes of the failure to have real accountability have been identified, the individual or group might spend time identifying what can be done to change these causes and solve the problems.

Suggestions for the Use of Activity 10.3

We suggest that you first do Task 1 individually; however, it can also be done in a full-group discussion. If the activity is being done in a group, it is very helpful if the conditions for accountability can be refined down to no more than three to five that nearly everyone can agree on. You are then ready to move to Task 2. The fishbone tool (or at least its principles) has been recommended for analytical work in various organizational change strategies including organizational learning (see, for example, Senge and others, 1994)

Figure 10.3. Sample Beginning to Fishbone Analysis of Accountability

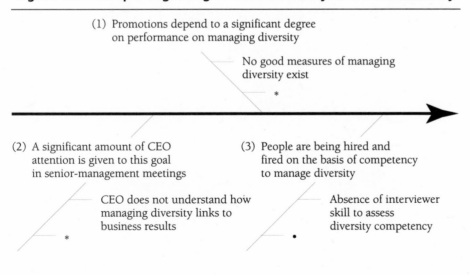

(1) Promotions depend to a significant degree on performance on managing diversity

No good measures of managing diversity exist

*

(2) A significant amount of CEO attention is given to this goal in senior-management meetings

(3) People are being hired and fired on the basis of competency to manage diversity

CEO does not understand how managing diversity links to business results

Absence of interviewer skill to assess diversity competency

*

•

* Reasons why this is not happening; an example is shown for each condition.

and reengineering (Hammer & Stanton, 1995). You might want to produce (or ask the group to produce) a completed detailed fishbone diagram as a "deliverable" from the work session. Several small groups could each take a condition (main bone) for explosion (to define contributing causes) or, if there is more time, all groups could work on all conditions and then compare notes.

TAKING ACTION
Leadership

In order to facilitate continuity in our learning process with the work done on leadership in Activity 10.1, we have created another activity dealing with the management philosophy dimension of leadership. Whereas the previous activity challenged the way we think about diversity, Activity 10.4 asks you to actually make a decision about a management philosophy for your organization.

Activity 10.4
DEVELOPING A PHILOSOPHY FOR MANAGING DIVERSITY

Objectives
1. To facilitate discussion and understanding about different management philosophies on diversity
2. To aid in thinking through the implications of different management philosophies for diversity and in reaching consensus about a management philosophy for your organization

Procedure
Task 1
Working alone, read the following descriptions of some prevalent philosophies regarding diversity:

1. *Discouraging and minimizing diversity:* "It is in our best interest to minimize diversity in work groups because diverse work groups are more difficult to manage and the management of diversity saps energy from other managerial activities that have higher potential payoffs."

2. *Ignoring diversity:* "Diversity is not an issue worthy of significant attention because the similarities among people dwarf their differences. At this point in our history, the work experiences of our work force are seldom affected by things like gender, race, nationality, and age differences, and we are getting better every day at handling other kinds of differences like work function and work style."

3. *Valuing diversity:* "Diversity is a reality in today's organizations. Not only are 'group identity' differences real and potent influences on an individual's work experiences but work groups that are diverse (on gender, race, nationality, and other dimensions) enjoy performance advantages over more homogeneous work groups. Diversity not only is inevitable but also adds value to the organization if it is effectively managed. Therefore, we should not only pursue equal opportunity for workers but also proactively achieve or sustain diversity in order to increase the performance capacity of the organization."

4. *Acknowledging and accommodating diversity:* "Diversity is a reality in today's workforce, and 'group-identity' differences do have an effect on people's work experiences. Therefore, it is important to avoid discrimination and take proactive steps to ensure equal opportunity. In addition, we should help managers to become more knowledgeable about, and accepting of, differences of all kinds."

Task 2
Working alone, identify the managerial philosophy that best describes your current (honest) view about diversity in the workplace. If you have a different philosophy that you prefer to work with, add it in.

Task 3
Working alone or (preferably) in a group of two or more, complete a worksheet for managerial philosophies on diversity like the one shown in Exhibit 10.1 with some of your first thoughts about the behavioral implications of each of the four (or more) philosophies. Note that these implications could concern either personal or organizational policies or practices. Before writing anything, discuss the issues and try to come to consensus. Answer the following three questions:

1. What are the behavioral implications of each philosophy?
2. What arguments can be made in favor of and against each philosophy?
3. What is the right or best managerial philosophy for your organization to adopt at this time and why?

If you are working in a group, be prepared to share some of your worksheet entries and points of discussion with the facilitator and/or the larger group.

Suggestions for the Use of Activity 10.4
Based on the premise that what we believe ultimately determines our behavior, this activity should be used early on in the work with leaders of change efforts. In debriefing the activity, you might want to point out that beliefs about diversity can be inferred from behavior. For example, not actively managing diversity suggests a philosophy of ignoring diversity. When

EXHIBIT 10.1. Worksheet for Managerial Philosophies on Diversity

Philosophy	Behavioral Implications
Discouraging and minimizing diversity	
Ignoring diversity	
Valuing diversity	
Acknowledging and accommodating diversity	
Other	

we focus attention on legal requirements and affirmative action, we are acknowledging certain forms of diversity but not necessarily valuing it. Valuing diversity is the only one of the four listed philosophies that suggests that we might want to actively seek out diversity in the absence of legal pressures or concerns about cost increases that result from unmanaged diversity.

Research and Measurement

In our experience, most managers involved in organizational change work are keenly interested in measurement of results. Unfortunately, when it comes to managing people, this interest is not always pursued as diligently as it should be. There are a variety of reasons for this. So-called "soft" measures like survey data have low legitimacy for some managers. Others fear that the numbers won't look good and will undercut support for the change initiative just when it is gaining much-needed momentum. Still others are reluctant to measure because the implementation of the change strategy is so anemic that it presents a low probability of actually finding any measurable progress, and the list goes on. None of these reasons (one might say excuses) justifies inattention to measurement by people who are serious about organizational change. If you agree, we propose that you spend considerable time on Activity 10.5 early in the change process.

● ● ●

Activity 10.5
DEVELOPING A MEASUREMENT
PLAN FOR MANAGING DIVERSITY

Objective

1. To create a tentative plan for measuring organizational diversity competency

Procedure

Imagine that you are a member of a diversity steering committee or task force and that you have been assigned the task of developing a measurement plan for your organization or work unit with the strategic objective of managing diversity. Using the material in Reading 10.1 as a guide, develop a proposed measurement plan to present to the senior management team for approval.

Suggestions for the Use of Activity 10.5

The following list contains some items to keep in mind when developing measurement plans for managing diversity; they may assist you in using Activity 10.5 to create or evaluate a measurement plan.

- Develop metrics within a conceptual and analytical framework that is derived from, or at least linked to, the vision for diversity that has been adopted in your organization.
- Make sure that the metrics are comprehensive.
- Pay attention to timing.
- Carefully address adjustments for globalization.
- Be diligent about follow-up and assign specific accountability for reporting of the collected data.

A *conceptual framework* is useful to provide some organization to the metrics and to facilitate linking the measures to the vision for change that has been created. For example, the model for the multicultural organization offered by Taylor Cox, Jr., in Chapter Fourteen of *Cultural Diversity in Organizations* (Cox, 1993) is one way of defining a vision for diversity in organizations. This same framework can then be used to plan corresponding metrics. In this way, leaders are assured of developing a comprehensive and organized set of measurements that tie directly to the goals of the change process.

Comprehensiveness requires that attention be given to all four of the stages of measurement discussed in Figure 10.2 with appropriate attention to (1) the extent to which other variables may interfere with assumptions about the effect of diversity-related interventions, (2) the comprehensiveness of the action plans, and (3) timing.

Two areas in which timing becomes important are *baseline contamination* and *premature closure.* Baseline contamination occurs when interventions designed to change the culture are already well under way before the first comprehensive measurement of diversity climate is taken. When this happens (and it occurs frequently), organizations run the risk of understating the progress made at the time of the first update on the metrics.

Premature closure refers to the common mistake of expecting results too soon. There is no sense in taking follow-up measurements when 80 percent of the action plan has yet to be implemented. Also, as we have already noted, results in different stages of measurement occur in successively later time periods. We therefore have to carefully match the measures being observed to the time frame that has elapsed since implementation.

Globalization requires that measures be insightfully adapted to reflect differences in language, cultural norms, and legal structures around the world. For example, certain EEO-related measures that work very well in the United States would not be appropriate in Japan or Saudi Arabia. Organizations should carefully think through all survey measures to ensure not only that the items are translated, but also that the questions themselves have the same interpretation in the various countries.

Finally, no plan is worth much unless it is implemented. We have seen more than one company invest untold hours of time and thousands of dollars of the company's money in the development of well-conceived measurement plans that remain unused years later. It helps to be specific about whose responsibility it is to collect the required data and to integrate the reporting of the metrics with the existing reporting structure for operations results in the company.

EDUCATION

No aspect of the change process is more important than the quality of education provided to help people learn the new skills, behaviors, and values that are needed to succeed in the new culture. In the realm of organization development, training is without question the most widely used intervention strategy to manage diversity. Although the need for training is undeniable, our experience, as well as recent empirical research (see Rynes & Rosen, 1995), suggests that much of this training is ineffective.

Because there appears to be more resistance to diversity training than to many other types of work-related education, extraordinary care must be given to the design and implementation of this training. Even then, achieving consistently effective training is difficult. Nevertheless, after years of learning by doing, we now have mostly very good results in efforts to teach about diversity, both in our consulting work and in our university teaching. Some of the things that we've learned were communicated in Reading 10.2. We suggest Activity 10.6 to give you more help and to take the learning process into the action phase.

●●●

Activity 10.6
ISSUES IN THE DESIGN OF DIVERSITY TRAINING

Objective
1. To think through and make decisions about how several critical issues relating to diversity training should be handled

Procedure
Read the following list of ten critical issues that occur in the design of diversity training:

1. Time allocated
2. Breadth of employee population to attend the training
3. Cross-sectional versus level-stratified attendees
4. Voluntary versus mandatory attendance
5. External versus internal facilitation
6. Stand-alone workshops versus integration with existing training
7. Emotion versus cognition versus behavior as the points of focus in the learning objectives and methods
8. How to follow up initial awareness training
9. Curriculum structure (for example, identity-group based versus topic-based content formats)
10. How to promote commitment from members of the dominant culture to support the training effort

After reading over the list, work alone or with group members on the following two tasks.

Task 1
Discuss the various options for handling each issue. Identify the advantages and disadvantages of each option (for each issue).

Task 2
Try to come to consensus (or, if working alone, make a personal decision) about how each issue should be handled in your organization, and be prepared to defend your decisions.

Suggestions for the Use of Activity 10.6

A wide range of time and depth can be devoted to this activity. The time can be shortened by identifying only one advantage and one disadvantage for only two alternatives for each item in the list. If more time is available, the learning can be deepened by pushing for as many pros and cons as a person or group can come up with.

The best approach on each of these design factors can only be determined in the context of a specific organization and with specific parameters, such as the objectives of the training or the level of internal facilitation expertise. With this in mind, we have nevertheless offered some comments and opinions about each of these items, shown in Table 10.2. Keep in mind that each option has both advantages and drawbacks, and that a recommendation for a particular approach is not meant to obscure the point that tradeoffs are being made.

TABLE 10.2. Comments on the Training Design Issues of Activity 10.6

Issue	Comment or Suggestion
1. Time allotted	This must be matched to learning objectives; a rule of thumb is to plan no less than two hours for each narrowly defined topic or key learning.
2. Breadth of population	Ideally, everyone should have all training for basic competency, with additional coverage for leaders on strategic issues.
3. Cross-sectional or level stratification	Usually cross-sectional is best.
4. Voluntary versus mandatory participation	Mandatory is usually the best option and always for supervisory personnel.
5. External versus internal facilitation	When possible, the best approach is a combination of the two.
6. Stand-alone versus integration into other courses	Stand-alone is seldom the best choice once a day or two of initial awareness has taken place.

**TABLE 10.2. Comments on the Training
Design Issues of Activity 10.6, cont'd.**

Issue	Comment or Suggestion
7. Emotion versus cognition versus behavior	Some combination of these may work best, but be careful to match the time available with choices made here and on item 5.
8. How to follow up on initial awareness training	Create understanding and identify behaviors and action steps; there is also a need for more on awareness.
9. Curriculum structure	Both identity-group and topic-based formats have their place; in many cases, topic-based designs are preferred.
10. Handling low commitment to learn among majority-group members	Build an explicit business case for managing diversity as a critical competency; include learning activities that reinforce the message that adversity is not a pseudonym for members of minority groups.

Systems Alignment

Earlier, in the "Creating Understanding" section, you were asked to think through and write some ideas on using staffing and rewards to drive organizational change. Staffing and rewards link roughly to the items listed for the systems alignment component of the change model, as shown below:

Staffing	*Rewards*
Recruiting	Performance appraisal
New-hire orientation	Compensation
Promotion	Development

In this section, we want to take the learning from Activity 10.2 a step further by asking you to do a preliminary assessment of alignment for your organization.

Activity 10.7
PRACTICE ON SYSTEMS ALIGNMENT

Objective
1. To learn how to do systems alignment by creating the beginnings of an assessment for your own organization

Procedure
Complete the following two tasks.

Task 1
Working alone or in groups as assigned by a facilitator, complete the worksheet in Exhibit 10.2, listing one or two current practices of your organization— or of organizations for which you or your members have recently worked— that strongly support the goal of diversity competency, and one or two practices that tend to work against this goal.

Task 2
When Task 1 has been completed (and if time permits), you or your team should next discuss and come to consensus on steps that could be taken to (1) further leverage the facilitators of diversity competency in the organization and (2) overcome or diminish the barriers to diversity competency that were identified.

Suggestions for the Use of Activity 10.7
It is important to emphasize that this activity merely gets one started on the process of doing a full assessment of the human resources system. One of the failures in this area of change is that the alignment of systems is fragmented, with some policies and practices supporting the strategic goals and others not. A half-baked approach to analyzing systems can contribute to this kind of fragmentation.

EXHIBIT 10.2. Worksheet on Systems Alignment

System Area	Supports Managing Diversity Competency	Hinders Managing Diversity Competency
Recruiting		
Orientation		
Promotion		
Performance Appraisal		
Compensation and Benefits		
Training and Development		

Most groups will not have difficulty identifying one or two items for each cell of Exhibit 10.2. Scholarship programs targeting women for careers in manufacturing and engineering are supportive in recruiting; all-male college recruiting teams represent misalignment. The inclusion of diversity competency in performance appraisal forms helps alignment; the absence of specific measures of competency is a barrier. The use of orientation films that feature people of different identity groups is a plus; failure to have a substantive treatment of diversity issues in the content of orientation is a minus, and so on.

In terms of leveraging current facilitators, this often can be as simple as extending a practice (such as including content on diversity issues in training interviewers) to cover more people. In terms of overcoming barriers, practices or policies often can be modified, but sometimes they need to be eliminated.

Follow-Up

The diversity competency model for organizations in Figure 1.3 gave thirteen conditions that must be present in the organization in order for diversity competency to be fully supported. It takes time for all of these conditions to be put into place, and achieving them is certainly a matter for extensive follow-up activity on plans. In view of this, we believe that the thirteen conditions specified for organizational diversity competency also define what it means to institutionalize the change process for managing diversity. When they are in place, diversity competency has become a way of life, ingrained in the way that the organization is run.

Activity 10.8 will help you to assess where your organization stands on its follow-up to institutionalize the change process.

● ● ●

Activity 10.8
INSTITUTIONALIZING DIVERSITY COMPETENCY

Objective
1. To assess the status of your organization on follow-up in the change process and its progress toward institutionalizing the changes necessary for organizational diversity competency

Procedure
Using the worksheet provided in Exhibit 10.3, do an analysis of your organization on the thirteen requirements of organizational diversity competency. The following three steps are required:

1. Indicate whether or not each of the thirteen conditions shown in the exhibit are currently in place.

2. For each item that was indicated as not being in place during step 1, identify the first one or two actions that must be taken in order to move your organization in the direction of achieving that condition.

3. For each action specified in step 2, indicate the people who are or should be assigned the responsibility to make this action happen.

Suggestions for the Use of Activity 10.8
If this activity is done in a group, the facilitator may ask for teams to share one or two of their best ideas for action steps on each work activity area shown in Exhibit 10.3. A full discussion of ideas that might be given to help participants complete and use Exhibit 10.3 is well beyond the scope of this book. This is a place where some external expertise may prove quite useful. Two general points that a facilitator may wish to cover are: (1) setting priorities and (2) the quality test.

1. *Setting priorities.* If this activity is done honestly, the action plan created will require not months but years to complete. It will therefore be necessary to prioritize the steps. This is best done by reference to internal data on the critical diversity issues for a particular organization. For example, creating

EXHIBIT 10.3. Institutionalizing Diversity Competency

Area of Work Activity	Present Now		Steps to Make This Happen	Person Responsible
	Yes	No		
1. Managing diversity is integrated into the organization's strategic planning process.				
2. The value of diversity as an organizational resource is included in statements of mission, values, or vision.				
3. The organization is seeded with strong change agents committed to working on managing diversity.				
4. Formal plan for measuring success.				
5. Well-accepted plan for achieving or maintaining demographic diversity (a combination of gender, racioethnicity and nationality that is appropriate to the firm).				
6. Diversity competency is a criterion in hiring decisions.				
7. Diversity competency is addressed in new-hire orientation.				
8. All employees receive diversity-awareness training.				

EXHIBIT 10.3. Institutionalizing Diversity Competency, cont'd.

Area of Work Activity	Present Now		Steps to Make This Happen	Person Responsible
	Yes	No		
9. There is a process for ongoing education on diversity issues includ-ing a wide range of training courses.				
10. Diversity competency is a key factor in promotion decisions.				
11. Diversity competency is a key factor in succes-sion planning (defining pools and specifying development plans).				
12. Diversity competency is a key factor in perfor-mance appraisals.				
13. Diversity competency is linked to compensation.				

SOURCE: This material is taken from documents used in the consulting firm of Taylor Cox and Associates, Inc.

a more diverse demographic profile will generally be more important for U.S. firms than for Canadian firms.

2. *The quality test.* In addition to a yes/no checkoff, attention should also be given to the quality of the steps taken. For example, many firms have now included diversity in some fashion in performance appraisal forms, but this does not always signify that solid measurements have been developed for this appraisal factor or that performance on this item is heavily weighted in forming overall performance ratings.

11

The Continuing
Quest for Excellence

We have three objectives for this concluding chapter. First, we want to summarize our view of the main contributions of the book in terms of the subject of diversity competency. Second, we will offer some activities designed to assist you in planning to continue the learning process beyond the book. Finally, we will make some brief comments about our view of the future of work on managing diversity.

SUMMARY OF MAJOR CONTRIBUTIONS

In this book we have given our perspective on developing competency to manage diversity. We have analyzed diversity competency on two levels, individual competency and organizational competency. The conceptual framework for the book has three main components. First, we have defined competency to manage diversity not as acquiring a list of skills, but rather as an ongoing learning process in which individuals and organizations progress through the three phases of awareness, understanding, and action. Competency is achieved when a person or organization has successfully worked through these three phases with regard to the broad spectrum of everyday tasks and responsibilities that are carried out in doing organizational work. This conception of competency was given more specificity by the presentation of two diversity competency models, one for the individual level of analysis and one for the organizational level of analysis. These models, which appeared in Figures 1.2 and 1.3, form the second main component of the conceptual framework of the book.

The third piece to the framework is the model for understanding how diversity affects organizational performance, which was presented in Chapter Three. This model summarizes the intellectual underpinnings of our approach to diversity in organizations and is taken directly from Taylor Cox's book, *Cultural Diversity in Organizations* (Cox, 1993).

The conceptual framework, consisting of the three components just described, is our effort to provide some intellectual foundations for developing diversity competency, and we hope it will be an important contribution to the practice of management in this arena. In order to clarify, reinforce, and illustrate our concept of diversity competency, the material in the book has been organized around the three-step learning process, with many activities that involve direct utilization of the diversity competency models. We hope that this organizing principle has given some coherence to our approach.

Another intended contribution of the book was to provide a broad scope of vehicles for learning in terms of both types of vehicles (readings, cases, and activities) and the dimensions of diversity addressed. Despite this goal, we know that some subjects did not receive the depth of treatment that they deserve. This recognition of the limitations of the book reminds us to repeat a point made in the Preface, that we view this work as ongoing and expect to build on and improve this beginning effort in the future.

TOWARD A FUTURE OF CONTINUOUS LEARNING

Having worked through the material in the book, you may now be wondering, "Where do I go from here?" As a partial answer to that question, we will suggest some final learning activities that are geared toward continuing the learning and development process for building diversity competency.

Activity 11.1
"ME" AS THE AGENT OF CHANGE

In this day of empowerment, delayering, and reengineering, it is increasingly valid to focus attention on the accountability of each member of the organization to make organizational change happen. All too often, we dismiss or shirk our personal responsibility for change by pointing to real or imagined organizational barriers to change. The importance of organizational support for change, and the need for top management to lead the effort, cannot be denied. At the same time, we believe that every individual can and should be an agent for positive change and that the most successful organizational change efforts will have dozens, if not hundreds, of strong champions for change distributed throughout the organization. In recognition of this, Activities 11.1 and 11.2 are suggested as tools for creating a plan for continued learning and contribution in the area of managing diversity. Because these two activities are closely linked, our suggestions for using them are combined and presented at the end of Activity 11.2.

Objective

1. To challenge yourself to make a personal commitment to be accountable for change in your organization in connection with the effort to achieve or enhance diversity competency

Procedure

Answer the following two questions as honestly as you can. This is not to be shared unless it is done voluntarily. The most important person to know this information right now is you.

1. When it comes to managing diversity, am I willing to be accountable for promoting the process of change in my organization?

(yes _____ no _____ not sure _____)

2. Why did I answer as I did? If I answered "not sure," what is the basis of my uncertainty? If my answer was "yes," what does this mean in behavioral terms for me right now?

Activity 11.2
CREATING A PERSONAL DEVELOPMENT PLAN FOR CONTINUED LEARNING

Objective
1. To help you to create a personal development plan for continued learning toward diversity competency

Procedure
1. Think about various actions that you could personally take to improve your own competency for managing diversity.

2. Choose three or four specific developmental actions that you are willing to implement within the next year.

3. Break down the items listed in step 2 into actions that can be taken:
   a. Within the next thirty days
   b. Within the next ninety days
   c. Within the next twelve months

4. Use the following questions to help clarify and solidify your commitment to a specific plan of development:
   a. Why did I select these steps?
   b. How will I measure my performance?
   c. What assistance or support from others (or my employer) will I need?
   d. What obstacles may hinder me from fulfilling the plan (personal, interpersonal, organizational, or societal)?
   e. How will I benefit from completing the plan? How will my employer benefit?

Suggestions for the Use of Activities 11.1 and 11.2
Although there is some overlap in these two activities, they ask for different results and we suggest that you do them both. Honest answers to Activity 11.1 from everyone in the work unit will go a long way toward assessing the probability for success of a change effort on diversity in your organization.

The reasons for uncertainty or reluctance to accept personal responsibility for change are numerous: a fear of the unknown, the full-plate problem, doubts about the ability to really measure results, and so on. Getting these doubts out on the table will help to either move the change process forward or make an enlightened decision that the effort should be abandoned or postponed. A poorly done change effort is worse than none at all.

Activity 11.2 should result in an actual development plan for the next twelve months. Of course, this should be determined in agreement with your supervisors and, if appropriate, it should be made a part of the regular individual development process done annually in your organization.

The ideas for personal development shown in Exhibit 11.1 should be discussed following Activity 11.2 (we suggest that they not be discussed before doing the activity). You may want to incorporate some of the specific ideas in Exhibit 11.1 into your development plan.

PLANNING THE NEXT STEPS FOR ORGANIZATIONAL DEVELOPMENT

The previous two activities focused on the individual level of development. We now want to shift attention to the organizational level. Activity 11.3 is not intended to replace any of the plans that you may have already created by using the activities in the earlier chapters; however, we want to focus more on the steps to be taken in the immediate future to move your organization forward in the change process.

EXHIBIT 11.1. Creating Competency for Managing Diversity: A Career Development Approach

Ideas for Individual Development Plans

Development Objective: Enhance Competency
for Working in and Supervising Diverse Work Groups

Planned Activities for the Year _____

Individual Responsibility	*Organizational Responsibility*
1. Attend awareness training	1. Provide awareness training
2. Volunteer as an in-house trainer	2. Provide opportunities for in-house trainers
3. Community work with organizations of a predominantly different identity	3. Create interorganizational relationships with organizations with different dominant identity groups
4. Participate in off-site dialogue meetings on diversity	4. Provide partial or full support for off-site dialogue meetings on diversity
5. Participate in on-site dialogue-group discussions	5. Provide partial or full support for on-site dialogue groups
6. Read _____ number of books or articles on diversity	6. Provide a library or reading list on diversity
7. Actively support and participate in cultural diversity celebration events	7. Sponsor cultural diversity celebration days or events.
8. Develop a mentoring relationship with someone from a different identity group	8. Sponsor events to facilitate mentor-protégé matchups or (if internal research warrants it) create a targeted mentoring plan
9. Volunteer for an overseas assignment	9. Provide opportunities for overseas assignments
10. Travel to countries with different cultures	10. Sponsor travel or allow time off for travel as career development

EXHIBIT 11.1. Creating Competency for Managing Diversity: A Career Development Approach, cont'd.

Individual Responsibility	*Organizational Responsibility*
11. Invite at least one person (of difference) to lunch each month	11. Sponsor a culturally diverse set of events to bring employees together socially
12. Volunteer to serve on a diversity task force or planning committee	12. Create one or more diversity task forces or planning committees and provide them access to the CEO
13. Enroll in college courses on diversity	13. Provide tuition support for formal college study of diversity
14. Volunteer for community outreach activities related to diversity education	14. Provide logistical support for educational activities on diversity which target the community
15. Attend a national conference on managing diversity	15. Provide financial support for a limited number of line managers to attend national conferences on diversity
16. Organize an annual diversity roundtable for your organization	16. Provide logistical support for a diversity roundtable
17. Integrate diversity issues as an ongoing topic in staff meetings at the work-unit level	17. Integrate cultural diversity issues as a topic in regular staff meetings at the executive council level
18. Author or coauthor an article or case study on a diversity-related topic	18. Provide logistical support and publicity for authors of articles on diversity
19. Learn a new language	19. Provide tuition or fee reimbursement for language courses
20. Pursue a job assignment in a work unit with a substantially different demographic profile or a job involving managing-diversity duties	20. Support the employee in obtaining the requested job assignment

Activity 11.3
TAKING THE NEXT STEPS

Objective
1. To determine the next steps to be taken by your organization toward creating organizational diversity competency

Procedure
Working alone or in groups as assigned by a facilitator, address the following tasks:

1. Reflecting back on what you have learned about what it takes to achieve organizational diversity competency, write a statement that summarizes where you believe your organization is now in the process.

2. Identify one to three next steps that should be taken during the next six months to move the change process forward.

3. In order to help clarify and solidify your plans, respond to the following questions:
   a. What specific tasks are involved in these steps and who will perform each of them?
   b. How will our effectiveness or achievement of the steps be measured?
   c. What resources exist inside the organization that can assist with these tasks (people, policies, technology, and so on)?
   d. What obstacles may get in the way? How can they be avoided or overcome?
   e. Will external assistance be required for any of the next steps?

Suggestions for the Use of Activity 11.3
This activity is the organization-level corollary to Activity 11.2. If it is desired, the same time-line breakdown can be applied for this activity as was used for Activity 11.2, but we have omitted it here because we want to focus on the very next thing to be done rather than on creating a one-year development plan. Clearly it is a good idea to do both.

The idea behind this activity is to answer the question: Given where we are now and where we need to go, what is the most important thing for us to be doing as an organization in the next few months? Possible answers include: developing an awareness training plan, conducting an assessment of the culture of the organization, getting an initial reading on the content and intensity of the diversity-related issues from the point of view of the employees, creating a measurement plan, and making explicit the business rationale for managing diversity to further clarify the relevance of this work to the business strategy.

Given the work that was done in the earlier portions of the book, this activity could also be approached by deciding which of the various action steps previously discussed should be set as priorities for the next three to six months.

THE FUTURE OF WORK ON DIVERSITY

In these final paragraphs, we would like to comment briefly on our thoughts about the future of organizational change in the area of managing diversity. After a decade of intense activity, we see work on managing diversity as undergoing a transition. It is no longer the latest buzzword in corporations; instead, we are now entering the life stage in which managing diversity will either become a part of the ongoing work of organizations seeking to improve performance results or die on the vine as one more halfhearted, poorly understood, and relatively unsuccessful organizational transformation effort. For our part, because of the number of organizational leaders we see, in both the private and public sectors of the U.S. economy and around the world, who understand the full spectrum of legal, moral, and organizational performance motivations for continuing the work, we are cautiously optimistic that the work will continue at a high level of attention in the future.

As we continue this important work, several things strike us as particularly important. First, it is critical for managers to understand that continuing the work on managing diversity is aided by, but does not depend upon, the legal structure that surrounds affirmative action programs in the United States. The future of the legal basis for affirmative action in the United States is an important issue in its own right, but, as an accurate understanding of the content of this book makes clear, organizations will need to manage diversity regardless of what happens to these laws.

Second, we see a trend toward more integration of work on diversity with other strategic processes in organizations such as strategic planning, total quality, high-performance work teams, and organizational learning. If it is done with integrity, this integration should make the work stronger and give it longer life than if it does not occur.

Third, the "director of diversity" position will probably begin to disappear in the future, a step that has already taken place in some companies, like Eli Lilly. This development will also be positive if, and this is a big if, true accountability is established among line managers and employees for performance results on managing diversity, and the change process for diversity competency is institutionalized in the organization.

Fourth, while the need for external expertise in this area will continue for some time, organizations are increasingly developing in-house expertise on managing diversity; consequently, consulting partnerships on diversity involving one or more external people with internal experts should become stronger in the next five years.

Another prediction is that work on racioethnicity and nationality will increase in the United States while work on gender will take center stage in Europe and Japan. This prediction is based largely on worldwide labor-force demographics. The participation of women in the workforce is nearing a plateau in the United States (nearly 50 percent of the total workforce and around 33 percent of management), while many of the other highly industrialized nations are much further behind in their utilization of women, especially in managerial and professional jobs. At the same time, tensions and conflict based on racioethnic and nationality differences continue to grow in the United States in general, and these tensions will inevitably be enacted to some degree in the workplace.

Finally, we think that much more attention will be paid to education and other forms of intervention in schools in the future than has occurred to date. We certainly hope that this will be the case. Questions remain, however, as to whether change processes that have been successfully used in business firms can be transferred for use in schools. How, for example, does one achieve a mandate for broad-scale cultural change in a university engineering or business school? More attention to change related to diversity must also take place at the primary and secondary levels of education.

These are just a few of the many areas that will require our diligent attention if diversity competency is to become widespread in the world. We hope that this book has made some contribution toward that goal.

References

Abrams, D., & Hogg, M. A. (1990). *Social identity theory.* New York: Springer-Verlag.

Adler, N. J. (1983). Cross-cultural management research: The ostrich and the trend. *Academy of Management Review, 8,* 226–232.

Adler, N. (1986). *International dimensions of organization behavior.* Boston: Kent Publishing.

Akridge, R. (1985). Rehabilitation, career development and self-awareness. *Journal of Rehabilitation, 51,* 24–30.

Alderfer, C. P., & Smith, K. K. (1982). Studying intergroup relations embedded in organizations. *Administrative Science Quarterly, 27*(1), 35–65.

Allport, G. W. (1958). *The nature of prejudice.* Reading, MA: Addison-Wesley.

American Society for Training and Development. (1986, September). *Design productive mentoring programs.* Info-Line Publication Issue 609. Alexandria, VA: Author.

Antal, A. B., & Kresbach-Gnath, C. (1987). Women in management: Unused resources in the Federal Republic of Germany. *International Studies of Management and Organization, 16,* 133–151.

Asante, M. K., & Asante, K. W. (Eds.). (1985). *African culture.* Westport, CT: Greenwood Press.

Asher, J., & Asher, J. (1976, October). How to accommodate workers in wheelchairs. *Job Safety and Health,* pp. 3–35.

Ashforth, B., & Mael, F. (1989). Social identity theory and the organization. *Academy of Management Review, 14*(1), 20–39.

Bandura, A. (1969). *Principles of behavior modification.* New York: Holt, Rinehart & Winston.

Bandura, A., Ross, D., & Ross. S. A. (1963). Vicarious reinforcement and initiative learning. *Journal of Abnormal and Social Psychology, 67,* 601–607.

Barker, R. G., & Wright, B. (1954). Disablement: The somatopsychological problem. In E. Wittkower & R. Cleghorn (Eds.), *Recent developments in psychosomatic medicine* (pp. 419–435). Philadelphia: Lippincott.

Barnett, J. (1994). *Understanding group effects within organizations: A study of group attitudes and behaviors of engineers and scientists.* Doctoral dissertation, The Fielding Institute, Santa Barbara, CA.

Barrera, M., & Ainlay, S. L. (1983). The structure of social support: A conceptual and empirical analysis. *Journal of Community Psychology, 11,* 133–143.

Bartlett, C. A., & Ghosal, S. (1987). Managing across borders: New strategic requirements. *Sloan Management Review, 28,* 7–17.

Bell, E. L. (1990). The bicultural life experience of career-oriented Black women. *Journal of Organizational Behavior, 11,* 459–477.

Berkeley Planning Associates. (1982). *Study of accommodations provided by federal contractors.* Washington, DC: U.S. Department of Labor, Employment Standards Administration.

Berkowitz, E. (1984). Professionals as providers: Some thoughts on disability and ideology. *Rehabilitation Psychology, 29,* 211–216.

Berry, J. W. (1980). Social and cultural change. In H. C. Triandis & R. W. Brislin (Eds.), *Handbook of cross-cultural psychology* (pp. 211–279). Boston: Allyn & Bacon.

Berry, J. W. (1983). Acculturation: A comparative analysis of alternative forms. In J. Samunda & S. L. Woods (Eds.), *Perspectives in immigrant and minority education* (pp. 66–77). Lanham, MD: University Press of America.

Berry, J. W. (1984). Cultural relations in plural society: Alternatives to segregation and their sociopsychological implications. In N. Miller & M. Brewer (Eds.), *Groups in contact.* New York: Academic Press.

Biernacki, P. (1986). *Pathways from heroin addiction: Recovery without treatment.* Philadelphia: Temple University Press.

Birkman & Associates. (1988). *Relational management system.* Houston: Author.

Birkman & Associates. (1991). *Self study guide: An introduction to the Birkman Method.* Houston: Author.

Black, J. S., Gregersen, H. B., & Mendenhall, M. E. (1992). Toward a theoretical framework of repatriation adjustment. *Journal of International Business Studies, 23,* 737–760.

Black, J. S., Mendenhall, M. E., & Oddou, G. (1991). Toward a comprehensive model of international adjustment: An integration of multiple theoretical perspectives. *Academy of Management Review, 16,* 291–317.

Blumenfeld, W. J. (1992). *Homophobia: How we all pay the price.* Boston: Beacon Press.

Bowe, F. (1983). *Demography and disability: A chartbook for rehabilitation.* Fayetteville, AR: Arkansas Rehabilitation Research and Training Center, University of Arkansas.

Boyacigiller, N. (1995). The international assignment reconsidered. In M. Mendenhall & G. Oddou (Eds.), *Readings and cases in international human resource management* (pp. 149–157). Cincinnati: South-Western College Publishing.

Breton, R., Burnet, J., Hartmann, N., Isajiw, W., & Lennards, J. (1975). Research issues on Canadian cultures and ethnic groups: An analysis of a conference. *Canadian Review of Sociology and Anthropology, 12,* 81–94.

Brewer, M. B. (1995). Managing diversity: The role of social identities. In S. Jackson & M. Ruderman (Eds.), *Diversity in work teams* (pp. 47–68). Washington, DC: American Psychological Assocation.

Buono, A. F., & Bowditch, J. L. (1989). *The human side of mergers and acquisitions: Managing collisions between people, cultures, and organizations* (1st ed.). San Francisco: Jossey-Bass.

Campbell, J. (1985). Approaching affirmative action as human resource development. In H. McCarthy (Ed.), *Complete guide to employing persons with disabilities* (pp. 14–30). Albertson, NY: Human Resources Center.

Carnevale, A. P., & Gainer, L. J. (1989). *The learning enterprise.* Washington, DC: U.S. Department of Labor.

Cattan, P. (1988). The growing presence of Hispanics in the U.S. workforce. *Monthly Labor Review, 111*(8), 9–14.

Center for Public Resources. (1982). *Basic skills in the U.S. work force: The contrasting perceptions of business, labor, and public education.* New York: Author.

Chatman, J. (1989). Improving interactional organizational research: A model of person-organization fit. *Academy of Management Review, 14*(3), 333–349.

Chen, C. C., & DiTomaso, N. (1996). Performance appraisal and demographic diversity: Issues regarding appraisals, appraisers, and appraising. In E. E. Kossek & S. A. Lobel (Eds.), *Managing diversity: Human resource strategies for transforming the workplace.* Cambridge, MA: Blackwell Business.

Clawson, R., & Kram, K. (1984, May–June). Managing cross-gender mentoring. *Business Horizons, 27*(3), 22–32.

Colbert III, C. R., & Wofford, J. G. (1993, Summer). Sexual orientation in the workplace: The strategic challenge. *Compensation and Benefits Management,* pp. 1–18.

Collins, N. W. (1983). *Professional women and their managers.* Englewood Cliffs, NJ: Prentice Hall.

Collins, S. M. (1989). The marginalization of Black executives. *Social Problems, 36*(4), 317–331.

Conte, L. (1982). Manpower policy and the disabled person: An international perspective. *Rehabilitation Literature, 43,* 130–135.

Copeland, L. (1988, June). Valuing workplace diversity. *Personnel,* pp. 52–60.

Cox, T. H., Jr. (1991). The multicultural organization. *The Executive, 5*(2), 34–47.

Cox, T. H., Jr. (1993). *Cultural diversity in organizations: Theory, research and practice.* San Francisco: Berrett-Koehler.

Cox, T. H., Jr., & Blake, S. (1991). Managing cultural diversity: Implications for organizational competitiveness. *The Executive, 5*(3), 45–56.

Cox, T., Jr., & Finley, J. (1995). An analysis of work specialization and organization level as dimensions of workforce diversity. In M. Chemers, S. Oskamp, & M. Costanzo (Eds.), *Diversity in organizations* (pp. 62–90). Newbury Park, CA: Sage.

Cox, T., Jr., & Finley-Nickelson, J. (1991). Models of acculturation for intra-organizational cultural diversity. *Canadian Journal of Administrative Sciences, 8*(2), 90–100.

Cox, T. H., Jr., & Nkomo, S. M. (1990). Invisible men and women: A status report on race as a variable in organizational behavior and research. *Journal of Organizational Behavior, 11,* 419–431.

Cox, T. H., Jr., & Nkomo, S. M. (1992). Candidate age as a factor in promotability ratings. *Public Personnel Management, 21*(2), 197–210.

Crewe, N. M., & Zola, I. K. (Eds.). (1983). *Independent living for physically disabled people.* San Francisco: Jossey-Bass.

Daniels, S. (1985). Attitudinal influences on affirmative action implementation. In H. McCarthy (Ed.), *Complete guide to employing persons with disabilities* (pp. 31–47). Albertson, NY: Human Resources Center.

Davis, J., & Rodela, E. S. (1992). Mentoring for the Hispanic: Mapping emotional support. In S. Knouse, P. Rosenfeld, & A. Culbertson, *Hispanics in the workplace* (pp. 137–150). Newbury Park, CA: Sage.

De Anda, D. (1984). Bicultural socialization: Factors affecting the minority experience. *Social Work, 39*(1), 101–107.

Denison, D. R. (1984). Bringing corporate culture to the bottom line. *Organizational Dynamics, 13*(2), 5–22.

Denison, D. R. (1989). *Corporate culture and organizational effectiveness* (Working Paper). Ann Arbor: University of Michigan.

Domino, G., & Acosta, A. (1987). The relation of acculturation and values in Mexican Americans. *Hispanic Journal of Behavioral Sciences, 9,* 131–150.

Domm, D. R., & Stafford, J. E. (1972). Assimilating Blacks into the organization. *California Management Review, 25,* 46–51.

Dunn, R. A. (1981). *Management science: A practical approach to decision-making.* New York: Macmillan.

Dunphy, D. (1987). Convergence/divergence: A temporal review of the Japanese enterprise. *Academy of Management Review, 12,* 445–459.

Eckstrom, R. B., French, J. W., & Harmon, H. H. (1979). Cognitive factors: Their identification and replication. *Multivariate Behavioral Research Monographs, 72,* 3–84.

Eisenberg, M., Griggins, C., & Duval, R. (Eds.). (1982). *Disabled people as second-class citizens.* New York: Springer.

Eisenberger, P., Fasolo, P., & Davis-LaMastro, V. (1990). Perceived organizational support and employee diligence, commitment, and innovation. *Journal of Applied Psychology, 75*(1), 51–59.

Ellien, V., & Vandergood, D. (1985). *A supported work approach: Employer-based rehabilitation facilities services.* Washington, DC: National Association for Rehabilitation Facilities.

Epstein, C. F. (1988). *Deceptive distinctions: Sex, gender and the social order.* New York: Yale University Press; New Haven and London: Russell Sage Foundation.

Fagenson, E. A. (1988). The power of a mentor: Protégés' and non-protégés' perceptions of their own power in organizations. *Group and Organizational Studies, 13,* 182–194.

Fagenson, E. A. (1993). Is what's good for the goose also good for the gander? On being white and male in a diverse workforce. *Academy of Management Executive, 7*(4), 80–81.

Ferdman, B. M. (1992). The dynamics of ethnic diversity in organizations: Toward integrative models. In K. Kelley (Ed.), *Issues, theory and research in industrial/organizational psychology* (pp. 339–384). Amsterdam: North Holland.

Fernandez, J. P. (1981). *Racism and sexism in corporate life: Changing values in American business.* Lexington, MA: Lexington Books.

Finkelstein, V. (1980). *Attitudes and disabled people* (Monograph No. 5). New York: World Rehabilitation Fund.

Frideres, J. S. (1989). *Multiculturalism and intergroup relations.* New York: Greenwood Press.

Frieden, L. (1980). Independent living models. *Rehabilitation Literature, 41,* 169–173.

Frieden, L. (1984). From independent living to interdependent living: The future for people with disabilities. *American Rehabilitation, 10,* 23–26.

Fullerton, H. N. (1987, September). Labor force projections: 1986–2000. *Monthly Labor Review,* pp. 19–29.

Fullerton, H. N. (1989). New labor force projections, spanning 1988 to 2000. *Monthly Labor Review, 112*(1), 3–11.

Ghosal, S., & Bartlett, C. A. (1988). Creation, adoptions and diffusion of innovations by subsidiaries of multinational corporations. *Journal of International Business Studies,* pp. 365–388.

Glass, L. (1992). *He says, she says: Closing the communication gap between the sexes.* New York: G. P. Putnam's Sons.

Gonsiorek, J., and Weinrich, J. (1991). The definition and scope of sexual orientation. In J. Gonsiorek and J. Weinrich (Eds.), *Homosexuality: Research implications
for public policy.* Newbury Park, CA: Sage.

Gray, J. (1992). *Men are from Mars, women are from Venus: A practical guide for
improving communication and getting what you want in your relationships.* New York:
HarperCollins.

Greenberg, S. B. (1985). *Report on democratic defection.* New Haven: The Analysis
Group.

Griffith, J., & Villavicencio, S. (1985). Relationships among acculturation, socio-
demographic characteristics and social supports in Mexican American adults.
Hispanic Journal of Behavioral Sciences, 105, 175–178.

Habeck, R., Galvin, D., Frey, W., Chadderdon, L., & Tate, D. (1985). *Economics and
equity in employment of people with disabilities: International policies and practices.*
East Lansing: Michigan State University Center for International Rehabilitation.

Hahn, H. (1984). *Equality and disability: European perceptions of employment policy.*
New York: Work Rehabilitation Fund.

Haire, M., Ghiselli, E. E., & Porter, L. W. (1966). *Managerial thinking: An international study.* New York: Wiley.

Hammer, M., & Stanton, S. (1995). *The reengineering revolution: A handbook.* New
York: HarperCollins.

Hampton, D. R., Summer, C. E., & Webber, R. A. (1987). *Organizational behavior
and the practice of management* (5th ed.). Glenview, IL: Scott, Foresman.

Harris, L., & Associates. (1986). *The ICD survey of disabled Americans: Bringing
disabled Americans into the mainstream.* New York: Author.

Haugen, S. E., & Meisenheimer, J. R. (1991). U. S. labor market weakened in 1990.
Monthly Labor Review, 114(2), 3–16.

Hazuda, H., Stern, M., & Haffner, S. M. (1988). Acculturation and assimilation
among Mexican-Americans: Scales and population-based data. *Social Science
Quarterly, 69*(3), 687–706.

Helgesen, S. (1990). *The female advantage: Women's ways of leadership.* New York:
Doubleday.

Henderson, J. C., & Nutt, P. C. (1980). The influence of decision style on decision
making behavior. *Management Science, 26,* 371–386.

Hofstede, G. (1979). Value systems in forty countries: Interpretation, validation,
and consequences for theory. In L. H. Eckensberger, W. J. Lonner, & Y. H.
Poortinga (Eds.), *Cross-cultural contributions to psychology* (pp. 398–407). Lisse,
Netherlands: Swets & Zeitlinger.

Hofstede, G. (1980). *Culture's consequences: International differences in work-related
values.* Newbury Park, CA, and London: Sage.

Hofstede, G. (1983). Dimensions of national cultures in fifty countries and three regions. In J. B. Deregowski, S. Dziurawiec, & R. C. Annis (Eds.), *Expiscations in cross-cultural psychology* (pp. 335–355). Lisse, Netherlands: Swets & Zeitlinger, 1983.

Hofstede, G. (1984). The cultural relativity of the quality of life concept. *Academy of Management Review, 9*(3), 389–398.

Holloway, F. A. (1989). What is affirmative action? In F. Blanchard & F. J. Crosby (Eds.), *Affirmative action in perspective* (pp. 9–19). New York: Springer-Verlag.

Hosmer, L. (1995). Affirmative action in Birmingham, Alabama, Case. In L. Hosmer, *Moral leadership in business* (pp. 178–189). Burr Ridge, IL: Irwin.

House, J. S. (1983). *Work stress and social support.* Reading, MA: Addison-Wesley.

Janus, S., & Janus, C. (1993). *The Janus report on sexual behavior* (pp. 69–71). New York: Wiley.

Jencks, C. (1985, May 9). How poor are the poor? *New York Review of Books,* pp. 41–49.

Johnson, S. D. (1980). Reverse discrimination and aggressive behavior. *Journal of Psychology, 104,* 11–19.

Johnston, W. B., & Packer, A. H. (1987). *Workforce 2000: Work and workers for the twenty-first century.* Indianapolis, IN: Hudson Institute; Washington, DC: U.S. Department of Labor.

Jones, E. (1986). Black managers: The dream deferred. *Harvard Business Review, 64,* 84–93.

Jung, C. G. (1923). *Psychological types or the psychology of individuation.* London: K. Paul, Trench, Trubner; Orlando, FL: Harcourt Brace Jovanovich.

Kallen, H. M. (1924). *Culture and democracy in the United States.* New York: Boni & Liveright.

Kanter, R. M. (1977). *Men and women of the corporation.* New York: Basic Books.

Kanter, R. M. (1983). *The change masters.* New York: Simon & Schuster.

Kanungo, R. N. (1982). *Work alienation and the quality of work life: A cross-cultural perspective.* Paper presented at the 20th International Congress of Applied Psychology, Edinburgh, Scotland.

Kiefer, C. (1974). *Changing cultures, changing lives.* San Francisco: Jossey-Bass.

Kizilos, P. (1990). Take my mentor, please. *Training, 27*(4), 49–55.

Klein, G. D. (1980). Beyond EEO and affirmative action. *California Management Review, 22*(4), 74–81.

Kluegel, J. R., & Smith, E. R. (1986). *Beliefs about inequality: Americans' views of what is and what ought to be.* Hawthorne, NY: Aldine-de-Gruyer.

Kobrin, S. J. (1988). Expatriate reduction and strategic control in American multi-national corporations. *Human Resource Management, 27,* 63–75.

Kochman, T. (1981). *Black and white: Styles in conflict.* Chicago: University of Chicago Press.

Kram, K. (1983). Phases in the mentor relationship. *Academy of Management Journal, 26,* 608–625.

Kram, K. (1985a). *Mentoring at work.* Glenview, IL: Scott, Foresman.

Kram, K. E. (1985b). Improving the mentoring process. *Training and Development Journal, 39*(4), 40–43.

Kram, K., & Hall, D. T. (1996). Mentoring in a context of diversity and turbulence. In E. E. Kossek & S. A. Lobel (Eds.), *Managing diversity: Human resource strategies for transforming the workplace* (pp. 108–136). Cambridge, MA: Blackwell Business.

Kram, K., & Isabella, L. (1985). Mentoring alternatives: The role of peer relationships in career development. *Academy of Management Journal, 28,* 110–132.

Lambert, W. E., & Taylor, D. M. (1988). Assimilation versus multiculturalism: The views of urban Americans. *Sociological Forum, 3,* 72–88.

Leonard, J. (1984a). The impact of affirmative action on employment (Working Paper No. 1310). Washington, DC: Bureau of Economic Research.

Leonard, J. (1984b). What promises are worth: The impact of affirmative action goals. (Working Paper No. 1346). Washington, DC: National Bureau of Economic Research.

Likert, R. (1967). *The human organization, its management and value.* New York: McGraw-Hill.

Loden, M., & Rosener, J. B. (1991). *Workforce America! Managing employee diversity as a vital resource.* Homewood, IL: Business One Irwin.

Lynch, F. R. (1991). *Invisible victims: White males and the crisis of affirmative action.* New York: Praeger.

Malekzadeh, A., & Nahavandi, A. (1990). Making mergers work by managing cultures. *Journal of Business Strategy, 11,* 55–57.

Mank, D., Rhodes, L., & Bellamy, T. (1985). Four supported employment alternatives. In W. Kiernan & J. Stark (Eds.), *Pathways to employment for developmentally disabled adults.* Baltimore: Paul H. Brookes.

Maslow, A. H. (1954). *Motivation and personality.* New York: HarperCollins.

Massey, D. S., & Denton, N. A. (1988). Suburbanization and segregation in U.S. metropolitan areas. *American Journal of Sociology, 94,* 592–626.

Massey, D. S., & Mullan, B. P. (1984). Processes of Hispanic and Black spatial assimilation. *American Journal of Sociology, 89*(4), 836–872.

May, L., & Houston, P. (1985, July 22). Affirmative action finally wins grudging acceptance. *Los Angeles Times.*

McCarthy, H. (1986). Corporate social responsibility and services to people with disabilities. *Journal of Rehabilitation Administration, 10,* 60–67.

McCarthy, H. (1988). Attitudes that affect employment opportunities for persons with disabilities. In H. E. Yucker (Ed.), *Attitudes toward persons with disabilities* (pp. 246–261). New York: Springer.

McLeod, K. A. (1979). *Multiculturalism, bilingualism and Canadian institutions.* Toronto: Guidance Centre, University of Toronto.

McLeod, P. L., Lobel, S. A., & Cox, T., Jr. (1996). Ethnic diversity and creativity in small groups. *Small Group Research, 27*(2), 248–264.

Mefferd, R. B. (1975). *The Birkman Method: Reliabilities and validities for business and industry.* Houston: Birkman-Mefferd Research Foundation.

Mendenhall, M. E., Dunbar, E., & Oddou, G. R. (1987). Expatriate selection, training and career pathing: A review and critique. *Human Resource Management, 26,* 331–345.

Mischel, W. (1977). The interaction of person and situation. In D. Magnussen & N. S. Endler (Eds.), *Personality at the crossroads* (pp. 333–352). Hillsdale, NJ: Erlbaum.

Mitroff, I., & Kilman, R. (1984). *Corporate tragedies: Product tampering, sabotage and other catastrophes.* New York: Praeger.

Morrow, P. C. (1983). Concept redundancy in organizational research: The case of work commitment. *Academy of Management Review, 8,* 486–500.

Mulkowsky, G. P., & Freeman, M. J. (1979). The impact of managerial orientation on implementing decisions. *Human Resource Management, 18,* 6–14.

Nahavandi, A., & Malekzadeh, A. (1988). Acculturation in mergers and acquisitions. *Academy of Management Review, 13*(1), 79–90.

Navin, S., & Myers, J. (1983). A model of career development for disabled adults. *Journal of Applied Rehabilitation Counseling, 14,* 38–43.

Nemeth, C. J. (1985). Dissent, group process, and creativity. *Advances in Group Processes, 2,* 57–75.

Nkomo, S. M. (1992). The emperor has no clothes: Rewriting race in organizations. *Academy of Management Review, 17,* 487–513.

Noe, R. A. (1988). An investigation of the determinants of successful assigned mentoring relationships. *Personnel Psychology, 41,* 457–479.

Oddou, G. R. (1991). Managing your expatriates: What the successful firms do. *Human Resource Planning, 14,* 301–308.

Olian, J. D., Carroll, S. J., Giannantonio, C. M., & Feren, D. B. (1988). What do protégés look for in a mentor? Results of three experimental studies. *Journal of Vocational Behavior, 33,* 15–37.

Olivares, F. (1987). Women in management in Italy: More than an emerging issue. *Equal Opportunities International, 6*(1), 6–10.

Padilla, A. (Ed.). (1980). *Acculturation theory, models, and some new findings.* Boulder, CO: Westview Press.

Parello, V. (1985). Strangers to these shores: *Race and ethnic relations in the United States*. New York: Wiley.

Pascale, R. (1985). The paradox of corporate culture: Reconciling ourselves in socialization. *California Management Review, 27*(2), 26–41.

Pettigrew, T. F., & Martin, J. (1987). Shaping the organizational context for Black American inclusion. *Journal of Social Forces, 43,* 41–78.

Phillips, R., & Smith, R. (1982). Improving communications between counselor and employers. *Journal of Rehabilitation, 48,* 54–56.

Prahalad, C. K. (1990). The core competence of the corporation. *Harvard Business Review, 90*(3), 79–91.

Ragins, B. R. (1989). Barriers to mentoring: The female manager's dilemma. *Human Relations, 42,* 1–22.

Ramcharan, S. (1982). *Racism: Nonwhites in Canada*. Toronto: Butterworths.

Renshaw, J. R. (1987). Women in management in the Pacific Islands: Exploring Pacific stereotypes. *International Studies of Management and Organization, 16,* 152–173.

Rice, A. K. (1969). *Learning in groups*. London: Tavistock.

Rickard, T., Triandis, H., & Patterson, C. (1963). Indices of employer prejudice toward disabled applicants. *Journal of Applied Psychology, 47,* 52–55.

Rodela, E. S. (1990). *A training model: The stressor-strain as a heuristic to promote the understanding of cross-cultural issues and the Hispanic Vietnam veteran*. San Antonio, TX: Readjustment Counseling Service, Department of Veterans Affairs.

Russell, J. S., Terborg, J. R., & Powers, M. L. (1985). Organizational performance and organizational level training and support. *Personnel Psychology, 38,* 849–863.

Rynes, S., & Rosen, B. (1995). A field survey of factors affecting the adoption and perceived success of diversity training. *Personnel Psychology, 48,* 247–270.

Sales, A. L., & Mirvis, P. H. (1984). When cultures collide: Issues of acquisition. In J. R. Kimberly & R. E. Quinn (Eds.), *Managing organizational transition* (pp. 107–133). Homewood, IL: Irwin.

Sandroff, R. (1988). Sexual harassment in the Fortune 500. *Working Woman, 13*(12), 69–73.

Schein, E. D. (1984). Organizational socialization and the profession of management. In D. A. Kolb, I. M. Rubin, & J. M. McIntyre (Eds.), *Organizational Psychology* (pp. 7–21). Englewood Cliffs, NJ: Prentice Hall.

Schein, E. H. (1990). Organizational culture. *American Psychologist, 45*(2), 109–119.

Schneider, B. (1988). *Facilitating work effectiveness*. Lexington, MA: Lexington Books.

Schneider, B., & Bowen, D. E. (1985). Employee and customer perceptions of service in banks: Relocation and extension. *Journal of Applied Psychology, 70*(3),l 423–433.

Schroedel, J., & Jacobsen, R. (1978). *Employer attitudes towards hiring persons with disability: A labor market research model.* Albertson, NY: Human Resources Center.

Schweitzer, N., & Deely, J. (1981). The awareness factor: A management skills seminar. *Journal of Rehabilitation, 47,* 45–50.

Schweitzer, N. J., & Deely, J. (1982, March). Interviewing the disabled job applicant. *Personnel Journal,* pp. 205–209.

Scull, A. (1981). Deinstitutionalization and the rights of the deviant. *Journal of Social Issues, 37,* 6–20.

Senge, P. M., Roberts, C., Ross, R. B., Smith, B. J., & Kleiner, A. (1994, July). *The fifth discipline fieldbook: Strategies and tools for building a learning organization.* New York: Doubleday.

Shapiro, G. L., & Farrow, D. L. (1988). Mentors and others in career development. In S. Rose & L. Larwood (Eds.), *Women's careers* (pp. 25–39). New York: Praeger.

Siegel, S., & Kaemmerer, W. (1978). Measuring the perceived support for innovation in organizations. *Journal of Applied Psychology, 63*(5), 553–562.

Siehl, C., Ledford, G., Silverman, R., & Fay, P. (1988). Preventing culture clashes from blotching a merger. *Mergers and Acquisitions, 22,* 51–57.

Solomon, C. M. (1994). Success abroad depends on more than just job skills. *Personnel Journal, 73,* 51–54.

Steinhoff, P. G., & Tanaka, K. (1987). Women managers in Japan. *International Studies in Management and Organization, 16,* 108–132.

Stubbins, J. (1982). *The clinical attitude in rehabilitation: A cross-cultural view.* New York: World Rehabilitation Fund.

Stubbins, J. (1984). Rehabilitation services as ideology. *Rehabilitation Psychology, 29,* 197–202.

Szasz, T. (1961). *The myth of mental illness.* New York: HarperCollins.

Tajfel, H. (Ed.). (1978). *Differentiation between social groups: Studies in the social psychology of intergroup relations.* San Diego, CA: Academic Press.

Tajfel, H., & Wilkes, A. L. (1963). Classification and quantitative judgement. *British Journal of Psychology, 54,* 101–113.

Tannen, D. (1990). *You just don't understand: Women and men in conversation.* New York: William Morrow.

Tannen, D. (1995). *Talking from 9 to 5. Women and men in the workplace: Language, sex and power.* New York: Avon.

Taylor, S., Fiske, S., Etcoff, N., & Ruderman, A. (1978). Categorical and contextual bases of person memory and stereotyping. *Journal of Personality and Social Psychology, 36*(7), 778–793.

Thomas, R. R., Jr. (1990, March–April). From affirmative action to affirming diversity. *Harvard Business Review, 68*(2), 107–117.

Triandis, H. C. (1976). The future of pluralism revisited. *Journal of Social Issues, 32,* 179–208.

Triandis, H. C. (1995). A theoretical framework for the study of diversity. In M. Chemers, S. Oskamp, & M. Costanzo (Eds.), *Diversity in organizations* (pp. 11–36). Newbury Park, CA: Sage.

Triandis, H. C., Hall, E. R., & Ewen, R. B. (1965). Member heterogeneity and dyadic creativity. *Human Relations, 18,* 33–55.

Trice, H. M., & Beyer, J. M. (1993). *The cultures of work organizations.* Englewood Cliffs, NJ: Prentice Hall.

Tsui, A., Egan, T., & O'Reilly III, C. (1992). Being different: Relational demography and organizational attachment. *Administrative Science Quarterly, 37,* 549–579.

Tung, R. L. (1987). Expatriate assignments: Enhancing success and minimizing failure. *Academy of Management Executive, 1,* 117–125.

Turner, J. C., & Giles, H. (Eds.). (1981). *Intergroup behavior.* Oxford: Blackwell.

U.S. Commission on Civil Rights. (1983). *Accommodating the spectrum of individual abilities.* Washington, DC: Author.

Valentine, C. A. (1971, May). Deficit, difference, and bicultural models of Afro-American behavior. *Harvard Educational Review, 41,* 137–157.

Van Maanen, J., & Barley, S. R. (1984). Occupational communities: Culture and control in organizations. *Research in Organizational Behavior, 6,* 287–365.

Vander Zanden, J. (1980). *American minority relations* (4th ed.). New York: Knopf.

Vandergood, D., Jacobsen, R., & Worrall, J. (1977). *New directions for placement-related research and practice in the rehabilitation process.* Albertson, NY: Human Resources Center.

Vernon, S. W., & Roberts, R. E. (1985). A comparison of Anglos and Mexican Americans on selected measures of social support. *Hispanic Journal of Behavioral Sciences, 7,* 381–399.

Vertinsky, I. (1976). *Implementation II: A multi-paradigm approach.* Working paper presented at the International Conference on the Implementation of Management Science in Social Organizations, University of Pittsburgh.

Walker, B. A., & Hanson, W. C. (1992). Valuing differences at Digital Equipment Corporation. In S. E. Jackson & Associates, *Diversity in the workplace: Human resources initiatives.* New York: Guilford Press.

Weiner, Y. (1988). Forms of value systems: A focus of organizational effectiveness and cultural change and maintenance. *Academy of Management Review, 13,* 534–545.

Werther, W. B., & Davis, K. (1993). *Human resources and personnel management.* New York: McGraw-Hill.

Whetten, D. A., & Cameron, K. (1991). *Developing management skills.* New York: HarperCollins.

Williams, J. (1987). *Eyes on the prize*. New York: Penguin Books.

Wong-Rieger, D., & Quintana, D. (1987). Comparative acculturation of Southeast Asian and Hispanic immigrants and sojourners. *Journal of Cross-Cultural Psychology, 18*(3), 345–362.

Wright, P., Ferris, S. P., Hiller, J. S., & Kroll, M. (1995). Competitiveness through management of diversity: Effects on stock price valuation. *Academy of Management Journal, 38*(1), 272–287.

Young, J., Rosati, R., & Vandergood, D. (1986). Initiating a marketing strategy by assessing employer needs for rehabilitation services. *Journal of Rehabilitation, 52,* 37–41.

Name Index

Subject Index

Internal Revenue Service (IRS): and benefits, 133; and discrimination, 127

Intuitive strategy, 64, 67, 69, 70

Iowa, University of, benefits at, 132

Iran, and quality of life, 152–153

Iraq, and quality of life, 152–153

Israel, and quality of life, 152–153

Italy: and diverse workforce, 203; and quality of life, 152–153

J

Jamaica, and quality of life, 152–153

Japan: and cultural differences, 152–153, 157, 197–198; and diverse workforce, 203; and expatriate managers, 172; and gender equity, 29, 36, 332

K

Kaiser Permanente, benefits at, 132

Kentucky Fried Chicken, in Japan, 197–198

Kenya, and quality of life, 152–153

Korea, Republic of, and quality of life, 152–153

Ku Klux Klan, 266, 277

Kuwait, and quality of life, 152–153

L

Laguna Beach, benefits in, 132

LCA Video/Films, film from, 197

Leadership: concept of, 284; in organizational change, 284–291, 306–309; for workplace equity, 135–137

Lebanon, and quality of life, 152–153

Lesbian and Gay Civil Rights Act (Massachusetts), 126

Lesbians. *See* Sexual orientation

Levi Strauss and Company: benefits at, 132; and diversity, 36; support groups at, 134

Libya, and quality of life, 152–153

Local ordinances, on discrimination, 126–127

Los Angeles, and discrimination, 104, 127

Lotus Development Corporation, benefits at, 132, 133

M

Malaysia, and quality of life, 152–153

Managers, expatriate, 171–191

Management philosophy, and organizational change, 284, 288–291, 307–309

Managing diversity: action on, 25–28; affirmative action distinct from, 15–19; aspects of, 13–47; awareness of, 14–19; business strategies for, 29–47; defined, 2, 13–14; discussions on, 19, 22, 24–25, 27–28, 46–47; and economic issues, 35–38; films on, 46–47; and organizational performance, 35–42; practices in, 17–18; rationale for, 29; responsibility for, 20–22; understanding of, 19–25; with whites and males, 23–25

Marketing, and diversity, 35–36

Maryland, and discrimination, 127

Masculinity/femininity, and quality of life, 151, 153, 156–158

Massachusetts, laws in, 125, 126, 132

Massachusetts Commission Against Discrimination, 126

MCA, Inc., benefits at, 132

Measurement, in organizational change, 291–293, 302–303, 309–312

Mediators, for socialization, 218, 223

Melting pot socialization, 218

Mental models, for diversity, 288–291

Mentoring: defined, 249; and emotional support, 250–252; for expatriate managers, 178–179, 185; findings on, 255–257; and organizational structure, 248–260, 281–282; planned use of, 249–250

Mergers, and acculturation, 204–205, 206, 207, 208

Mexico, and cultural differences, 152–153, 197

Michigan, University of, Institute for Social Research at, 251

Minneapolis, and discrimination, 127

Minnesota, laws in, 125, 126

Minnesota Communications Group, benefits at, 132

Minorities: and bicultural socialization, 214–224; mentoring for, 248–260, 281–282

Models, for socialization, 218–219, 223

The Authors

Taylor Cox, Jr., is associate professor of organization behavior and human resource management at the University of Michigan Business School, where he teaches MBA courses on organizational consulting, managing diversity, and leveraging human resources as a competitive advantage. He is also founder and president of Taylor Cox & Associates, Inc., a research and consulting firm that partners with clients for the design and execution of organizational change processes. The twenty-plus clients of the firm have included Exxon, General Motors, General Electric, Alcoa, Phelps Dodge, and Eli Lilly.

His teaching experience spans twenty-five years and ten colleges and universities, including MBA and executive teaching at the Fuqua Graduate School of Business at Duke University and executive teaching at the New York School of Industrial and Labor Relations at Cornell University, in addition to the University of Michigan, where he has spent the last nine years. His work experience also includes nine years in middle management positions encompassing both the private and public sectors.

Dr. Cox has published more than twenty-five articles and books on management-related topics. His previous book, *Cultural Diversity in Organizations*, was cowinner of the National Academy of Management's best-book award, signifying its selection as "the book contributing the most to the advancement of the state of knowledge in management" for the years 1993–1994.

Ruby L. Beale is currently on the faculty of the Department of Psychology and the School of Business Administration and has a research scientist appointment at the Center for the Education of Women at the University of Michigan. She is also a principal in a human resource management firm specializing in managing and enhancing work productivity and job and school performance with diverse populations.

Dr. Beale has designed and implemented workshops on the psychological, interpersonal, organizational, and societal factors that can inhibit or facilitate the performance of employees and students. She is a specialist in diversity and multicultural programming and trains trainers to successfully implement programs with a diverse audience. She has provided consultation on organization development to corporations, educational institutions and programs, professional associations and networks, municipalities, public and private social service agencies, and grass-roots community organizations.

Her research includes examination of the effects of the stress of sexism and racism at work on the physical and psychological well-being of working women of all cultures. She received her Ph.D. and M.A. degrees from the University of Michigan.